PRINCE OF DARKNESS

Also by Alan Weisman

Lone Star: The Extraordinary Life and Times of Dan Rather

PRINCE OF DARKNESS:
RICHARD PERLE

The Kingdom, the Power,
and the End of Empire in America

Alan Weisman

UNION SQUARE PRESS
An imprint of Sterling Publishing Co., Inc.

New York / London
www.sterlingpublishing.com

Grateful acknowledgement is made for permission to reprint the following:

"Political Science" words and music by Randy Newman © 1972 (renewed)
Unichappell Music Inc. All rights reserved. Used by permission of Alfred Publishing Co., Inc.

"Richard Perle: Whose Fault Is He?" © 2002 by Calvin Trillin; "On the Resignation of
Richard Perle, Captain of the Sissy Hawk Bridge, from the Chairmanship of the
Defense Policy Board" © 2003 by Calvin Trillin; "On Richard Perle, Lobbyist
Businessman and, Perhaps Not Coincidentally, Chairman of the Defense Policy Board"
© 2003 by Calvin Trillin. All poems originally appeared in *The Nation*. This usage granted
by permission of the author c/o Lescher & Lescher, Ltd. All rights reserved.

"A Few Words in Defense of Our Country" words and music by Randy Newman
© 2006 Randy Newman Music. All rights outside the U.S. and Canada administered by
WB Music Corp. All rights reserved. Used by permission of Alfred Publishing Co., Inc.

STERLING and the distinctive Sterling logo are registered trademarks of
Sterling Publishing Co., Inc.

Library of Congress Cataloging-in-Publication Data Available

10   9   8   7   6   5   4   3   2   1

Published by Sterling Publishing Co., Inc.
387 Park Avenue South, New York, NY 10016
© 2007 by Alan Weisman
Distributed in Canada by Sterling Publishing
c/o Canadian Manda Group, 165 Dufferin Street
Toronto, Ontario, Canada M6K 3H6
Distributed in the United Kingdom by GMC Distribution Services
Castle Place, 166 High Street, Lewes, East Sussex, England BN7 1XU
Distributed in Australia by Capricorn Link (Australia) Pty. Ltd.
P.O. Box 704, Windsor, NSW 2756, Australia

Manufactured in the United States of America
All rights reserved.

Sterling   ISBN-13: 978-1-4027-5230-8
            ISBN-10: 1-4027-5230-X

For information about custom editions, special sales, premium
and corporate purchases, please contact Sterling Special Sales
Department at 800-805-5489 or specialsales@sterlingpublishing.com.

For Lee—I hope I have made you proud.

Author's Note

Prince of Darkness is the product of independent research by the author, including numerous interviews of a wide range of sources and a review of documentation over the course of more than a year. No promises, assurances or agreements as to tone, content or conclusions were made to any of those interviewed.

—Alan Weisman
June 27, 2007

Contents

No one likes us—I don't know why
We may not be perfect, but heaven knows we try
But all around, even our old friends put us down
Let's drop the big one and see what happens

—Randy Newman, "Political Science"

I.
PROLOGUE

HE CLAIMS ALL this Prince of Darkness business is a case of mistaken identity, the fault of a confused, misinformed member of the Fourth Estate (naturally), and a European to boot (emphatically).

"He was a British reporter writing a piece for the *Observer* in the 1970s," he says. "And he got that statement from Denis Healey, a former British defense minister. Healy was a very clever, amusing guy. And he was asked about me by this British reporter and he said, 'Yeah, in Washington he's known as the Prince of Darkness.' Well, he *meant* Robert Novak, and in those days I looked a little bit like Novak. But you know how lazy some journalists are. Once it's in the file, that's it. And so the next piece picked it up, and the next, and the next, and now I'm stuck with it. And I've seen a dozen different explanations for how I got that label, and they're all wrong."

That is Richard Perle's story, and he is obviously sticking to it. But the moniker would not have stuck for good had it not meshed comfortably with the persona, had there not been some empirical evidence that made it plausible. Mistake or not, the damn shoe fit.

"That dark thing under his eyes," says a man who knew him as a teenager and has watched his career for decades, "it's like something out of a 1920s horror movie. You don't get the Prince of Darkness thing laid on you if you look like John Edwards." The fact is that Richard Perle *is* a creature of the night. Even as a young staffer on Capitol Hill, his workday would begin hours after his colleagues' had started and would end many hours after they had gone home. "Chronically, he would not work in the mornings," said a former coworker. "Often he would not appear at all." Perle's looks and work habits aside, there is this from the former president of the United States, Jimmy Carter: "I never thought I

1

had much hope that I could convince Richard Perle that we needed a SALT II Treaty, or that we should negotiate *any* treaty with the Soviet Union."

This last remark is an extraordinary admission from the leader of the free world about a man unknown to most Americans, a man not elected by anyone to anything, a man who claims to be troubled by his sinister-reputation.

"It's upsetting to be perceived as some dark and mysterious figure," he says. "All I do is talk to people." Indeed. But whom does he talk to? To presidents, senators, congressmen, prime ministers, sultans, princes, chancellors, dictators, arms dealers, exiled dissidents, lobbyists, journalists, spooks, kooks, gourmands, wonks, gadflies, and remoras of every stripe. And when Richard Perle talks, people not only listen but often cringe. In fact, the very mention of his name among my friends, colleagues, and business associates evokes a visceral reaction that goes beyond fear and loathing. A case in point was a recent conversation I had with a senior vice president of a large multinational corporation. Our chat had nothing whatsoever to do with my work, but the woman felt compelled to inquire anyway.

"So, what are you up to?"

"Another book," I said.

"Am I allowed to know what it's about?"

"It's a biography of a man named Richard Perle."

The woman, a handsome, middle-aged socialite, threw her shoulders back as though she had been zapped by a Taser. Her face hardened and she fairly hissed at me.

"I have always *hated* Richard Perle," she said.

"Oh. Have you met?"

"No. And I have no desire to."

Some months later, a friend who works in the construction business was driving me to a meeting and asked about my next book.

"It's about a man named Richard Perle."

My friend took his eyes off the road and stared at me.

"They should have hung that bastard with Saddam."

"You mean 'hanged.' "

"What?"

"I believe the word is 'hanged.' "

"Whatever."

Perhaps the most benign label hung on Richard Perle is King of the Neocons, that rowdy collection of former liberal Democrats, Wilsonian globalists, and Trotskyites who soured on the New Left for its wimpy, weak-kneed response to the adventurism of the Soviet Union, and for its aversion to the use of military force regardless of the consequences. In fact, Perle did note vote for a Republican for president until Ronald Reagan. He remains a registered Democrat to this day, out of respect for his mentor, Senator Henry "Scoop" Jackson, Democrat from Washington State. If being the most visible member of that group were his only appellation, Richard Perle would be of minor interest. But Google his name and you find …

The Whore War Monger.

He should be hanged by his balls. [Note the correct verb form.]

A man who would rather burn down a hut just to boil some eggs.

An American tragedy.

A fascist bloodsucker.

Only the Evil One himself hates humanity more than Richard Perle does.

As a journalist, I have always been attracted to men and women whose lives and work fall on the periphery, just outside the mainstream. They are not misfits, exactly, but contrarians, provocateurs, resisters of the status quo who stand out by not joining in. Hence my profiles over the years of Jackie Gleason, John Malkovich, Sean Penn, Daniel Day-

Lewis, violinist Nadja Salerno-Sonnenberg, inventor Dean Kamen, Marine Corps commandant Al Grey, and baseball team owner Marge Schott, and my recent biography of anchorman Dan Rather. As my former colleague Morley Safer once said, "I'm only interested in people whose lives are more interesting than their work." With Richard Perle, I had little idea of what his life was about before I began my research, but his work I knew quite well. I had been following his career since the Reagan administration and its clashes with Soviet leaders Andropov, Chernenko, and ultimately Mikhail Gorbachev. The issues at that time were the abandonment of détente as a foreign policy and the aggressive engagement of the Soviets on a broad range of fronts: political, economic, and most chillingly, military.

The United States had limped through the humiliation of gasoline lines and hostages in Tehran and was now moving upright on the world stage, affecting a "Don't Tread on Me" swagger. In accounts of the internecine policy battles within the administration, the name Richard Perle kept popping up. He was characterized in the press as a kind of hit man for Secretary of Defense Caspar Weinberger, a dour rejectionist who played to Ronald Reagan's long-held fears regarding the sinister intentions of the Soviets and their many surrogates throughout the world. After all, Reagan was himself a neoconservative, although his liberal credentials were highly suspect among the Left. Even when Gorbachev, this youthful salesman, came calling with his bag full of perestroika, glasnost, and Communism Lite, Ronald Reagan, with Richard Perle perched on his shoulder whispering "nyet" in his ear, would not be seduced. I watched with fascination as Perle and his acolytes diverted the affable president with a beguiling vision of an outer-space-based shield that would protect America from nuclear missiles, a legerdemain so powerful that it demolished an arms control agreement of historic dimension and hastened the inevitable collapse of the "evil empire." If Ronald Reagan's Russian mantra was *Doveriai, no proveriai* (Trust, but verify), Perle's rejoinder was "No *doveriai*...ever!"

This guy is just a third-level bureaucrat. How can he be having such an effect?

Through the years of Bush 41 and Clinton I and II, Richard Perle continued to make his provocative views felt from behind a duck blind of think tanks, ad hoc committees, foreign policy forums, and talking-head spots on network TV. He thumbed his nose at the UN Security Council by advocating overt military aid to the Croats and Bosnian Muslims being slaughtered by rampaging Serbs. He is listed as a co-author of a blueprint for conquest addressed to the newly elected prime minister of Israel, a hellish litany of must-do's including forced regime change in Syria and the abandonment of peace agreements with the Palestinians. He and others in his circle are persistently accused of being Zionist agents carrying water for right-wing Likudniks in Tel Aviv and Jerusalem, and he has made a habit of falling into ethical quagmires in his business dealings, leading a casual observer to suspect either that he is a shameless profiteer or that he has an odd blind spot concerning conflicts of interest.

Like Woody Allen's *Zelig*, Perle appears in every foreign policy snap-shot, a rumpled, haughty presence, usually with his mouth open and his index finger pointing toward some unseen target. The French news agency Agence France-Presse apparently delights in running the exact same picture of Perle in every article about him, a particularly unflatter-ing moment when its nemesis appears to have had lemon juice squirted in his eye. The Gaullists are no doubt galled by the fact that he vacations at his home in Provence, while damning their government at every turn.

By the late nineties, Perle and his like-minded friends had ratcheted up their rhetoric, first in a manifesto called *Project for the New American Century* and then in an open letter to President Clinton. Both declared that the United States was on the cusp of a new imperium, a time for the nation to exercise its unmatched military and economic power to reshape the world in its image, relying not on global institutions or partnerships but on its manifest destiny as the purveyor of freedom and democracy for a malnourished world. The eyebrow-raising subtext detailed a benevolent hegemony in which the regimes of "rogue states" would be rolled back, the specified target being Saddam Hussein. "American policy cannot continue to be crippled by

5

a misguided insistence on unanimity in the UN Security Council," the open letter concludes.

Nowhere between the lines, or above, below, or through them, is the burden of empire fully addressed, the cost not just in dollars and blood, but also in spirit. Did Americans want their country to be an activist arbiter, a globo-cop? Would they be willing to downsize their aspirations, at least for a time, and accept the near certainty of chronic conflict as the price for their "exceptionalism"? It is not fun to be king, as previous empires have discovered.

The campaign continued through the start of the new millennium, with Perle preaching of dire consequences if and when Iraq acquired a nuclear bomb to add to its presumed arsenal of chemical and biological weapons. In statements like the following before the Senate Armed Services Committee, Perle invoked the memory of fallen Soviet satellites as a template for U.S.-backed regime change in Iraq: "The principal objection to a plan like this is that it cannot succeed because the Iraqi opposition is weak and ineffective. Of course it is. So was the opposition to Ceausescu, right up to the very day he was brought down. Skeptics too easily discount the empowerment of the opposition that would flow from western support."

Then came 9/11 and its echo, "It changed everything." In fact, all it changed was the casus belli. The goal of removing Saddam was now folded into a worldwide War on Terror, which in turn meshed nicely with the New American Imperium, which would be championed by a president so shallow and unlettered that an adviser had to inform him that Germany was indeed a member of NATO and had been for some time. (The advisor was Richard Perle.) In the eyes of the beholder this was either a divinely inspired alignment of moon and planets or a perfect storm that would shake the republic to its foundation. The game plan was sketched; the players were all in position. But at the eleventh hour, there was some movement in the dark, a courier of sorts with a message from Saddam himself: Call off your force and you can have everything you want. Everything, that is, except my resignation. The message was delivered not to the Pentagon or even to the CIA, but to Richard Perle, that rumpled bureaucrat caught once again in the snapshot. He relayed the offer to an appropriate party but did not have to wait long for a reply.

"Tell them we'll see them in Baghdad."

And so it began.

Unlike many of his posse who prefer the relative safety of academia and policy boards, Richard Perle is a highly visible and mobile target. He accepts invitations to speak before hostile groups knowing full well he will be heckled or worse. At a debate with Democratic Party leader Howard Dean in Portland, Oregon, a protester threw a shoe at Perle before being dragged away, screaming, "Liar! Liar!" Was this, I wondered, some sort of masochistic delight in placing himself in harm's way? Was it unbridled narcissism? Does he really enjoy being the Prince of Darkness, regardless of how the nickname was bestowed? The answer, I would learn, is that Richard Perle has always and will always believe in the bulletproof integrity of his arguments; he always believes he can win people over. He has never denied or hidden who he is or what he hopes to achieve.

After some preliminary research, I telephoned Perle in the summer of 2006 at his home in the Washington, D.C., suburbs. We had never met and my name meant nothing to him. After assuring him I was not a stalker or a hero worshiper, I asked for his e-mail address so I could send him what I called my bona fides—my record as a journalist over the past three decades. After he had read the CV, I asked if I could make my pitch in person regarding a biography, requesting just fifteen minutes of his time.

"How can I refuse?" he said. "Come on over."

I took the Amtrak from New York to Washington, and then a taxi to Perle's comfortable home in Chevy Chase. As I waited in his living room, I panned the memorabilia on the walls and coffee table: photos of the wife and child, of the moms and dads, books on wine and great vineyards, nothing that would reflect a life spent in the bare-knuckled world of global politics.

Perle greeted me in an open-necked shirt and worn cardigan, faded jeans and sandals. He did not cut the swath of a Prince of Darkness; as one of his colleagues remarked, "He's more like a Jewish koala bear." I was dressed in a pin-striped business suit and English wing-tipped shoes, standard CBS issue. The outfit was meant to send the message that I was a serious person on what I considered to be serious business.

"Espresso?" he offered, in what would become a ritual greeting.

I declined, and for the next ten minutes he listened as I outlined my plan. I told him I intended to write this book because I had decided he was an interesting person, that I was neither an ideologue nor a polemicist, that I was not, in fact, even a registered voter. There was no agenda, hidden or otherwise, except the pursuit of a good story. I was not requesting his "authorization," and would not accept it even if offered. I was requesting only his time, spread out over months, and his willingness to answer questions on whatever subject I chose. I would make no promises as to the tone or style I would adopt, or the conclusions I might draw. He would not be allowed to review any material prior to publication and I would not inform him of other interviews I would be conducting, but I would accept his help in contacting individuals I could not reach myself.

Now it was time to sum up. "You know people. Check me out. I don't do Kitty Kelly but I don't write valentines either. The bottom line is: There's nothing in this for you."

Throughout my monologue Perle sipped his demitasse and studied me with a hint of a smile. "I'm just a footnote," he said. "Why would anyone want a book about me?"

"That's my call, isn't it? If I'm wrong, it's my fault."

"Well then, why not?"

Over the next six months, I kept Amtrak in business, wearing out the path between New York and Washington, following Perle on speaking engagements to various cities, and visiting him at his home in Provence. On each occasion, he was as his friends had described him: kind, courteous, witty, and inquisitive.

This is not a book for foreign policy scholars or political partisans. It is the story of a man who, through a combination of luck, timing, and inherent intellectual brilliance (unquestioned even by his legion of critics), found himself at the epicenter of power in a volatile and threatening world, and tried to remodel it to match his ecumenical ideal. It is an attempt to retrace the steps of a man's life to better understand how he arrived at this place and this time and with his fully formed worldview, regardless of whether that view is shared and celebrated or derided and condemned.

It is a book about Good versus Evil; at Perle's Place, the menu is short.

As so many things go so horribly wrong in Iraq, both Richard Perle and his Weltanschauung become scrumptious targets for the hubris police. "I'm so damned tired of being called the architect of the Iraq War," he says. "Huge mistakes were made, but they were not made by neoconservatives. We had almost no voice in what has happened."

That does not cut any ice with at least one high-ranking administration official. "You had this constant goading that came from Richard, and if he now says, 'I had nothing to do with Iraq,' he means he had nothing to do with the planning for it or how many divisions we needed. But his steady drumbeat about how we had to deal with these things, and his constant—*constant!*—appearances on television in Europe were a source of major distraction. He single-handedly did more to foul up our relations with Europe than any other single human being. And then he would decamp to his house in France!"

"Yes, I think he is hurt," says friend and vice presidential adviser David Wurmser, "because the overall theory Richard and I and a lot of others had converged in Iraq. And if it was done incompetently, then it reflects on the whole theory of the endeavor. Behind what Richard and I and others were advocating was a revolutionary idea in which stability and condominium, the status quo, are not the foundations for a foreign policy. It's the spreading of freedom and democracy, and anchoring your foreign policy to those values. And if you implement it incompetently, the whole concept is indicted."

For Richard Perle, this is a new and painful experience...being linked not only with failure but with a disaster of incalculable proportions. For it wasn't so long ago that his name was joined with spectacular victories, when his ideas and his endless hours of rigorous debate changed the world for good. After all, he had come so far and learned so fast, it seemed as though the streak would never end. But that was a different time and a different place, back when his world was young.

II.
THE IMP OF THE PERVERSE

HE BARELY REMEMBERS New York City, where he was born in September of 1941. Two years later, his father, Jack, a high school dropout who went into the wholesale textile business, moved his family to Southern California, where the climate and the business were more agreeable. There was Martha, an elegant, gracious woman; Richard, a somewhat shy three-year-old, and then a younger brother, Robbie, who was born brain damaged. To this day, no one understands precisely how it happened, but negligence on the part of the hospital was the chief suspicion. The boy could walk and play but was undisciplined and unpredictable. "For a long time, my parents, particularly my mother, simply couldn't accept the reality that this was irreversible," Perle said. "She kept taking him from specialist to specialist. They were devastated, of course."

The end of the war had left a severe housing shortage in Los Angeles. So, for about nine months, the family lived in a hotel in Palm Springs. It was called the Lone Palm for the solitary plant that floated on an island in the middle of the pool. "What I loved about that place was room service. Pancakes for breakfast every morning! And horseback riding. A guy used to take me to his stable for lessons. Remember, in those days Palm Springs was just desert."

The Perles found a house at 320 Fuller Avenue near La Brea and Fairfax, an area sprinkled with synagogues and delicatessens. Perle recalls having no difficulty making friends in what for him was a mostly uneventful childhood. Thus he was highly puzzled by this little ditty published in the *Nation* several years ago by Calvin Trillin:

> Consider kids who bullied Richard Perle—
> Those kids who said Richard Perle threw just like a girl,

11

Those kids who poked poor Perle to show how soft
A Mama's boy could be, those kids who oft-
Times pushed poor Richard down and could be heard
Addressing him as Sissy, Wimp or Nerd.
Those kids have got a lot to answer for,
'Cause Richard Perle now wants to start a war.
The message his demeanor gets across:
He'll show those playground bullies who's the boss.
He still looks soft, but when he writes or talks
There is no tougher dude among the hawks.
And he's got planes and ships and tanks and guns—
All manned, of course, by other people's sons.

"I honestly have no idea where he got that," Perle told me. "I certainly don't remember ever being bullied. I sent him an e-mail about it. He claims to know some people I went to school with, but I don't recall any of them."

When the veracity of Trillin's doggerel was challenged in a letter to the editor by a woman who claimed to have been in little Richard's class, Trillin responded, "I suppose Rocco Guntermann, the classmate whose existence you deny, did not say to me just last week, 'We can settle this if Perlie Girl meets me near the swings at 5 o'clock on Friday—and tell him not to bring two teachers and his mother this time!' Would it surprise you to learn that Rocco is now a psychotherapist in Sherman Oaks?"

A check of relevant telephone books and professional organizations revealed no Rocco Guntermann. So I phoned Trillin for an explanation. "Yeah," Trillin laughed, "Rocco was the guy I made up. The really astonishing thing was I literally had no idea where Perle had grown up. I just made up the whole thing that he'd been pushed around in grade school." Trillin said he was further astonished when a friend's wife, who claimed to have gone to grade school with Perle, called to ask how Trillin knew that Perle had indeed been bullied. Trillin said he replied, "You mean it's true? It's getting so you can't even invent a slander in this country anymore."

While Perle insists he has no recollection of such incidents, the protagonist of his one novel, *Hard Line*, who bears an uncanny resemblance to Perle, is described as a somewhat troubled youth: "He was…different. And so his classmates picked on him in the instinctive, impersonal cruel way of preadolescents, and he withdrew like a turtle inside an emotional shell."

The Perles' was not a religious household. Richard became a bar mitzvah but never did memorize his Hebrew. Politics was rarely discussed, although Perle would occasionally taunt his father, a registered Democrat and devotee of FDR, by pretending to espouse radical left-wing causes. Jack Perle was a good-time guy who enjoyed golf and card playing for money, activities that held no interest for Richard. It would be years before the son would come to appreciate what a mensch his father was, how his simple live-and-let-live outlook was both noble and admirable.

"He was very smart," Perle told me. "Self-taught. Left school. He read a lot and he knew a lot, but he wasn't an intellectual. By the time I was in high school I was interested in ideas and people who were interested in books and music and so forth. Yes, he was a mensch. And one of the things I am eternally grateful for is that I came to appreciate him while he was still alive. And as I got older, I began to realize he was really a terrific person."

As a teenager, Perle's idea of a good time was a spirited set-to with his friends over the issue du jour, be it the congressional resolution making "In God We Trust" the national motto, or the Soviets' resolution to invade Hungary. For junior high, he was sent to a boarding school called Chadwick, which he described as a beautiful campus on a hillside. He was an indifferent student and, worse, racked up so many demerits for various infractions that he was usually kept at school every other weekend, while his friends were allowed to go home.

"So I got thrown out of there and I ended up at Hollywood High School. Now, I should have gone to Fairfax, which was a much better school, but I picked Hollywood for the most stupid and immature reason: The kid next door went to Hollywood too, so I knew I could always get a lift."

This was Southern California of the late 1950s, where teenagers would gather at coffeehouses, such as Positano in Malibu, and affect the personae of Jack Kerouac and Lenny Bruce. "I would consider us Bohemian middle class," said law professor Franklin Zimring, a classmate of Perle's. "The parents were a lot of people who worked in the industry...attorneys or lesser screenwriters, very much to the left of center. One kid's father was a lawyer for the Hollywood Ten. These were not the kids who were going to Harvard or the University of Chicago."

Zimring and Perle were also members of the debate team, which in those days was a special and highly competitive enterprise, with National Forensic League competitions throughout Southern California. Perle invented a particularly effective tactic that disarmed and often embarrassed his opponents. "During a debate, there was a session in which you could ask the other team a question," recalls composer Russell Horton, who was a member of the Perle-Zimring team. "And they would ask them a question in which the operative word was a ten-dollar word that most sixteen- or seventeen-year-olds wouldn't understand, but which the judges and debate coaches would. Like, 'Tell me, would your proposal be applied ubiquitously?' At this point, the other team had a choice. They could say, 'I don't understand what that word means,' which makes them look pretty bad, or they could just try to bullshit their way out of it. And so you watched them going further and further down the toilet. You just keep saying, 'But I don't understand how that is ubiquitous!' It was really very clever."

Clever, cunning, artful, adroit. Perle did not have the body, the skills, or the interest for sports, but he had a nimble mind and he used it as a weapon to impress and disarm. On the debate stage rather than the football field, Perle was ten feet tall and bulletproof. His fictional alter ego, Michael Waterman, had all the right stuff: "He learned to stand straight, look his opponents in the eye, and beat the intellectual bejesus out of them—and he did it with zeal."

Harry Major witnessed young Perle's entire repertoire. Every high schooler had a teacher like Harry Major, the craggy but benign idealist out of *Goodbye, Mr. Chips*, *Mr. Holland's Opus*, *Dead Poets Society*, and *Stand and Deliver*. He is eighty-two now, but little about his student Richard Perle has been lost in the fog of time. "He and I were rather close at one time. I admired his mind, but he was a contrarian. I remember one day in my senior writing class he was reading a book during a lesson. I said, 'Richard, put the book away and pay attention.' And he said, 'I'm reading Robert Frost's poems and they're wonderful. You'd think that you as an English teacher would have some respect.' He tried to turn it around and make me seem like an anti-intellectual. He was cagey that way and I rather liked that"

As Major thought back through that time and began to connect the dots, he could imagine an arc forming, beginning, as Major saw it, with the young and foolish and spiraling downward to the old and tragic. "There was what Edgar Allan Poe called 'the imp of the perverse' about him. Poe said, 'We have the imp of the perverse in all of us and you know it's there because if you go to a dinner party and you're standing at the table and a very fat lady is about to sit down on a chair, you know what thought crosses your mind.' And Richard had the imp of the perverse. And he would end up laughing when I would say, 'This is just blatant nonsense!' And he would admit it, you know. He was always challenging the status quo, but it annoyed me because it was usually more on protocol than on principle. I guess he just liked being different.

"He was part of my life, and I think it's very sad now. This whole business in Iraq has been an incredible blunder and Bush is fighting hard to be the worst president we ever had. And to think that Richard Perle would be enhancing, promoting, encouraging, philosophizing for and with this man makes me shudder. Frankly, I would prefer that no one paid him any attention. Maybe he'll get an appointment to the Supreme Court."

There was no epiphany that caused Perle to question what were then his immature, unformed beliefs, just a nagging feeling that although people seemed well off and optimistic at the dusk of the Eisenhower era, they also seemed, well, ungrateful. Perle could not understand why any American would find anything admirable about socialism and so much to criticize about a free-market society. It was not the theory of the worker state that bothered him as much as the practice; to him, tyranny was tyranny no matter how the intellectuals tried to pretty it up. When Perle would visit the homes of his classmates, he was struck by the disparity between the idyllic lifestyle of the parents and their chronic discontent. "Now, these were all very successful people...doctors, lawyers, there was a trade union leader, and they all lived very well. They had houses in the hills with housekeepers and swimming pools, and yet they expressed communist views and sympathy for the Soviet Union. And that troubled me. The incongruity of it troubled me." Perle hoped to become a university English teacher. "It seemed like the ideal life...discussing Joyce and Yeats with all my graduate students. But then I got involved with a whole new set of issues."

While dating a classmate, Perle met the girl's father, Albert Wohlstetter. Technically, Wohlstetter was a mathematician, but that description is profoundly inadequate. Wohlstetter was an intellectual giant in the emerging growth field of strategic nuclear war. He was part of an eclectic band of theorists who had nested comfortably at a military think tank known as the RAND Corporation ("RAND" stands for "Research and Development"). This curious entity came into being as a line item in the budget of the newly formed Department of the Air Force in 1947, and RAND set up shop near a beach in Santa Monica, California. Wohlstetter and his wife, Roberta, became the Nick and Nora of the cold war, re-forming and reshaping the then amorphous wisdom of the time, introducing such concepts as "first strike" and "fail-safe." At RAND, they and their colleagues worked diligently on their theories, ceding the spotlight to the ostentatious Herman Kahn, known both for his girth and his record-setting twelve-hour lectures. Kahn, who became at least part of the inspiration for the Dr. Strangelove character in Stanley Kubrick's classic send-up of the nuclear nightmare, became a star of sorts with the publication in 1960 of *On Thermonuclear War,* a six-hundred-plus-page bit of bombast that included answers to such existential questions as "Will the survivors envy the dead?" Kahn's response: Don't worry; be happy. "Despite a widespread belief to the contrary, objective studies indicate that even though the amount of human tragedy would be greatly increased in the postwar world, the increase would not preclude normal and happy lives for the majority of survivors and their descendants."

Such existential mud puddles were of little interest to Albert and Roberta Wohlstetter. Their focus was firmly on creating a system that would allow the United States to deploy its nuclear and conventional forces in a flexible, devilishly ingenious array, thereby creating a variety of response options of varying intensity. The point was to move conventional thinking away from the ham-fisted notion of "massive retaliation," the policy in place at the time, formally unveiled by Eisenhower's secretary of state John Foster Dulles in a speech in 1954.

Sitting by the Wohlstetters' pool one day, Albert showed Perle a paper he had written called *The Delicate Balance of Terror,* It was a treatise on tactics to avoid total nuclear war; why Wohlstetter thought a seventeen-year-old would be interested in such matters is perhaps a tribute to Perle's driving curiosity. The thesis, considered a classic to this day, challenges the most basic assumption of the cold war: that if both sides possessed the capacity to annihilate the other, nuclear war would be senseless. This belief, known as mutually assured destruction, or MAD, was the guiding principle of the day and had gone unchallenged for decades. In language more suited to the skillful essayist or impressively persuasive debater, Wohlstetter objected to MAD not only on moral grounds (of course, a widely held position) but on tactical and practical grounds. Wohlstetter asked, as Perle explained it, What if the Soviets struck with one nuclear weapon? Would we unleash hundreds? And if they struck with one and still had many more, would it make sense for us to retaliate? Wohlstetter defined six major hurdles that must be overcome in designing and deploying forces to meet a multiplicity of threats, and he added, "Prizes for a retaliatory capability are not distributed for getting over one of these jumps. A system must get over all six."

Wohlstetter then proffered a discriminating mixture of offensive and defensive systems, some existing only in his mind, and concluded on a pessimistic note:

> [These decisions] are hard, involve sacrifice, are affected by great uncertainties, concern matters in which much is altogether unknown and much else must be hedged by secrecy; and, above all, they entail a new image of ourselves in a world of persistent danger. It is by no means certain that we shall meet the test.

This last point offered a glimpse of a broader and more profound vision that eclipsed the nuts and bolts of strategic warfare. It raised the question at the very heart of the nation's character and sense of purpose: We have the power; how shall it be used? In Wohlstetter's view, it should be used to project America's values and aspirations, to superimpose its ethics and morals toward a righteous end, to provide safety and security to the vulnerable by guaranteeing its own, and ultimately to defeat evil. Once when Wohlstetter was asked why the United States should intervene in Bosnia when civilians were being slaughtered in many other parts of the world, he replied, "We should start by ending the genocides in which we are complicitous." Alternatively, he would scowl, then smile and remind his audience, "This is genocide, not another 'lifestyle choice.'"

In later years, the Wohlstetters would troll for sympathetic technocrats and operatives to join their cause. In his book, *The Politics of Truth*, former ambassador Joseph Wilson, husband of exposed CIA agent Valerie Plame, describes one such incident involving the Wohlstetters and Colonel W. Patrick Lang, a Middle East intelligence expert during the first Bush administration.

> Lang described to me a visit from an elderly couple who dropped in on him unannounced one afternoon at his Pentagon office….They began to probe the colonel for his views and

beliefs. Mrs. Wohlstetter pointed out sections in books they had written and asked for his views on theories espoused in them. It became apparent to Lang that he was being auditioned—though, apparently not to the satisfaction of the Wohlstetters. They soon packed up their books and left.

But what had failed to persuade Colonel Lang in 1992 had long since become gospel to Richard Perle, who found in *The Delicate Balance of Terror* a prelude to a new sense of purpose. "I was probably too young to be drawn to that kind of material," Perle recalled. "But what I liked about it was how rigorous the argument was. It was just very elegant, systematic, and orderly," Perle said, "and I am none of those. It was so beautifully argued, and I've always been attracted to rigorous argument."

For Perle, politics had little to do with any of this. This was a study in systems: what are the most effective and efficient means to achieve the desired result. Perle's political maturation came in no small measure from reading Hans Morgenthau's *A Realistic Theory of International Politics*, written in 1948. This was the main text of a political science course Perle took at the University of Southern California (USC), where he began his undergraduate studies in 1960, a manifesto about power, the virtually fundamental, Darwinian inevitability of power that Morgenthau believed existed in the DNA of the human race.

> The struggle for power is universal in time and space and is an undeniable fact of experience. It cannot be denied that throughout historic time, regardless of social, economic and political conditions, states have met each other in contests for power. Even though anthropologists have shown that certain primitive peoples seem to be free from the desire for power, nobody has yet shown how their state of mind can be recreated on a worldwide scale so as to eliminate the struggle for power from the international scene.... International politics, like all politics, is a struggle for power. Whatever the ultimate aims of international politics, power is always the immediate aim.

"It's a very well done argument for what is called the 'realistic' school of international relations theory," Perle explained. "It always amuses me when I'm referred to as an ideologue as opposed to a realist because I grew up with Morgenthau. And his book had the same quality as Wohlstetter's paper; he lays out an argument and then thinks of all the counterarguments and analyzes each one of them. So, his view is that the world is a Hobbesian world...it's basically everyone against everyone."

Perle did some minor campaign work for John Kennedy, regarding the option of Richard Nixon "appalling." "I was never a fan of Richard Nixon and never became a fan of his, although I came to regard him as pretty shrewd and intelligent." Their paths would cross repeatedly in the years to come.

In 1962, Perle got his first glimpse of what the dark side of power looked like when he visited Berlin during summer vacation. He arrived shortly after a young East German named Peter Fechter had been shot while trying to climb the Berlin Wall, and then bled to death in the no-man's-land between the East and West German guards. Perle stayed at a small hotel near the spot where Fechter had died and where thousands of floral arrangements had been laid. Fechter had been twenty-one years old, the same age as Perle. At that time an American could take a train into East Berlin and safely return, and Perle was eager to see what was on the other side of the Wall. He took with him a copy of the *International Herald Tribune*, the German newspaper *Die Welt* (although he could not read German), and a *Peanuts* cartoon book, which the East German guard confiscated.

He sat on a park bench and opened the *Herald Tribune*, hoping someone would see him reading this English paper and speak with him. When no one did, he opened *Die Welt* and pretended to be reading it when he saw a man walk slowly past him. No contact. The young American was too naive to realize that the stroller might well be a Stasi officer on patrol. The man returned, walking now from Perle's right to his left. Still no contact. On the third stroll the man sat down next to Perle and began to speak to him in fractured English. The two used hand signs and body language to communicate, and when the man,

Walter, felt it was safe, he fetched his wife and daughter, who Perle figured to be about seven or eight years old.

They said they lived in Mecklenburg, an agricultural area in the northern part of the country, and had come to Berlin on a holiday. Their transportation was a motorcycle with a sidecar for the mother and daughter. Walter explained that they had come to Berlin so they could eat decently. There was little food in their town, even though it was located in rich farm country. Perle invited the trio to lunch at a nearby café, and when the check came, Walter insisted on paying. "I don't want you to give them a single mark," he told Perle. The Germans were astonished to learn that Americans could travel from state to state without a passport or permission from anyone. They had required approval to travel from their home to Berlin. The daughter had never met a man who did not speak German, and as Perle kept leaning close to Walter to ascertain what he was saying, the girl probably assumed the American was hard of hearing. They walked and talked throughout the day and well into the night, arriving at the station where Perle could get the last train out at eleven p.m. Walter handed Perle a piece of paper with his address and said, "Please send me books and magazines." The wife, seeing this, grabbed Perle and said, "Please, he's been in trouble before. I beg you…don't send anything!" As the train approached, the little girl began crying. It was a scene from a movie, and Richard Perle cries at sad movies. "It was a very emotional moment, because I knew I would never see them again. So that was my first encounter with life in a totalitarian state."

He earned his BA in international politics at USC, and later an MA in politics at Princeton. For his doctoral work, Perle applied to the London School of Economics (LSE) and was accepted despite his lackluster academic performance. At LSE, he made friends easily, including documentary film producer Brian Lapping, a Brit who would remain a friend and eventually a neighbor at their vacation homes in Provence.

"Richard was doing his PhD, which, typically, he never finished," Lapping recalled. "And he asked this girl, Ann, to go out with him. She replied that she was engaged." She was engaged all right, to Lapping.

"So Richard said, 'Why don't you and your fiancé come and have a meal with me?' He was sharing a flat with Edward Luttwack (a Romanian-born Jew of breathtaking knowledge and conceit who would become a forceful strategic thinker both in and out of government) and typically, Richard went into the kitchen and cooked a wonderful supper, (an appreciation of good wine and good food being two more gifts from Albert Wohlstetter). But Luttwack talked without cease. We had to invite Richard back so we could get to know him. And the thing we talked about with most enthusiasm and shared vision was how it was stupid to be soft on foreign policy."

Among Perle's professors at LSE was the Marxist theoretician Ralph Miliband, creator of the *New Reasoner*, the *New Left Review*, and the *Socialist Register*, none of which would ever make Perle's required reading list. Lapping calls Miliband "one of those dreadful Left figures whom Richard was pretty contemptuous of." Perle remembers the bright side. "The best thing that happened to me in Ralph Miliband's class was a lifelong relationship with the girl who sat next to me. That was Ann Lapping. So I'm grateful to Miliband for that."

Just a month into the semester, the Cuban missile crisis brought the world to a standstill. The students organized an emergency debate and Perle signed up to speak, not realizing that debates in the UK often resemble question time for the prime minister, with its attendant hooting and hollering. "I had no idea what to expect when I got up on that stage," Perle told me. "So I got shouted at and heckled, but I was pretty confident in my argument." There would be no war, Perle insisted, pipe in hand, because the United States had the overwhelming local advantage. As for deterrence, the Soviets would be outnumbered in missiles by fifty to one, plus they were burdened with the added disadvantage of having a very long supply line while the United States was right next door. "The Russians will back down," Perle said as the room became quiet. It was pure Perle, staring down the naysayers, beating the intellectual bejesus out of them.

Former assistant secretary of state Richard Burt, a man who jousted with Perle throughout his career, told me, "Richard Perle can take a really bad idea and make it sound almost plausible and reasonable, even brilliant. And I came to admire his ability to read an audience, understand what people want to hear or need to hear, and couch his argument in terms that sounded so completely sensible." For Perle, the missile crisis was a cautionary lesson in the vagaries of empirical wisdom; what you believe you see is not always what is there...a reality that would come back to haunt him many decades later over the war in Iraq.

"I don't recall being afraid at the time," he said. "I recall being puzzled that no less than Bertrand Russell had packed up and gone to Scotland. There was pretty damn close to a panic that there was going to be a nuclear war, and I was pretty sure there wasn't going to be. But the subsequent history suggests the situation was graver than I thought it was. I was too young and inexperienced to take into account miscalculations and errors and misperceptions."

Perle returned to the United States in 1964 in time to watch the Johnson landslide over Barry Goldwater, and the slow but steady military escalation in Vietnam. "I was doubtful about the war from the beginning," Perle said, "because I didn't think we could win. But I didn't believe it was immoral and I certainly didn't sympathize with the North Vietnamese or the Vietcong." And as America's fortunes began to sour in Southeast Asia, so did Perle's life back in the states. First, he married a young Danish girl who suffered a nervous breakdown just one week after the marriage. For two years he stayed with her in Denmark, hoping she would recover while trying to finish his thesis in the meantime. In the end, they thought it best that he return to the United States; he went back to Princeton but continued to speak with her long after their divorce and his second marriage.

Second, between 1969 and 1971, both his mother and his father died of cancer. Now it would be just Richard and the impaired Robbie, who was being moved from place to place like an unwanted guest. "Richard would buy him LA Dodger tickets," said longtime friend Howard Feldman. "Robbie loves baseball. It's been a very difficult thing for Richard with his parents gone and all. I know it weighs pretty heavily on him." Of his brother, Perle would say only, "He's alive. I talk to him on occasion, usually when he's in some sort of desperate trouble. And then for months at a time I won't hear from him."

Another man might well have drowned in despair, but Perle was saved by a chance meeting with a man who would become both his mentor and his surrogate father; Senator Henry "Scoop" Jackson, Democrat from the state of Washington. Of Jackson, Perle told me, "He was my father when I still really had a father. He would counsel me on things fathers counsel kids about. And because he was not my father, I was probably more willing to take his advice."

It would be the start of a beautiful friendship, a marriage made on Capitol Hill.

III.
THE SORCERER'S APPRENTICE

ONE COULD STOCK a midsized library with books about the origins of the neoconservative movement. Why this genesis should generate almost as much scrutiny as the Almighty's is no doubt a sign of the times. As the neocons achieved cult status as a shadow government during the Clinton years, their bloodlines became a source of fascination among those who analyze how the new players evolved from the old. Machiavelli, Hobbs, and Leon Trotsky are often cited as the holy trinity for their belief that only an enlightened elite can bring order to the mindless chaos of the masses. What appeared to be this decidedly un-American view was promulgated by Leo Strauss, a German-Jewish immigrant professor at the University of Chicago in the 1950s and 1960s. As the lineage is usually described in the media, Strauss begat philosopher Allan Bloom, who begat political theorist Irving Kristol, the self-described "liberal who was mugged by reality," and they in turn begat a young Paul Wolfowitz and a tribe of true believers who would dominate the George W. Bush administration and bring about the Iraq War.

But as lapsed neocon Francis Fukuyama put it, "More nonsense has been written about Leo Strauss and his connection to the Iraq War than any other subject." Perhaps, but that is because Strauss's disciples, most notably Wolfowitz, are unapologetic in their allegiance to Strauss's writings and teachings, as least as they interpret them. Decades after Strauss's death in 1973, scholars continue to argue over whether Strauss was, as the *New York Times* wondered, "Democracy's Best Friend or an Anti-Democratic Elitist."

If Richard Perle's tag as the Prince of Darkness was a case of mistaken identity, his label as a Straussian is guilt by association. True, Wolfowitz and most other proud Straussians are friends and colleagues, but Perle insists he is neither a Strauss acolyte nor a Wilsonian, the other adjective usually paired with his name. Woodrow Wilson believed America's role in the world was the spreading of democracy through mostly peaceful means, making him, in the minds of neocons, half right, and leaving Perle with yet another label—"a Wilsonian in combat boots," as one wag put it.

Perle resists any attempts by friend and foe to pigeonhole or typecast him. "I don't think in grand historical terms," he once said to me. "I have only a passing acquaintance with Woodrow Wilson's writing and thinking and I would not have identified with him. If you develop along the lines of people you admire, I hugely admired Churchill and his refusal to accept defeat."

Far less esoteric and more to the point is the view that neocon flora sprouted in early January 1953, in suite 1428 on the fourth floor of the Old Senate Office Building, the home of freshman senator Henry Jackson of Washington. Jackson, a six-term congressman, was considered something of a maverick even in a time when sharp ideological differences divided postwar America. He pilloried President Eisenhower for not spending enough to fight communism, yet resigned from Senator Joseph McCarthy's Subcommittee on Government Operations in 1953 in protest over McCarthy's anticommunist "witch hunts." He twice introduced resolutions calling for across-the-board arms cuts with the Soviet Union but later did everything in his power to try to scuttle the 1972 Anti-Ballistic Missile Treaty.

Scoop Jackson was a libertarian, human rights activist, social conservative and persistent advocate of American military might, and over the next three decades he would become one of the most respected figures ever to walk the halls of the U.S. Senate. By himself, Jackson was a formidable presence, but his stature and effectiveness were enhanced even further by a supporting cast admired and feared for its tenacity and tactical brilliance.

Jackson's most significant early recruit was a diminutive dynamo named Dorothy Fosdick. "Dickie," as she was known, had already compiled an extraordinary résumé by the time Jackson met her in 1954.

Even her pedigree was impressive: daughter of Harry Emerson Fosdick, the pacifist pastor of New York City's magnificent Riverside Church, built for him by John D. Rockefeller, Jr., She had come to the State Department in 1942 to work on the optimistically-named Postwar Planning Division. Over the next decade Dickie would assist an all-star cast of U.S. foreign policy Brahmins, including George Kennan, Paul Nitze, General George C. Marshall, and Eleanor Roosevelt, with whom Fosdick helped draft the Universal Declaration of Human Rights for the newly launched United Nations.

Fosdick's worldview was rooted in the philosophy of her father's contemporary and rival, Reinhold Niebuhr, who managed to find the square root of the two dominant doctrines of the day: the cynical realists—the biblical "children of darkness"—and the idealists—the "children of light." In Niebuhr's view, both were dangerously misguided.

> The children of darkness are evil because they know no law
> beyond the self. They are wise, though evil, because they under-
> stand the power of self-interest. The children of light are
> virtuous because they have some conception of a higher law
> than their own will. They are usually foolish because they do
> not know the power of self-will. They underestimate the peril of
> anarchy in both the national and international community.
> Modern democratic civilization is, in short, sentimental rather
> than cynical…it does not know that the same man who is
> ostensibly devoted to "the common good" may have desires and
> ambitions, hopes and fears, which set him at variance with his
> neighbor.

Written in 1944, Niebuhr's *The Children of Light and the Children of Darkness* is both an admonition and a warning to a world community that had not yet recognized the full horror of the Nazi reign. "Realism" without a moral sense, without humanity, is corrosive and destructive. He who worships self-interest inherits the wind. "Idealism" without a full understanding and acceptance of man's baser instincts leads to subjugation and defeat. The blueprint for survival and growth lies in between and must include common cause against those who would impose their will borne of self-interest upon others. The shorthand: Both America's cynicism *and* its naïveté made it blind to the demonic fury of Nazism, and it must not make the same mistake with the Soviet Union.

For Fosdick, this view was a moral imperative, and it meshed seamlessly with Jackson's. In April of 1945, he and seven other congressmen were invited by General Eisenhower to visit the just-liberated death camp at Buchenwald. Jackson was said to have dismissed rumors of atrocities as anti-German propaganda, recalling that similar reports had also been heard during World War I. But seeing led to belief and acceptance. "The atrocities are the most sordid I have ever imagined....It is impossible to describe adequately in words the condition of these prisoners," he wrote.

In an oral history project recorded years after Jackson's death, Fosdick described that moment in Jackson's life as a true epiphany. "In some ways, this was his most profound experience, because the Holocaust was, from his point of view, not only a tragedy for the Jews but was the utter breakdown of law and order and justice and politics and humanity. And it also underscored the inability of the West to appreciate the dangers of totalitarianism and the horrors it could invoke if it was left to run riot and not withstood early."

Jackson's major theme throughout the Eisenhower years and into the New Frontier was that the Soviet Union could not and should not be trusted, and that institutions such as the United Nations are an unreliable substitute for strong, independent governance. Jackson said precisely that in a speech to the National Press Club in 1962, a speech coauthored by Dickie Fosdick: "The hope for peace and justice does not lie with the United Nations. Indeed the truth is almost exactly the reverse. The best hope for the United Nations lies in the maintenance of peace, and peace depends on the power and unity of the Atlantic community and the skill of our direct diplomacy."

The UN-as-piñata would become a neocon theme, echoed a decade later by Daniel Patrick Moynihan and still later by George W. Bush's almost-ambassador to the UN, John Bolton. Their attitude was, essentially, Why even play in a game in which the deck is stacked? Let the corrupt diplomats double-park in Manhattan with impunity and dine on the dole at Le Cirque. America can handle itself. Adlai Stevenson, America's UN ambassador at the time of Jackson's broadside, called the speech "a grave mistake." In his mind it was Dorothy Fosdick getting even for their love affair that had gone sour, a liason that had been an open secret in Washington at the time. Stevenson's appeals to educate Jackson on the importance of the UN and America's role in it were rebuffed.

As the Democrats tore themselves apart over the Vietnam War, Jackson stuck by Lyndon Johnson, not so much out of loyalty to his party's leader as from sheer conviction that the domino theory was real, and that withdrawal would embolden the Soviet Union. His support of the war caused some of his constituents to question both his judgment and his sanity, but he continued to be reelected by wide margins.

The backdrop against which Vietnam and other international skirmishes played out was the growing nuclear arsenal of the Soviet Union and the emergence of China as a nuclear power. Johnson's defense secretary, Robert McNamara, favored capping U.S. nuclear forces at a level that he believed would maintain the stability of MAD but not necessarily assure nuclear superiority. When word surfaced that the Soviets were attempting to build a missile shield around Moscow, McNamara convinced the president that an increase in either offensive or defensive weapons would be a waste of money and would, he believed, actually make America less secure.

Thus began debate on what would become the great chimera of the U.S.-Soviet arms control saga: the anti-ballistic missile shield.

In 1969, doctoral student Richard Perle was invited to Washington by his old friend Albert Wohlstetter to attend a meeting of great importance. Also in attendance was Wohlstetter's prize student, Paul Wolfowitz, along with former secretary of state Dean Acheson and former secretary of the navy Paul Nitze.

At the time, Congress was hotly debating an antiballistic missile system, known as Safeguard, which would much later morph into the Strategic Defense Initiative (SDI), or Star Wars, during the Reagan administration. Under the Safeguard proposal, both the United States and the Soviets could expand from two to twelve defensive sites at which missiles could be launched to intercept an enemy's incoming missiles. (When the treaty was finally signed in 1972, it allowed only two sites each, and that number was reduced to one in 1974.) Never mind that the systems probably wouldn't work. The fantasy of a missile shield had been peddled almost nonstop since the end of World War II by various tub-thumpers including Daniel Graham, a director of the Defense Intelligence Agency, and Edward Teller, the self-proclaimed "father" of the hydrogen bomb. Among their more arcane proposals was a fleet of small, one-man space cruisers orbiting Earth in search of stealth missile launches, and the construction of a gigantic warhead that could destroy many enemy missiles as they arced through space. Although Safeguard was a relatively modest attempt at missile defense, President Nixon's support of it was strongly opposed by liberal senators such as J. William Fulbright, (D-Ark.), Stuart Symington, (D-Mo.), and Edward Kennedy (D-Mass.) on the grounds that it would spur the arms race and damage any hope of a new arms limitation agreement with the Soviets.

To formulate a powerful response to the doves, Wohlstetter directed young Perle and Wolfowitz to go around Washington and interview senators on their knowledge of and views on the issue. "One of the people we interviewed was Scoop Jackson," Perle said. "It was love at first sight. Here we were, a couple of graduate students, sitting on the floor of Scoop's office, reviewing charts on the ballistic missile defense and listening to his views on the subject...At one point, Scoop said, 'You're never really going to understand how this government works until you have direct experience. So why don't you come to work for me for a year and you can work on your thesis in your spare time?' But there was never any spare time with Scoop, and I was there for eleven years."

Jackson led the fight for Safeguard funding and won it largely because the charts prepared for him by Perle and Wolfowitz were bigger and more impressive than the charts used in debate by Symington and the liberal opposition. As Wolfowitz recalled, "What impressed me was that he insisted on understanding the results we got on the graphs. He sat on the ground with two twenty-nine year old graduate students to master them."

While Wolfowitz took a different but parallel path, Perle stayed with Jackson and Fosdick. His education would include discipline in the necessary but mundane habits of being a good citizen (such as remembering to file income tax returns, paying parking tickets, and balancing one's checkbook, which they taught him) as well as the finer art of Capitol Hill gamesmanship. The latter included knowing how and when to leak to the press information favorable to one's cause or unfavorable to the opposition's; knowing how to draft a "killer amendment" that would thwart unwanted legislation; knowing when to have your man enter a meeting to gain an advantage (the last man in usually wins); and knowing how to rearrange chairs at a committee hearing so that a hapless opponent cannot hear the stage prompts from his staff. "I did that to Cy Vance," Perle recalled with a smile about some long-ago battle with Jimmy Carter's secretary of state. "I knew that he simply didn't know what he was talking about. The real policy was being made by people way below him. And if I could put him in a position where he was separated from his staff, he would flounder more or less immediately, and that's exactly what happened."

"And this gave you great pleasure?" I asked.

"We thought he was doing the wrong thing, and in fact didn't understand in any reasonable level of detail what he was doing and it was important to expose that to the other senators."

Perle quickly became known as something of a pit bull in the corridors of Congress, considered a gentlemanly but consummate infighter wielding a velvet shiv, who could kill softly by employing his virtues of patience and curiosity. "He doesn't browbeat people," Richard Burt said. "He just asks questions and bides his time. He very quickly tries to assess a situation and figure out who his allies are and who his adversaries are. Most people in government don't do that." Those who liked

Scoop Jackson but disagreed with some of his positions often blamed Perle for provoking adversarial relationships. In fact, a former cabinet member said Perle's symbiotic relationship with Jackson affected the teacher more than the pupil. "I ran into Scoop in the late seventies after Perle had left his staff and it was like having an old friend back. He was relaxed and comfortable and funny, like he used to be."

"Complete rubbish," Perle responded when the story was relayed to him. "Scoop didn't change. That's really absurd."

Jackson himself was known as a tough but reasonable consensus builder, who could cajole a fence-sitting senator to climb down on his side. "I remember telling Scoop we needed a vote and that [Jacob] Javits just might go our way," Perle said. "And Scoop said, 'I'll get him in the gym.' Well, three days go by and Javits didn't go to the gym. But when he did, sure enough, Scoop got him."

Jackson also taught Perle how to lose a hand but still win the pot. As Richard Nixon lobbied hard for Senate ratification of the ABM Treaty, Jackson realized he could not muster the votes to block it. But before the vote on the ABM Treaty, there would be a vote on an Interim Agreement (later known as SALT I), a kind of corollary to the treaty that dealt strictly with offensive missiles and which would require only a simple majority to pass. That made it vulnerable to manipulation.

Jackson agreed to an idea Perle suggested: an amendment to the Interim Agreement strongly recommending that in any future agreements with the Soviets the United States should not be limited to an inferior level of strategic forces. Now, who could oppose that? It was a slap-down to the administration, and to make sure everyone got the message, Jackson got Republican Hugh Scott to cosponsor it and had Perle leak a draft to William Beecher of the *New York Times*. Passage of the Interim Agreement was the responsibility of Arkansas senator J. William Fulbright, chairman of the Foreign Relations Committee, a fan of arms control and a foe of Jackson.

As Perle recalls, during the Interim Agreement debate, California senator Alan Cranston came rushing to the floor to ask Fulbright, "Mr.

Chairman, are you aware there's a story by William Beecher that the senator from Washington is going to introduce an amendment highly critical of the administration and that Senator Scott is cosponsoring it?"

"Fulbright says he knows nothing about it and orders his assistant to look into it," Perle laughed. "So the guy comes back and confirms it, and Fulbright says, 'I can't believe they would do this.' And just then Scoop says, 'We're just asking for equality in these arms agreements.' And then he turns to Fulbright, who was still a racist in those days, and says, 'Senator, I think we're entitled to equality in *all* matters.' So we passed it, both houses, overwhelmingly."

Perle then leaned forward, relishing the memory. "That was a very clever amendment, but the germ of the idea was not mine, although I would love to have you write that it was. The idea came from Fred Ikle, the director of the Arms Control Agency. He quietly said to me one day, 'You know, to stiffen them in future negotiations an injunction might be a good idea.' So I wrote it up as an amendment."

The amendment had no legal authority; it was pure oratory. Nixon and future presidents could ignore it, but they could not ignore its powerful political impact. Even Henry Kissinger admitted that the amendment created a new reality in which larger deals that sought to balance many elements would be impossible. In fact, it would rear its head a decade later during an intense nuclear arms negotiation with the Soviets that would frame Perle's career.

What began incubating in Scoop Jackson's office was the embryo of a political cadre that would have a profound effect on U.S. foreign policy for decades to come, a band of brothers (with den mother Fosdick) who would move the United States away from negotiation and accommodation with the Soviet Union and other adversaries, to a position of aggressive confrontation. This group included Elliott Abrams, a former member of Harvard's Young Socialist League who became a special counsel to Jackson and later was convicted of withholding information from Congress in the Iran-Contra Affair; a summer intern named Douglas Feith, another Harvard man, who as assistant secretary of defense for George W. Bush would supervise a special unit designed to buttress the case for the Iraq War; Frank Gaffney, who would become the Defense Department's leading cheerleader for the Star Wars missile defense shield; Jim Woolsey, whom Perle and Jackson met at a dinner party, later becoming one of Bill Clinton's CIA directors; scholar Michael Ledeen, a National Security Council (NSC) consultant who also became embroiled in the Iran-Contra Affair; and a handful of other important players, each revolving around Richard Perle, who, in turn, revolved around Jackson. These were salad days indeed for young and restless conservatives out to change the world.

"Richard helped make Jackson more effective than Jackson otherwise would have been," recalled Feith. "Now, that's a big deal. For a senator to appreciate the value of a staffer who can be incisive and skillful at argumentation like a well-trained lawyer who is also careful about his facts, that's a very big deal."

Because Perle was the star of the company, the players had to indulge his eccentric work habits. The Prince of Darkness did not function by the dawn's early light. "You could not get him into the office," Howard Feldman said. "He not only slept late; he perfected the art of answering the phone at home as if he was really alert."

"The desk I was seated next to was often vacant because Richard was not often in the office," said Frank Gaffney with a laugh. "He would materialize as though the Messiah had been brought back to Earth. He would not work the morning shift and often would not appear at all. But, when the chips were down, he would pull an all-nighter to get something done that could have easily gotten done in the daytime." Perle's nocturnal habits would travel with him a decade later when he worked for the Pentagon. "He wouldn't come in until nine thirty or so, after he had had his usual espresso, which was not the Pentagon way," Perle's friend and former aide Bruce Jackson told me. "There, if the boss showed up at seven a.m., you showed up at six thirty just to beat him, like a guts poker game. Richard wouldn't play that at all. [Caspar]Weinberger would say when his staff was supposed to meet, and Richard would say, 'Well, then I'm not coming because it's too early for me.' That was pretty amazing."

Perle almost never attended Jackson's morning staff meetings either. He would write the senator's speeches and position papers at home at night and leave them in his mailbox outside his Capitol Hill apartment. Dickie Fosdick would pick them up and review them until eleven thirty or so, when Perle would wander into the office. "This was a holdover from my student days," Perle admitted. "The reason partly is that things are quieter at night. The phone doesn't ring and you can concentrate."

In the early years of Perle's apprenticeship with Jackson, their biggest headaches were President Nixon and his national security advisor, Henry Kissinger. Jackson's relationship with them was complex, with the senator supporting the administration on Vietnam and on wage and price controls, but staunchly opposing them on the broad policy of détente with the Soviets. The Jacksonites believed that détente was a weak and cowardly position to adopt against an implacable and relentless foe, a form of appeasement. They claimed it was Kissinger, not Perle, who held a dark view of America, perceiving it as a nation in decline whose least painful option was an accommodation with Moscow and an acceptance of the Soviets as equals.

"Kissinger had illusions that he was this great statesman who would be able to make deals with the Russians," Fosdick recalled. "He was used to coming up the Hill and wowing them and having his way. But in Scoop he found his equal. Scoop was no less the strategist and global-minded statesman, and he had just as much self-confidence as Kissinger."

To agree to bargain at all is to place one's adversary on an equal moral footing, a concession that Jackson, Perle, and their team found abhorrent. They believed that because of the Soviets' deplorable human rights record, their numerous treaty violations, and their incessant mischief-making around the world, they should be confronted only from a position of strength and only when the outcome of talks would be in America's interest, that is, *not* mutually beneficial. The longer the United States continued to negotiate with the Soviets, they insisted, the longer the corrupt, evil empire would threaten America and the rest of the world. So the battle between the concept of détente and the concept of no retreat, no compromise, and no negotiation was joined, with staffer Richard Perle riding shotgun. He used every weapon in his arsenal to sway public opinion and move Jackson's Senate colleagues away from the Kissinger–State Department embrace of the status quo and toward the more assertive, even obstreperous positions he and Jackson believed in. Provocative memos and position papers (described by one aide as "works of art"), plants and leaks in the columns of friendly journalists, horse trades with aides to committee chairmen; all this and more Perle orchestrated with a self-confidence uncommon for one in his early thirties.

Ken Adelman, who would join Perle in the arms control effort during the Reagan administration, still marvels at Perle's talent for making something big out of something quite modest. "It's his ability to use an otherwise forgettable office in an unforgettable way," Adelman told me. "You know, a staffer on the Hill is considered one of the lower forms of life. And usually they do some things and then they move on. But Richard made it into such an important position that Henry Kissinger at the height of his powers as national security advisor was thinking about what Richard Perle would do next."

Figuring out what Perle would do next became something of a spectator sport in Washington. Adelman recalled that when Perle went to work at the Pentagon during the Reagan years, his immediate boss, Frank Carlucci, would often call to share his bewilderment. "He'd call me up and say, 'Ken, I just heard this story about what Richard did. He said this, and he leaked that, and he did this. What do you think?' And I would say, 'That sounds about right to me. But it's worth it. It's worth having this guy.' And a few days later he'd call again and say, 'Ken, I just heard another story about Richard. He contacted this guy, and he didn't go to the morning meetings, and what do you make of this?' And I'd say, 'It's worth it, Frank. It's worth it.'"

Perle was already a star by the time Michael Ledeen met him in 1977, and their first substantive dialogue concerned not foreign policy but French food for fun and profit. "He had a scheme to start a soufflé restaurant. Either he or some friend had invented some kind of soufflé

oven in which you, the customer, came in and you got your little soufflé bowl and you picked a flavor…lemon, chocolate, whatever. And then
they'd pour the flavor in and you would stir it and then watch it rise in
this oven that had plastic windows. The big rumor around Washington
was that Kissinger had raised a lot of money to invest in this restaurant
just to get Richard off of Capitol Hill. He wanted to put him perma-
nently in the restaurant business."

While Jackson, Fosdick, and Perle were natural allies in their view of
the Soviet Union, Perle was something of a neophyte on Middle East
policy and the Israeli-Arab conflict. By his own admission, Perle had not
spent much time thinking about American policy in the region, and
whether the interests of the United States and Israel were always in harmony. Jackson, of Norwegian descent, developed an idealized view of
the Israelis as being much like his ancestors: intelligent, industrious,
independent, and as vulnerable as Norwegians were in 1940. He once
told Israeli prime minister Yitzhak Rabin, "We small people have to stick
together."

Once, during a fact-finding tour of Saudi Arabia, Israel, and Iran, the
Saudis initially refused to grant Perle and Fosdick visas because they
were believed to be Jewish. Jackson picked up the phone and called
Joseph Sisco, assistant secretary of state for Middle Eastern affairs. "If
those visas aren't here within 24 hours, we'll just spend more time in
Iran." The visas arrived promptly.

Fosdick's affinity for Israel grew from her liberal upbringing and her
work with Eleanor Roosevelt on the human rights manifesto for the UN.
Together, the two Protestants taught the Jewish kid from Hollywood
High that in support for Israel, America had not only a strategic motive,
but as they saw it, a moral imperative as well. And in one volatile issue,
the concerns of all three compatriots converged with an almost biblical
quality: emigration for Soviet Jews.

Following Israel's smashing victory in the Six Days' War of 1967, a
surge of pride among Soviet Jews led to demands for greater emigration.
The Soviets responded by allowing a trickle of Jews to leave, but in the
summer of 1972 Moscow declared that anyone wishing to leave would

have to pay an "education tax," supposedly to compensate the state for the money it had spent on their education. In reality, of course, the tax was imposed to stifle emigration entirely. At the same time, the Nixon administration was anxious to extend most-favored-nation trading status to the Soviets, more subsidized loans, and grain deals of epic proportions. The grain deals alone were so large that they accounted for 25 percent of the entire U.S. crop of 1972, causing domestic prices for grain products to spike.

The idea of linking Soviet Jewish emigration with the Nixon-Kissinger détente may not have originated with Jackson, Perle, and Fosdick, but they knew an opportunity when they saw one. This was perfect—an opportunity to push human rights, to infuriate the Russians, to help Israel, and to torment Kissinger and Nixon all at once.

As Perle recalled, "Several senators dispatched their top staffers to figure out a way to block the trade agreement. I was there for Scoop." The group knew that any trade agreement with the Soviets would require congressional approval, so the first clear option was to tack on an amendment that would be a quid pro quo: the trade deal in exchange for free emigration. They knew this would be a provocative move, since it was blatantly anti-Soviet legislation. Some advised "quiet diplomacy," a notion Perle would grow to detest as his many dustups with various administrations grew in intensity. No, it would have to be a straightforward, unambiguous, no-nonsense, in-your-face amendment, and if the Soviets balked, too bad.

Jackson agreed with the assessment and instructed Perle to immediately draft an amendment and work with the Senate lawyers to get the language just right. "Nowhere in the amendment did we insert the word 'Jew,'" Perle recalled. "Scoop knew of course that the principal demand for visas came from Soviet Jews, but he felt that any protection his amendment might offer should apply to Jews and non-Jews alike."

On October 4, 1972, they introduced legislation that denied trade concessions to *any* country that did not respect the right of its citizens to emigrate. Sponsoring the House version of the bill was a former judge from Cleveland named Charles Vanik, whose constituents in Ohio's

22nd district included a significant number of liberal Jews and émigrés from eastern Europe. Vanik, of Czech ancestry, traveled frequently to Prague to meet with dissidents, and used his position on the Ways and Means Committee to keep the dissidents' cause in the spotlight. Long after his retirement, Vanik was given a special award by Czech President Václav Havel in appreciation of his efforts. The so-called Jackson-Vanik amendment applied to all races, religions, and places of national origin but did not affect nonsubsidized trade or commercial lending. In other words, no cash, no deal.

Nixon and Kissinger were furious. They had devised a series of interlocking relationships with the Soviets, and Jackson-Vanik could topple the whole house of cards. Kissinger protégé Brent Scowcroft was then a member of the NSC staff. "We tried to explain to Jackson and Perle that the results of Jackson-Vanik would be to shut off emigration. And they said, 'Oh, no, no, no.' We were trying to accomplish what they wanted by cooperating with the Soviet Union and making an agreement that would allow a certain number to go. Well, they didn't want that. They wanted to clobber the Soviet Union."

"In other words," I asked, "Perle wanted either a whole loaf or no loaf at all?"

"Or better a loaf gained with a club than with a rose," General Scowcroft replied.

Privately, Richard Nixon vented about the meddling of what he called "professional Jews," but he was reluctant to antagonize Jewish voters in the upcoming elections. So, he and Jackson reached a compromise: Nixon agreed not to lobby Republican senators to kill the amendment if Jackson agreed not to make Jewish emigration a campaign issue. Nixon, ever the politician, figured the amendment would never pass the Senate anyway, and, even if it did, it probably wouldn't make it past the House Ways and Means Committee.

Then came an incident that sealed Perle's and Jackson's distrust of Kissinger. At the start of the 1973 Yom Kippur War, both the Soviets and the Americans expected the Israelis to win as easily and decisively as it had in 1967. But the attack by Egypt and Syria caught Israel by such surprise that for several days it appeared the Arabs might actually win, or at least claim a large chunk of territory in a settlement. Kissinger, who always put détente and relations with the Soviets ahead of all else, wanted Israel to win only a partial victory, just enough for Egyptian president Sadat to save face, and demonstrate to the Israelis how dependent they were on American aid and weaponry. "The best thing that could happen for us," Kissinger reportedly told Defense Secretary James Schlesinger, "is for the Israelis to come out ahead but get bloodied in the process."

As Egyptian and Syrian forces, egged on by the Soviets, began to cripple the Israelis, Tel Aviv sent an urgent request to the United States for a massive supply of arms and equipment. Kissinger stalled, still believing the Israelis would win and not wanting to antagonize moderate Arab states.

As Perle tells it, the Israeli embassy used him as a conduit to keep in constant contact with Scoop Jackson, who knew Kissinger was lying about the reasons for the stalled airlift. Perle had heard Kissinger make telephoned statements to the Israelis that directly contradicted the known facts, blaming Defense Secretary Schlesinger for the holdup. Finally, Jackson's good friend Admiral Elmo Zumwalt told Jackson that Israel would lose the war if it was not resupplied immediately. Jackson went directly to Nixon, who ordered Schlesinger and Kissinger to give Israel everything it needed.

Jackson told reporters he saw Kissinger's cynical actions as "a disastrous example of his version of détente. Without Soviet support and material encouragement, without Soviet training and equipment, the war would never have been started." And when the Soviets realized the Arabs just might win, Jackson said the Soviets began "pouring in all this stuff because the United States was not moving anything. Where in all this is détente?"

So it was no surprise that the Jackson-Vanik amendment, despite its long and arduous journey through Congress, contained an element of payback as regards Henry Kissinger. The amendment bounced back and forth between the Senate and the White House for several years. But in

1974, when it became clear that Jackson now had the votes in the Senate, Nixon flew into a rage, calling Jackson irresponsible for sacrificing so much business with the Soviets for the sake of its Jewish citizens, and musing that Jackson was courting Jewish voters for another run at the presidency. He predicted an anti-Semitic backlash if U.S.-Soviet relations deteriorated. But Nixon was still comforted by his assumption that the bill would die in the House; even an aide to House Ways and Means chairman Wilbur Mills predicted the amendment would be DOA.

But then fate interceded. In New York City, Jackson and Perle met a semiretired shoe manufacturer named David Hermann who knew both Mills and Mills' aide, since he frequently went before Mills' committee to testify about foreign imports. Perle asked Hermann if he could help them out with Mills, and, after a lengthy briefing by Perle, Hermann phoned the Ways and Means chairman while Perle waited back at his hotel. When Hermann called, he said, "I want you to hear this." He put Mills' secretary on the phone and she read a statement by the chairman endorsing the Jackson-Vanik amendment.

Perle was stunned. "How did you do it?"

"Oh," Hermann said, "I put aside all that stuff you told me. I said to Wilbur that during the Hitler period we stood by, and this may be another case. We have to get these people out."

The amendment, attached to a trade law, finally passed both houses in December of 1974 and was signed into law in January of 1975. The Soviets did everything they could to circumvent the restrictions but eventually conceded the inevitable exit of much of its Jewish population.

But nothing could end the animosity among Kissinger Jackson and Perle. During the 1976 presidential campaign, in which Jackson was a candidate, then vice president Nelson Rockefeller told a private audience in Georgia that communists might have infiltrated Jackson's campaign. Rockefeller specifically accused Dorothy Fosdick and Richard Perle of harboring communist sympathies, claiming that Fosdick had once served as Alger Hiss's chief assistant at the 1945 UN conference in San Francisco, which, in itself, was true. When Rockefeller's remarks became public, the furious Jackson wired

Rockefeller: "The remarks attributed to you are obviously false and malicious. I demand an immediate apology. Dorothy Fosdick has been an outstanding public servant for 30 years. You have apparently made a general accusation against another staff member with the result that you have impugned the integrity of every member of my staff."

Rockefeller refused to apologize, proffering the dubious claim that because he made his remarks off the record, they did not exist. He wired Jackson: "I have made no charge, so there is none to be withdrawn." Jackson and Perle suspected it was Rockefeller's old buddy Henry Kissinger who was behind the remarks. As columnist George Will wrote, "The most likely explanation of Rockefeller's exercise in slander is that he is serving his former servant Henry Kissinger, who is known to resent Dickie and Richard as he resents all of the few remaining pockets of independent foreign policy judgment in government."

Finally, amid rising pressure to either back up his statement or back down, Rockefeller apologized to the Senate and to Jackson in an address to the full Senate on April 27, 1976. Jackson responded, "On behalf of me and my staff, this is the end of the matter." There would be no statement from Kissinger, who, in one of his autobiographies years later, grudgingly conceded that the Jackson foreign policy shop had been both formidable and effective. "Jackson had carefully studied Soviet strategy and tactics; he was convinced that their goal was to undermine the free world, that any agreement was to the Soviets only a tactical maneuver to bring about our downfall. He proceeded to implement his convictions by erecting a series of legislative hurdles that gradually paralyzed East-West policy. He was aided by one of the ablest—and most ruthless—staffs that I encountered in Washington."

From time to time, either Perle or Jackson would pull Kissinger's beard from afar, usually in an op-ed column or on a television talk show. Once, as then-secretary of state Kissinger was returning from an African trip, he read a piece by Perle accusing him of refusing to officially protest a decision by Turkey to allow overflight rights to Soviet aircraft during the Yom Kippur War. When Kissinger demanded an explanation from Jackson, the senator allowed his aide to respond. After a furious exchange of memos, Kissinger complained to Perle, "We have reached an amazing state of affairs when *a Senate staff member* [emphasis added] can accuse the Secretary of State in writing not only of having acquiesced in but conniving in the transit of Soviet arms across the territory of a NATO ally."

Despite the failed smear campaign, it was Scoop Jackson, Dickie Fosdick, and Richard Perle who would have the last laugh. When dissident extraordinaire Alexander Solzhenitsyn visited Washington, Kissinger and President Gerald Ford refused to admit him to the White House out of fear of offending the Soviets. Jackson set up his own reception in the Capitol. Solzhenitsyn and Jackson walked arm in arm up the Caucus Room to the applause of senators and congressmen, and when the most prominent survivor and chronicler of the gulags later visited Jackson's office he asked through his interpreter, "Where are the staff who are working on this?" Jackson pointed to Fosdick, Perle, and their colleagues. Solzhenitsyn then asked for a favor. His former chauffeur and director of a fund for the families of prisoners, Alexander Ginsburg, was in trouble. "They are hounding him and I'm afraid they are going to get him," Solzhenitsyn said. "They will either finish him off in some way or send him to Siberia." He then asked the staff to arrange to have Senator Jackson call Ginsburg in the Soviet Union. Since the phones were bugged, the author wanted the KGB to hear that Scoop Jackson, the scourge of the Kremlin, was personally inquiring about his friend. Then, he believed, they would back off. Dickie Fosdick phoned so many times that within a week all of Moscow knew that Comrade Ginsburg was being paged by Senator Henry Jackson. Ginsburg got out eventually and joined Jackson on the campaign trail during the senator's 1976 run for the presidency. For both the émigrés and those who made their dream possible, Jackson-Vanik was a gift that kept on giving.

The effect of its passage made Perle realize that policy decisions had human consequences, that arguing noble intentions in the abstract and seeing flesh and blood results were two different things. Sadly, in light of events that would not occur until thirty years had passed, it was a lesson unlearned. "With most of the things you work on legislatively it's impossible to connect with real people. But with Jackson-Vanik, real people came out of not just the Soviet Union but other countries," Perle said. "We had a woman in our office who, full-time, collected information on people who had applied for visas and had been denied. Occasionally, people would wind up in the U.S. and come by to say hello. In this case, there were real people whose lives were saved."

"So, there was a touch of Schindler in this?" I asked.

"There was a touch of Schindler."

In a moving tribute to Jackson after his death in 1983, Perle wrote, "The Jackson-Vanik amendment would not go away. Instead, the Soviet Union went away. The amendment remains. The new leaders of Russia cling to their most-favored-nation status and have access to credit. However, if they ever attempt to shut the doors to emigration, both the credits and the MFN would be withdrawn. America has leverage over how Russia treats its citizens. That's what Scoop Jackson would have wanted. That is his legacy."

And to Richard Perle, *that* was winning.

IV.
EXILE ON MAIN STREET

OF COURSE RICHARD Perle believes Scoop Jackson would have made a great president. The what-ifs are intriguing. Had Senator John Kennedy not changed his mind about his running mate in 1960, a spot he had led Jackson to believe was his, a string of permutations and possibilities would have unspooled. But Jackson hid his disappointment by telling everyone who would listen that Kennedy had made the right move and would not have won the election without LBJ on the ticket.

Jackson ran twice for his party's nomination, getting swamped by the McGovern Death Wish in '72, and the post-Vietnam, post-Watergate trauma that produced Jimmy Carter in '76. The country looked at Henry Jackson and saw an old-time pol, a man who could be First Uncle. He wore off-the-rack suits from a Capitol thrift shop and pounded away at such off-the-rack themes as bigger defense budgets and less reliance on welfare.

Perhaps Jackson could have been repackaged and sold by a media Merlin like Roger Ailes waving his wand, but Perle doubts it. "During the campaigns there was talk about coaching him in various ways, but we all kind of gave it up. He had a few supporters in Hollywood who were eager to do that, but I don't think he ever went along with it."

For the two dreary years of the Ford presidency, Jackson and Perle maintained a holding action against the continuing détentism emanating from the White House and the Kissinger State Department. They had a key ally in Defense Secretary James Schlesinger, who shared Jackson and Perle's belief that the Soviet Union had embarked on a massive arms buildup that was being ignored by State and the NSC staff.

In November of 1974, Ford and Leonid Brezhnev concluded an agreement that imposed ceilings on some classes of missiles but not on the heavy ICBMs that were the Soviet specialty. Nor did the so-called Vladivostok Agreement, which was a prelude to a SALT II Treaty, address the Russian's new Backfire bomber, or allow the United States to produce unlimited numbers of cruise missiles of various ranges. Schlesinger, bucking his own boss, joined Jackson in opposing the deal, and together they helped to shelve a Senate vote on ratification for the rest of Ford's presidency. For his insubordination, Schlesinger was fired and replaced by Ford's staff coordinator, Donald Rumsfeld, who, to the pleasant surprise of Jackson and Perle, turned out to be more of a hawk than Ford had bargained for, as was Ford's new chief of staff, Dick Cheney.

While Jackson always gave Perle a much longer leash than any staffer would normally get, there were a few occasions in which the senator had to reign in his top dog. One time, for example, Perle appeared on *Face the Nation*, hosted by Martin Agronsky, and opined that Congress was so underwhelmed by Ford's initiatives that the president would do well to "be more careful with foreigners who drink vodka." The president did not take kindly to Perle's smart-ass remark and registered his strong objection to Jackson directly. After praising Ford's integrity and character, Jackson defended Perle, saying his remarks "cast no unfavorable reflection on the President and were made in a light mood." Still unaddressed was the issue of just how significantly the Soviets were rebuilding and expanding their forces and the motivation for such a buildup. The CIA, which is responsible for publishing the National Intelligence Estimates (NIE), which deal with such matters, refused to accept the premise that there was any buildup in the first place. That left the hawks frustrated. Hard-liners from yet another presidential advisory panel, the President's Foreign Intelligence Advisory Board (PFIAB), had been leaning on Ford to appoint an outside committee to review intelligence on the Soviets and draw its own conclusions. They saw the agency as infested with liberals who had grown comfortable with détente and were too lazy and too timid to look for evidence that did not come from their usual sources.

Some believe the liberal tag was hung on the CIA during the Watergate scandal, when the agency refused to cooperate in the cover-up. Whatever the case, dislike and mistrust of the CIA is not confined to the neocons. Lieutenant Colonel Lawrence Wilkerson, a longtime military intelligence officer and former chief of staff to Secretary of State Colin Powell, told me, "I never met anyone in the military, in any service, who thought the CIA was worth a damn. I once heard it characterized to a navy four-star as 'a bunch of old farts who sit around the world in the capital cities reading newspapers and reporting it back as finished intelligence.' And that's the kindest thing I ever heard about the CIA. During the first Gulf War, Schwarzkopf and Powell got so mad at the CIA that if they could have blown it up they would have."

The CIA's former chief of clandestine operations for Europe from 2001–2005, Tyler Drumheller, has heard all this before. "What they really hate is that we're the one group that comes in and says, 'No. What you're saying is bullshit. We have sources that say the opposite.' It drives them crazy."

To be sure, the members of the PFIAB were no friends of the CIA or of arms treaties with the Soviets; they included the ubiquitous Edward Teller, Claire Booth Luce, and Seymour Weiss, a longtime State Department operative and friend of Albert Wohlstetter. In a State Department memo by Weiss marked "Top Secret/Sensitive," Weiss described Paul Nitze as being so despondent over the terms of the original SALT agreement, terms Nitze felt gave the Soviets a dangerous first-strike advantage, that all he could offer were nightmare options:

Paul sees three possibilities for offsetting actions:

1) We might develop an effective first-strike capability of our own;

2) We might change our doctrine to one of 'launch on warning.' This has always been contrary to US strategic doctrine, but he acknowledges we could be forced into adoption of such a policy if our land force becomes as vulnerable to first strike as seems theoretically possible; and

3) We could abandon all land-based forces and move entirely to sea.

The traction for an ad hoc intelligence panel to produce an alternate NIE had been created by a provocative 1974 essay in *Foreign Policy* titled "Is There a Strategic Arms Race?" by Albert Wohlstetter, who concluded there was none because the United States was not competing. Trumpeting the same theme, PFIAB chairman Leo Cherne told the House Intelligence Committee, "Intelligence cannot help a nation find its soul. It is indispensable, however, to help preserve the nation's safety while it continues its search."

President Ford initially rejected the experiment after objections from CIA director William Colby, but relented after replacing Colby with George H.W. Bush who had no qualms about the so-called independent review. Bush, in fact, checked off the decision box on the authorization memo and wrote, "Let it fly!"

Of course, for such a review to have any meaning, those conducting the review should be as free from bias as humanly possible. Otherwise, the analysis will simply be skewed from a different vantage point, and the recipients will be substituting one set of biases for another. Nevertheless, when the panel, dubbed Team B to distinguish it from the CIA's Team A, began its work in the summer of 1976, it featured a cast with a decidedly starboard tilt: cold warriors William Van Cleave, General Daniel Graham, Paul Nitze, and young Paul Wolfowitz, whom Perle pushed for a spot on the panel. This group could hardly be considered dispassionate observers, nor was the group's chairman, a Harvard professor named Richard Pipes. Pipes, a Polish émigré whom Perle had introduced to Scoop Jackson and who had testified against the SALT Treaty at the Senate hearings, was a professor of czarist history with no background or training in strategic military affairs. He had published several papers on what he believed to be the true and ominous intentions of the Soviets, and they were just what Jackson, Perle, and their friends believed the president needed to hear.

If the panel was supposed to reflect an unbiased, objective view, no one apparently explained that to Pipes. "That was not the purpose," he told me. "We were to be a *counterpoint* to Team A. In other words, the authorities said, 'We are getting the same story all the time from the CIA, that the Russians share our view of nuclear weapons as a deterrent and so on. Let's get another group who have a different view, give them access to all of the evidence and see what they come up with.' So, this was deliberate. We were not to balance Team A, but come up with the strongest possible argument to prove they are right or they are wrong."

To no one's surprise, Team B produced not an independent analysis but a harsh critique of the CIA's findings, concluding the agency had shamefully underestimated the Soviets' military spending and had misread their intentions. Considering that Team B was working off of the same data that the CIA/Team A had, it appeared that one side or the other had constructed a parallel universe, a completely different picture drawn from the same information. In dramatic, if not overblown, prose, Team B's classified report declared that the Soviet economy was expanding, and with it, military spending to more than triple what the CIA was estimating. The report also claimed the Russians were making progress with a particle-beam weapon that could be used in a space-based missile defense system, and might have developed a submarine that could not be detected by sonar. (The panel explained that its failure to produce evidence of such a sub was a strong indication that it was probably out there somewhere.)

The bottom line: The Soviet Union believes it can fight and win a nuclear war.

I asked Richard Pipes whether Perle had taken part in Team B in any way. "No. This was a very secretive outfit and we did not discuss our work with anyone." But Perle, asked the same question, replied, "I knew everybody on the team so I was aware of their findings. And my sense is the report had real impact because it was very carefully done and persuasive." It was so secret that key portions of the report were leaked to the press in an effort to ratchet up defense spending and give President

Ford an issue he could use in his bid for election. "They were leaking all over the place," said one angry CIA official.

It was not enough to save Gerald Ford's presidency. Jimmy Carter moved in and ignored the tradition of carrying over the CIA director into the new administration, and also ignored Team B's conclusions. Perhaps it was for the best. Almost two decades later, following the collapse of the Soviet Union and the gradual release of once-secret Kremlin data, analysts discovered that not only were Team B's alarming conclusions mostly wrong, but even the CIA's more cautious estimates were far too cautious. The data indicated that the Soviet economy began to fall apart at about the same time Team B had taken up its analysis, and that Soviet defense spending had remained largely flat from the mid-seventies to the mid-eighties. They also found that Team B's guesstimate of Backfire bomber production had been overstated by half, that the facility allegedly building a particle-beam weapon was actually the site for tests on a nuclear-powered rocket engine, and that the infamous disappearing submarine had never appeared in the first place.

The B-Teamers might have noted as a caveat of sorts the strange defection of Viktor Ivanovich Belenko in October of 1976. Belenko flew his top secret MIG-25 Foxbat to an airstrip in Hakodate, Japan, and requested political asylum. The Foxbat had been billed by the Pentagon as a superplane that could hit Mach 3 and take out multiple targets simultaneously. But U.S. intelligence experts who took the plane apart before returning it to Russia were surprised to discover how poorly constructed it was. The wings were shriveled, hand welds were exposed, and rivets were not ground flush to reduce drag. Belenko complained he could not hit Mach 3, that the engines would explode first. Even at Mach 2.8, the Foxbat's engines would overheat and the missiles carried under the wings would vibrate dangerously. It had some impressive features, but it was not a superplane and thus not a superthreat.

To this day, Perle refuses to believe that Team B was a stacked deck with a biased view. "The critics argue that if you can inflate the threat you could argue for a bigger defense budget. I don't think Team B was part of that. In my experience the threat inflation came from the military. You just never met a commander who said he had enough to do his mission. You just always want more; it's as simple as that."

Even the mounting evidence that, in hindsight, the CIA's estimates of Soviet strength were a lot closer to the truth than Team B's does not mollify in the slightest Perle's dim view of the intelligence committee in general and the CIA in particular. "Albert Wohlstetter made a trip to Iran at around that time," Perle says, speaking of the period of protests against the shah of Iran before he eventually fled in January of 1979. "Before he left he ran into [CIA Director] Stansfield Turner and said, 'I'm going to Iran. Do you have a good man there?' And Turner said, 'A first-rate guy.' And Wohlstetter says, 'What's his name?' And Turner says, 'I'll have to get back to you.' Okay, so he didn't know the guy's name. But it turns out the first-rate guy in Tehran had been there for about three weeks after having been in Japan for four years. He was an expert on Japan but could not speak a word of Farsi. He knew nothing about the Gulf. And this is the guy we parachute in there in a moment of crisis?"

Although the Team B conclusions were filed away for posterity, just days after Carter's election, a group called the Committee on the Present Danger (CPD), which had been formed by some of Team B's members during the summer of '76, published its first manifesto, warning the new president that the Soviets had embarked on an arms buildup "reminiscent of Nazi Germany in the 1930s" and that unless the United States was prepared to spend plenty it would succumb to a "Communist World Order." The signatories included Richard Perle, Paul Wolfowitz, and thirty-one others who would find work in the Reagan administration. But for the next four years, they would have to contend with James Earl Carter, who did not take kindly to advice on foreign policy or much else.

Just weeks after the inauguration, Carter, whose victory in the Pennsylvania primary had knocked Scoop Jackson out of the race, invited him to the White House to discuss the still-unratified SALT II Treaty bequeathed to him by the Ford administration. Following the meeting, Jackson and Perle composed a twenty-three-page, single-spaced memo on the treaty's flaws, blaming the Nixon and Ford administrations for trying to win a deal for its own sake and allowing the Russians to set the agenda and the timetable. The memo included the Jackson-Perle version of what an acceptable treaty with the Soviets should look like, and concluded, "An unsound agreement now could make it difficult or impossible to obtain one later."

Carter sent copies of the memo to his secretaries of state and defense, Cyrus Vance and Harold Brown, and put his copy in a safe in the Oval Office. He said he would refer to it from time to time, trying to figure ways to get Jackson the kind of deal he wanted. In fact, Carter did try to make nice with Jackson, such as retaining hard-line and hard-headed General Edward Rowny, a Jackson favorite, as the Joint Chiefs' representative on the U.S. SALT II delegation, where he was widely assumed to be acting as a spy for Jackson and Perle. But, according to Perle, the Carter-Jackson relationship was neither close nor warm, and the causes went beyond policy differences. Governor Jimmy Carter had often expressed his disdain and disrespect for the Democratic presidential candidate in 1972, George McGovern. Then, after McGovern won the nomination, Perle remembers that Jackson received a phone call from Carter at 4 a.m. asking whether Scoop would talk McGovern into picking Carter as his vice president.

"Scoop could hardly believe his ears," Perle said. "Carter had spoken of McGovern with nothing but contempt, yet now he was willing to overlook all that in the hope of being selected. Whatever respect Scoop had for Carter went out the window with that call. Scoop could never think of Carter again without a certain feeling of revulsion."

But what really got under Jackson's skin, according to Perle, was Carter's appointment of Paul Warnke to head the Arms Control Agency. Warnke was the personification of everything Jackson and Perle loathed about the liberal approach to arms control, which was, in their minds, appeasement and accommodation. Warnke came out of the Clark Clifford school of diplomacy, which made him a "realist" in the crude labeling system of the media. The fact that he was a supporter of SALT and the arms control process was distasteful enough for Jackson and Perle, but an essay Warnke had written in 1975 titled

"Apes on a Treadmill" was the straw that broke the ape's back. Warnke characterized the United States and the Soviet Union as a pair of plodding, small-minded creatures stuck on a treadmill, making no progress toward what should be a common goal of nuclear arms reduction and a safer, more secure world. It was no surprise that Warnke dismissed the Jackson-Perle memo to Carter as "a first-class polemic." As the author of such an essay, he would know the genuine article when he saw it.

"Scoop and I found that essay truly offensive," Perle told me. "There were differences between the United States and the Soviet Union, and the arms race that Warnke believed was the fundamental problem was in fact not the product of mindless behavior by the United States nor was it simple, reciprocal imitation. It was much more complicated than that. So, the appointment of Warnke really shook Scoop up and he decided to fight."

Adding to Jackson and Perle's frustration was their belief that even if a substantive conversation with the president resulted in agreement on an issue, the Carter staff was incapable of following up and obtaining the desired result. "I remember him saying to me that Stu Eisenstadt [Carter's domestic policy advisor] was about the only person in the White House whom he had any confidence in."

Relations between the president from Georgia and the senator from Washington reached a breaking point in an incident involving Perle and the receipt of classified information. In 1977, a CIA analyst named David Sullivan compiled a report based on classified information that he believed confirmed numerous violations of existing arms treaties by the Soviets. The report was supposed to be published by the CIA in both long and short versions for government analysts and high-level policy planners. But Sullivan's superiors were so displeased with the report's conclusions, and were demanding so many revisions, that Sullivan feared it would never see the light of day. Sullivan vented his frustrations to Admiral Zumwalt, who told him to see Richard Perle, because Perle would understand the importance of the material and had the necessary security clearances to read it. Sullivan demurred, saying he feared going outside the agency. But after attending a CIA seminar on Soviet behavior at which Perle spoke, Sullivan approached Perle and mentioned his paper. According to Jay Winik in *On the Brink*, Perle looked Sullivan over and replied, "It sounds very interesting. I'll order a copy once it's published. Let's keep in touch."

Months later, Sullivan invited Perle to his home in the Virginia suburbs, where he handed Perle a copy of the report, which he had hidden in his trunk under a pile of books. Perle says he took the copy to Room 407 of the Senate office building, where classified information is stored, and had it logged in. But not before reading it. "Yes, I read it," he told me. "And I had the appropriate security clearances. Now, there was a CIA policy of which I was not aware that required an approval...on what level I'm not sure...before CIA material could be disclosed to senators or to Senate staff. But I wasn't governed by that policy; David Sullivan was. I just knew he was giving it to me so that if a decision was made to pulp the study there would be a copy. Of course I told Scoop about it immediately. He needed to know what was in there."

Among other things, the report detailed that the Soviets' SS-19 ICBM had been willfully designed to violate the SALT II Treaty and that work had already begun on a new high-tech radar facility that would be the centerpiece of an ABM system, also a violation of the ABM Treaty. Summarizing, Perle told Jackson the Sullivan report showed that not only were the Soviets cheating on existing treaties, but that they would agree only to new deals in which their developing weapons programs could proceed unencumbered while America's were restricted. "They were giving us nothing. Zero. We were accepting restrictions on various programs, but they always made sure that whatever they agreed to was consistent with a program they already had in the works."

The decision of how to use the material became moot when Sullivan came up for a routine polygraph test required of CIA employees. He told Perle he didn't think he could bluff his way through the questioning, and Perle told him, "Do what you have to do." When the polygraph technician asked Sullivan if he had ever disclosed information without authorization, he replied, "Yes," and then revealed what he had done.

In the ensuing brouhaha, Sullivan was not only fired by CIA director Stansfield Turner but vaguely accused of causing the death of a CIA double agent in Moscow, a false charge that would hound him for years.

Not satisfied with Sullivan's head, Turner demanded to see how Scoop Jackson would discipline his aide Richard Perle. When Turner arrived in Jackson's office and began wagging his finger about Perle, Jackson said, "If you want to talk about Richard, let's bring him in."

"So I walked in and Turner got all flustered," Perle recalled. "He was hemming and hawing and finally he blurts out what David Sullivan had done and that he'd been fired. And then he turns to Scoop and says, 'Frankly, I think it would be appropriate if you took similar action.' Scoop listened to what he had to say and then he replied, 'Mr. Perle is responsible for keeping me informed. He has the appropriate clearances. He stored the document in the appropriate manner. So I have no intention of firing him.' And that was the end of the meeting."

When Turner left, Jackson and Perle looked at each other and laughed. "Turner said I got dressed down for this, and that's not true." As for David Sullivan, Perle made sure he had a parachute, fixing a job for him on the staff of Texas senator Lloyd Bentsen, a move that further enraged the CIA director.

This was not the first time that Perle had been accused of either accepting or supplying classified information. A decade earlier, while still fresh on Jackson's staff, Perle was told he had been picked up on an FBI wiretap discussing classified information with someone inside the Israeli embassy in Washington. This story has been repeated as gospel over the years and still can be found on Google searches regarding Perle. But Perle claims he never knew about a wiretap, was never approached by the FBI or anyone else, and has never disclosed classified information to any unauthorized party.

"I first heard it from Sy Hersh," Perle said, referring to the investigative reporter who would become a constant irritant to Perle over the years. "He was writing a book on Kissinger and he wanted my cooperation. He believed I must have some dirt on Kissinger and he wanted me to help him. I said, 'I don't do that sort of thing.' And he said, 'Let me give you an incentive.' And he read to me a short statement that said that according to the Senate Foreign Relations Committee, Perle was revealed in a wiretap discussing classified information with someone at the Israeli embassy. And he said, 'If you don't cooperate, I'm going to put that in the book.' It was out-and-out blackmail."

The item does, in fact, appear in Hersh's *The Price of Power*, but the source is not attributed. Hersh did not respond to phone queries about this episode. In any event, no one questioned Perle about the alleged tap at the time, and no one has since.

"I make mistakes," Perle told me, "but I'm not stupid. If I were illegally discussing classified information, which I wouldn't do, I certainly wouldn't do it on the telephone."

Episodes such as the David Sullivan affair and the FBI wiretap that might or might not have happened, as well as Perle's penchant for leaks, raise the question, Would Perle be favorably disposed toward breaking the law if the outcome was, to him, a morally correct one? "That's a tough question," he replied. "Are we talking about international law?"

"United States law. It's interesting that you make the distinction."

"Yes, because there's no proper adjudication of issues in international law. It doesn't have the institutions surrounding it. So I can imagine taking action in a case where lawyers are divided, where it's a judgment call, which it invariably is in matters of international law. But on domestic law, if it says you can't do something when you're an official and you can't get the lawyers to help you find a way to do it that's legal, then I think you just don't do it."

According to Michael Krepon and Dan Caldwell's excellent collection of essays, *The Politics of Arms Control*, the single most effective organization inside the Washington Beltway opposing the SALT II Treaty was the Committee on the Present Danger, whose genesis was the 1969 ABM study group organized by Albert Wohlstetter and Paul Nitze, for which Perle and Wolfowitz had been recruited as researchers. Throughout the Carter years, the CPD flooded the airwaves and congressional hearing rooms with talking heads, distributed hundreds of thousands of pamphlets, and wrote reams of op-ed pieces hammering away at the treaty's perceived flaws. Members also formed ad hoc groups such as the American Security Council and the Coalition for Peace Through Strength. The Carter administration had spent so much political capital on its narrow victory on the Panama Canal Treaty that it had little left for the even more important fight over SALT II.

At one point, the administration decided to lay aside the treaty as negotiated by Nixon and Ford, and present the Soviets with what it called a "comprehensive proposal" calling for deep cuts in strategic forces and major concessions by the Russians on human rights. But because Carter, through secretary Vance, had sprung the proposal without prior warning or consultation, and because of its heavy emphasis on human rights, Moscow rejected it without discussion, insisting instead that the agreed-upon treaty be ratified.

In March of 1977, the CPD published its first pamphlet, *What Is the Soviet Union Up To?* from the predictable pen of Richard Pipes. The screed was basically a rewrite of the Team B conclusions, still technically classified, but which had largely been leaked to the press. It concluded once again that the Soviets were aligning their economy and their forces to fight and win a nuclear war. Months later, the committee publicly blasted the administration's new proposals even after the Soviets had rejected them. Leading members of the group, including Paul Nitze, Eugene Rostow, Jeanne Kirkpatrick, and Zumwalt, each received telegrams from Defense Secretary Harold Brown conveying the president's displeasure and inviting them to the White House to talk things over. From all accounts, the sit-down was a disaster, as guests left complaining that no amount of arguing could convince Carter that the treaty was a loser. As Rostow put it, "Carter just did not realize whom he was dealing with. He was McGovernism without McGovern."

The CPD and its offshoots had no counterparts in favor of the treaty, save for some religious groups such as the Southern Baptist Convention and the church of the Reverend Billy Graham. A pro-treaty group called

Americans for SALT got its act together too late to have any real impact on the debate and could not muster the funds or the clout of the opposition.

With the treaty all but dead, the Soviets themselves hammered the final nail in the coffin by invading Afghanistan in 1979. This flagrant act of aggression forced the White House to withdraw the treaty from consideration. Coupled with Carter's famous "malaise" speech, in which he essentially told the American people that *they* were largely to blame for at least some of the nation's ills, and gasoline lines across the country from a shortage contrived by Big Oil, it reinforced the image of Jimmy Carter as a wimp of the first magnitude.

Carter's supporters point out that during his presidency defense issues were not ignored. The Minuteman III ICBM had been "hardened," or made less vulnerable to nuclear blasts; a new submarine-launched ballistic missile, the Trident I, had been deployed in Poseidon submarines; B-52s had been revamped with cruise missiles; and work had begun on the Stealth bomber, a project not made public until 1980. Critics pointed to the cancellation of the B-1 bomber and the neutron bomb, a slowdown of the Trident submarine program, and the closing of the country's only ICBM production line. And if those critics needed an exclamation point on their indictment of the Carter administration, it came on November 4, 1979, when the U.S. embassy in Tehran was seized by supporters of the Ayatollah Khomeini, a humiliation that lasted for 444 days for America and its hostages.

Richard Perle recalled New Year's Eve 1978, when Carter and the shah clinked glasses in Tehran, and Carter praised Iran for being "a beacon of stability" in the Middle East. "During the cold war, a succession of administrations persuaded themselves that the Soviet threat was so overarching that we had to choose the lesser of two evils when we aligned ourselves with countries opposed to the Soviet Union. These were moral compromises, and we continue to make moral compromises. But Reagan didn't want to be seen clinking champagne glasses with Gorbachev; he was not ready to toast a Soviet leader."

Perle and his compatriots had gritted their teeth, held their noses, and bided their time through the Nixon, Ford, and Carter years, and they knew that as Jimmy Carter flew from California back to Plains, Georgia, on Election Day eve 1980, he would not fly over a single state he would carry the next day. Perle himself would vote Republican for the first time in his life.

He believed the time had come for America to prove to the world that it was more than a superpower in name only. All it would take was a president ready to pull the trigger.

V.
REVOLUTION

IN JULY OF 1977, Richard Perle married Leslie Joan Barr, then a staffer to New York's senior senator Jacob Javits, a member of an endangered species then as now: the liberal Republican. Barr is what Frank Sinatra would admiringly call "a real broad," a tough, no-nonsense woman with the street smarts one would expect from Barry Levinson's Baltimore. Her mother was a conservative homemaker who did not see the need for her daughter to go to college. Her father was a butcher who had been wounded in the hand at the Battle of the Bulge. Among the gifts he gave his daughter was a love of education and a love of food. His favorite expression was, "I may not be able to tell you every place I've been in Europe, but I can tell you what I ate when I got there." Their neighborhood, like many in the 1950s and early '60s, was a true melting pot where everyone gossiped and everyone knew their neighbors' business. That alone made Leslie Barr insist on attending college anywhere, anyplace but in Baltimore. She chose Simmons, a small women's school in Boston, where she majored in economics. As the first generation of her family to attend college, she had no fixed goals other than finding the best-paying job she could upon graduation.

Although politics did not play a role in her formative years, she, like many young Americans, was inspired by John F. Kennedy and the civil rights movement. But it was happenstance, not patriotism, that led her to the campus recruitment table run by the Central Intelligence Agency. The head spook gave her a test in which she was asked to decipher a made-up language in which the key is picking up patterns of letters. For instance, if many words end in "GZT," one may assume the word is a gerund ending with "ING," and so on. Although Barr had no ear for language, she did have a keen knowledge of grammar, which made the test easy for her. Her degree in economics perhaps led the CIA to put her on the desk responsible for monitoring trade to Eastern Europe and the Soviet Union, an area that would be of great concern to her future husband. Although Barr is matter-of-fact about where she first worked, attorney Howard Feldman, who has known the Perles for some thirty years and is still a close friend, expressed shock when I asked him if he knew.

"*What?*" he said after a long pause. "The CIA? I didn't know that. See, you never really know about your friends." Barr stayed at the agency for two and a half years, then moved first to a staff job on President Nixon's Council of Economic Advisors and then to research director for the Javits reelection campaign. With the campaign over, she decided to earn an MBA at the Columbia University Business School in New York.

Another friend of Perle's, Stephen Bryen, who was working for New Jersey senator Clifford Case, knew Barr was going through a divorce and encouraged Richard to take her out. Because Perle was too shy to make the overture, Bryen arranged for the two to be invited to the same party. Considering that Barr had been separated for only six weeks, the instant romance surprised her.

"He was really smart," she told me. "And we found we had an equal passion for food. I was raised on it. I had started cooking in my apartment when I was working for the agency. I cook by the book. I read the recipe and I follow it and it turns out perfectly. Richard is much more instinctive." Barr commuted from New York to Washington to spend time with Perle while she was earning her MBA, attending without a break for sixteen months.

Their wedding was held at Howard Feldman's newly purchased house in Chevy Chase, Maryland, and featured A-list guests: Scoop Jackson as best man, Congressman Les Aspin of Colorado, columnist George Will, AFL-CIO president Lane Kirkland, Perle's evil twin Robert Novak, Bernard Lewis, Paul Wolfowitz, former defense secretary Jim Schlesinger, General Ed Rowny, a balalaika band made up of Russian-Jewish émigrés, and a group of native Alaskans. "Howard was doing some legal work for Alaska," Perle recalled. "And late in the evening some of his clients had come. Intuits? Is that what they're called? Anyway, they all jumped in the pool. Schlesinger ended up in the pool too. Rowny was playing his harmonica and they were singing old socialist songs. It was a Fellini wedding."

Their son, Jonathan, arrived two years later, just as the Carter administration was in its last throes. At first, Perle was somewhat aloof around the baby, a reaction his wife had predicted. "I knew he would not have an affinity for an infant. But as soon as Jonathan became verbal, their relationship changed." A story that has been repeated endlessly in the press and on the Internet has Perle teaching his son to name the countries of the world, and instructing him to say "the bad guys" when pointing to the Soviet Union. Neither Perle nor his son recall anything even remotely like that, and for Mrs. Perle, it is just another example of why she rarely speaks to reporters. "There was a story in *Regardie's* magazine that said I went on a shopping spree while on an official trip with Richard to Tunisia. I just went berserk. I called Howard Feldman and said, 'I'm suing.' He asked, 'Why?' I said because that plane ended up in Tunisia but Richard and I had gotten off in Paris. I'd never been to Tunisia in my life. It just burns me up." Being the wife or son of Richard Perle would take some getting used to. "A lot of people ask me what it's like," said Jonathan, now a New York City attorney. "They really don't believe it. I've had some view me as the devil." Once, a girl he was dating decided to Google the name "Perle" and was somewhat shocked at what she read. "It took a little explaining to convince her that he does not, in fact, have horns."

As Scoop Jackson's go-to guy, Perle worked an eighty-hour week but found time for most of his son's major events, including the double-overtime championship basketball game that Jonathan's first-grade team lost. "Richard was there for the whole thing," Mrs. Perle said. "Was he there for the other ten games of the season? Probably not."

Leslie did not want her husband globetrotting for a senator or for anyone else in government; it was now the eighties, time for Richard to stay closer to home and make some real money. For about a year, Perle worked as a partner for a company owned by John Lehman, an old friend who would become Ronald Reagan's secretary of the navy. The company, Abington Corporation, was an international consulting firm that put buyers and sellers of technology and information together. Perle's salary and profit-sharing put him in the low six figures, a quantum leap from his pay as a Senate staffer. He recalls a trip to Paris with Lehman in which they had dinner with Lehman's cousin, Princess Grace of Monaco. "I remember two things: one, how beautiful she was, and two, how I picked up the check for one of the richest women in the world."

A Style section piece in the *Washington Post* at that time waxed poetic about the Perles' new $120,000 kitchen: two sinks, two dishwashers, fifty-five linear feet of butcher block kitchen counter, handmade oak cabinets, a restaurant-sized gas stove, four ovens, a gas grill with its own flue, and "enough copper pots and pans to cause a penny shortage."

"We had five linear feet of kitchen when we lived on Capitol Hill," Perle gushed. "So this is an improvement."

Perle's first clients for Abington were the Israeli arms merchants Shlomo Zabludowicz and his son Chaim, whose company, Soltam, Ltd., was trying to break into the U.S. market. Shlomo Zabludowicz was just the sort of man Perle idolized, a Polish Jew who walked out of Auschwitz with his wife, wearing only rags, and who within five years was the managing director of one of Finland's largest industrial companies. After starting Soltam in Israel, he came to Washington to try to accommodate some export license regulations and was introduced to Scoop Jackson. Jackson asked Perle to look into Shlomo's problem, and their relationship was born. Soltam paid Perle $50,000 and sent another $90,000 to Lehman's firm, a portion of which went to Perle. The money was channeled through Tamares, Ltd., a tiny company based in London and owned by another Zabludowicz son, Pojo, who is said to be worth several billion dollars. In addition to owning one of the world's finest collections of contemporary art, Pojo also owns a half dozen casino-hotels in Las Vegas and has been dubbed part of the Kosher Conspiracy an effort to influence foreign governments to support Israel.

Perle's interregnum in private life also included an effort that resulted in a U.S.-supported military coup in Turkey. The Soviet invasion of Afghanistan in 1979 raised concerns about stability in the region, particularly about the viability of NATO. That year, Perle's mentor Albert Wohlstetter organized a meeting in Istanbul to discuss with Turkish officials making Turkey a "U.S. staging post for Middle East contingencies and as a strategic ally of Israel." The options discussed at this meeting, which Perle attended, laid the groundwork for General Kenal Evren's 1980 coup, and the eventual establishment of Turgut Özal's pro-American Turkish government. In an article written two decades after the coup, Perle declared it was justified because the government had failed to restore order or to control "the rise of terrorism and widespread, random violence." It was later revealed that the coup had at least some assistance from the CIA; a note from NSC staffer Paul Henze to President Carter reading, "Our boys did it!" arrived just moments after the overthrow.

Perle would later go to work for Özal, after urging him to hire people who could effectively lobby for Turkish interests in Washington, to offset the clout of the Armenians and other anti-Istanbul groups. Strangely, an actor portraying Perle appears in a film released in Turkey in the spring of 2007 titled *Zincirbozan*, after the military camp where deposed politicians were sent after the coup. The Perle character is shown plotting political murders in the days and weeks before the junta makes its move, and meeting secretly with Özal to plan the post-coup elections. Perle himself finds it "inconceivable" that the CIA had any involvement in fomenting the violence that led to the coup since the government that was overthrown was not unfriendly to the United States.

For Özal, Perle had nothing but admiration. "I met him in 1981 in Istanbul on a trip with [Caspar] Weinberger," Perle recalled. "He was deputy finance minister at the time. And I remember saying to Cap that I had met this remarkable man, Özal, at a lunch, and that he was going to run the country some day. And he did. And whenever he came to Washington outside of his official schedule we would get together usually late at night in his hotel suite and talk until two or three in the morning. He was just full of ideas." Those ideas included a Turkish arms buildup that Perle would aid and abet in the early nineties after leaving government.

The lure of a new, like-minded administration began to play on Perle's ego and his imagination. He was recruited onto no less than three Reagan transition-team groups: State, Defense, and Export-Import bank. This was one of the opportunities that played to Perle's strength: his ability to place those who shared his views in positions that mattered. For more than a year, Perle had been part of a good-old-boy network that met every other Friday for lunch at the Madison Hotel. They were mostly top staff aides to conservative senators and congressmen including John Tower, Strom Thurmond, Jake Garn, Gordon Humphrey, and Malcolm Wallop. Money for the lunches and trips for the group was provided by the benignly titled Institute for American Relations, a tax-exempt entity formed by John Carbaugh, an aide to Thurmond and Jessie Helms. The Madison Group, as it came to be known, would plot ingenious ways to thwart their dovish counterparts, and blue-sky about the potential of a Reagan administration.

"It wasn't a collaborative organizational structure," Perle said. "It was an occasional lunch. I gave my views on some things and listened to what people had to say." Most of those in the group would end up on the Reagan transition team, and then as part of the administration. After Lehman was nominated as navy secretary, Perle pushed for Paul Wolfowitz, Elliott Abrams, and Mike Rashisi for major jobs in the dreaded State Department; Perle's friend and arms control mentor Fred Ikle was already ensconced at Defense, so the pieces were falling into place. While ideological opponents saw a dark conspiracy in this spreading network of like-minded bureaucrats, the fact is virtually everyone who lands a job of any import in Washington is part of some sort of cadre—political, ideological, fraternal, or social. Perle simply worked the connections better than most. "He's one of the few people I've known in or out of Washington," Michael Ledeen told me, "that when he tells you he's going to do something that is the *minimum* something he's going to try to do. He'll always try to do more."

Douglas Feith, whom Perle had hired as an intern, added, "There are people who are on the receiving end of networks and people who are on the giving end, and those on the giving end are like godfathers. And Richard for sure is a godfather. He would actively work to help anybody he had worked with and liked and admired and who he thought was useful to the overall cause of U.S. national security as he saw it. He would exert himself. He would send your résumé to people. He would call. So he had a tremendous number of people who felt grateful to him."

If gratitude was what Reagan's new secretary of state, Alexander Haig, thought he would receive when he offered Perle a job as under-secretary, he was mistaken. Perle had been tipped that the offer was coming, and both he and Jackson thought it would be an awful idea. Haig's personality was not a good fit for Perle, and the State Department was not his sandbox of choice. He told the general he preferred to remain in the private sector. Haig said he understood but was said to be outraged that Perle had turned him down. His outrage was Leslie Perle's delight; she had made it clear she wanted her husband out of government for good.

"I came home and told Leslie," Perle said. "She was ecstatic. And we thought that was the end of it." But weeks later, Perle was offered a post at the Pentagon, one closer to his area of expertise but apparently not close enough. He passed on that job as well. "I told them the job included things I'm not interested in and doesn't include the things I am interested in. It just wasn't the right job. So then they asked me to describe the right job." What Perle sketched out was a job that didn't exist: assistant secretary of defense for international security policy, a bit much for the marquee but just right for his needs.

Perle's decision was made easier by a blow-up in 1981 between him and John Lehman over the future of Abington. Perle understood that he would take over the company after Lehman was nominated for secretary of the navy, but Lehman decided to sell his interest, cutting Perle out. The two have not spoken since. That left the Department of Defense (DOD) spot and its $67,000 salary as Perle's only immediate venue. But, as is his wont, he moved aggressively to carve out jurisdiction on issues that were important to him, like export licensing of technology, an arcane field that traditionally had been the purview of the deputy director of engineering. "I thought that was a conflict of interest because the person who had that job is invariably the person involved in both promoting and controlling the sale of American technology," Perle said. "So, I took a run at that and it was resisted, as you can imagine. In the end, I went up to the deputy secretary, Frank Carlucci, and said, 'You should give me this responsibility because I want it and I'll do the right thing with it.' And he gave it to me. We reorganized the whole thing and set up a unit that became very aggressive in restricting exports. Now, I lost some battles, particularly on sales to Iraq. But my focus was on the stuff going to the Soviet Union. And that activity was set up under Steve Bryen, who was pretty tenacious in all of this. He did a great job."

In keeping with both his loyalty and his defiant nature, Perle's first major act, choosing Stephen Bryen as his deputy, was controversial not because Bryen had introduced the Perles to each other but because of Bryen's reputation. In March of 1978, Dr. Stephen Bryen, then a staffer on the Senate Foreign Relations Committee, was allegedly overheard at the Madison Hotel Coffee shop near the Capitol offering classified documents to some top Israeli officials, including a man identified as the Mossad station chief in Washington. The documents concerned the pending sale of F-15 fighter aircraft to Saudi Arabia, and included the locations where the aircraft would be based. The eavesdropper and whistleblower turned out to be a former executive director of the National Association of Arab Americans, who recognized Bryen as a Senate staffer. Bryen, who denied the allegation, was ousted from his job but went to work as executive director of the Jewish Institute for National Security Affairs (JINSA), one of the most aggressive lobbies in Washington. The Justice Department's lead investigator in the Bryen case failed in his attempt to impanel a grand jury when the Foreign Relations Committee refused to grant access to files needed by the prosecution. It also didn't hurt Bryen that the chief of the Justice Department's Criminal Division, Philip

Heymann, was an old schoolmate and fellow Supreme Court clerk of Bryen's attorney, Nathan Lewin.

Despite his past, and with Perle lobbying hard, Bryen received both top secret clearances, SCI (Sensitive Compartmented Information) and NATO/COSMIC (Control of Secret Material in an International Command). Perle knew the Bryen appointment would make his own nomination hearings even more difficult than they would have been in the first place. But he sat there and defended his friend, telling the senators, "I consider Dr. Bryen to be an individual of impeccable integrity. I have the highest confidence in his loyalty, patriotism, and character."

"What they put him through was awful, horrible," Perle told me. But it would not be the last time Bryen would end up in hot water over classified information. Perle's loyalty to friends caused him more trouble during his first year at the Pentagon, when he wrote a nasty note to army secretary John O. Marsh, Jr., on behalf of his old friend Shlomo Zabludowicz and his Israeli arms company, Soltam, for which Perle had lobbied before his DOD appointment. Zabludowicz had complained that the army was not giving him a fair shake on a contract for mortars, choosing a British company that Marsh was more familiar with. Perle was convinced that Marsh was simply using Soltam to make it appear that the bidding was competitive, and opposed Zabludowicz because he was friend of Perle's. "I am familiar with the documented and systematic suppression of the Soltam mortar, undertaken in the last administration to shield the UK from competition, [and] because the Soltam marketing organization was a client of mine." After much back-and-forth, the army concluded that the British deal was better when results were balanced against costs.

Because Perle received his payment for his original lobbying work on behalf of the Zabludowiczes after taking his Pentagon job, it appeared to some that he was representing a private company while holding a government job—a possible conflict of interest. Records show that while working for Lehman, Perle had retained his security clearance as a Senate staffer and was still being carried on the Senate payroll as a non-salaried worker. Nevertheless, an investigation by the Office of

Government Ethics found that Perle's work for the Zabludowiczes had indeed taken place before his confirmation as assistant secretary, that his 1981 disclosure statement included the payments, and that there was nothing improper in his memo to Secretary Marsh.

Perle's decision to pass up Al Haig's offer turned out to be the right one. The bombastic Kissinger pupil lasted a little more than a year in the job. He complained repeatedly of damaging leaks coming out of the Defense Department, and Richard Perle was frequently his top suspect. "Haig only lasted a year because he was not sufficiently deferential to the president, and the president didn't like that," Perle said. "Haig had to win every time, and he didn't. And he often lost because Reagan just didn't agree with him. And Al Haig found that very difficult to take."

By contrast, Perle's new boss could lose, accept it, and live to fight another day. Caspar Weinberger, a patrician lawyer who rarely smiled, always served his client's interest. His nickname, "Cap the Knife," was earned when he cut the budget as secretary of Health, Education and Welfare, but he was not in fact a budget-control freak. He simply understood that his clients, Richard Nixon and Gerald Ford, wanted to cut social programs, and he complied. Ronald Reagan, on the other hand, had pounded Jimmy Carter during the campaign on defense and security issues, and had promised to restore the U.S. military to competitive preeminence with the Soviet Union. That would mean the largest peacetime military buildup in history, and a lopsided battle against the State Department for Reagan's heart and mind. It mattered not a whit that Weinberger had no experience whatsoever in military or defense issues; he could take a policy directive and fight like hell to make it happen.

As an assistant secretary, Perle saw his main function as protecting his man's turf and "watching his six," as fighter pilots say. And this was more turf than Perle had ever grazed upon: a $300 billion budget and all the ships at sea. The immediate enemy was just across the Potomac in the person of his counterpart at the State Department, Assistant Secretary Richard Burt. The contrast between the two policy warriors was stark: Perle was short and paunchy and looked casually dressed even in a business suit. Burt was tall, dark, and handsome and looked every inch the Brahmin in his carefully tailored designer clothes. A product of the Fletcher School of Diplomacy and the International Institute for Strategic Studies in London, Burt had written a seminal study of the implications of the cruise missile while in his twenties. He first met Perle when he was a correspondent for the *New York Times* in Washington during the Carter years. It was not the job he wanted and he told Perle just that.

"Richard lived on Capitol Hill at that time," Burt recalled, "and I remember going up to his place for breakfast. I spent about an hour and a half just listening to him vent. And I realized then that this guy was really wired in, and that he had disaffected sources within the Carter administration. So he became a really good source for me."

Perle ended up doing more than that. When the Reagan team moved in, Burt received a phone call from Al Haig asking for a meeting about joining him as assistant secretary. "I was one of the first two or three people Haig hired," Burt said. "And I heard that Richard had had something to do with it."

But it was never too early for Perle to get the drop on Burt, who, throughout the Reagan years, would play Judy to Perle's Punch in behind-the-scenes policy battles. Tales of "the Two Richards," Shakespearean in their tragic-comic elements, were the talk of Washington. Once, when Burt and an aide were leaving the Pentagon after a briefing to the Joint Chiefs, they were stunned to see Perle coming toward them from the river entrance. "I didn't even know he'd been in the building," Perle laughed. "And there he was with these huge charts on an issue we had been quarreling about. And he turned bright red *because I could see all of his charts!*"

Burt's description of their relationship is one of contrasting philosophies in service of a common goal. "I represented not only the school of realism but also of greater continuity in U.S. foreign policy," Burt told me. "Richard, in that sense, was a radical and I wasn't. Richard was pursuing what he thought was in the national interest and I was as well. This is one of the differences between conservatives and neoconservatives, or realists and utopians. Richard is a Wilsonian with combat boots. He's one of those neocons who migrated from left of center to right of center and took that kind of utopian, ideological agenda with him."

Typical of their more substantive conflicts was an episode that began during a trip to Europe by Burt and his new boss, Secretary of State George Shultz. The Europeans were on edge because of the pending deployment by the United States of Pershing missiles among the NATO allies, and the administration was taking heat at home for being too hawkish. In a moment of inspiration, Burt suggested to Shultz that he propose a worldwide ban on chemical weapons. This way, the administration would appear less trigger-happy, and Shultz would get the credit.

"I was pushing to send signals that, hey, we *do* support arms control and we *do* look for agreements," Burt told me. "So, yeah, I sold Shultz on the chemical weapons thing." When news of the proposal hit Washington, Perle knew he had to work quickly to thwart any traction the move might gain in Congress; looking like wimps was the last message he wanted to send to the Europeans and, especially, to Moscow. He knew that the Russians would never agree to unannounced, on-site inspections of their warehouses and laboratories that any chemical weapons ban worth anything would require. So he had his aide, Douglas Feith, draw up a "killer amendment" to the proposal that would mandate draconian verification and force a "nyet" from Moscow.

"It was the height of cynicism," recalls Perle's friend and most-of-the-time ally Kenneth Adelman of the Arms Control Agency. "But two things need to be said about that. First, the Soviets *did* go along with it, later, under Gorbachev. And second, the United States and the Joint Chiefs would not. So this was a case of Richard outsmarting himself because we couldn't and Gorbachev could. The chemical industry said, 'We're not going to have Soviet inspectors looking through all our stuff.' So, we ended up proposing something that the other side could buy and we couldn't."

That was of little consequence to Perle; the proposal died, and that was that.

"Let me be clear," Perle told me. "I would not be above a killer amendment. But in this case, the inability to verify compliance was the killer."

In *Hard Line*, Perle's autographical novel, his character, Michael Waterman, describes his feelings about his counterpart, Daniel Bennett (obviously based on Rick Burt). "At first, Waterman had contempt for Bennett's ostentatious style and extravagant wardrobe. But he'd learned from experience that while Bennett's Savile Row suits, bold-striped Turnbull & Asser shirts with white collars and cuffs, floppy breast-pocket handkerchiefs and antique cufflinks gave him the look of a dandy, the man was a talented and deadly infighter who used the system, as well as his influence with the secretary of state, to full advantage." The memory makes Burt laugh. "The only goddamned thing about that book was that the supposed Burt figure is essentially a duplicitous traitor. I mean, I had people tell me, 'God, Rick, you ought to sue.' But thank God nobody read that book."

"I certainly don't think of Rick Burt as a traitor," Perle said with a broad smile. "Was he capable of duplicity? Of course! We all were in various situations."

Of all the secretaries of state who crossed Perle's path, perhaps the only one who thought of him without fear and loathing was George Shultz. But their relationship did not begin on a positive note. On their way to a meeting in Geneva with Soviet foreign minister Andrei Gromyko, Shultz had told his team, which included Perle from the DOD, he would not tolerate any press leaks. There were to be no conversations with reporters without Shultz's approval. Yet, Perle spent some of the flight to Geneva standing in the aisle at the rear of the cabin deep in conversation with author and journalist Dan Oberdorfer. The two were just whiling away the long hours of the flight, but when word of their chat spread up front to Shultz's cabin, the secretary was not pleased. The delegation checked into the Intercontinental Hotel and Perle decided to nap since he had not slept on the plane. He had just dozed off when his phone rang; a summons to Shultz's suite, and pronto. Perle, having no clue as to the reason for the demand, pulled himself together, took the elevator up, and walked into the secretary's massive living room. He was alone save for a huge confection of Swiss chocolate sitting on a table. It was a reproduction of a Swiss village, and Perle spent the next forty-five minutes staring at its roof and salivating. Finally, Shultz walked in with his NSC advisor, Robert "Bud" McFarlane in tow.

"He began by saying, 'I'm inclined to send you back on the next flight,'" Perle told me. "He said, 'I gave very clear instructions that there were to be no discussions with the press and you were seen talking to Don Oberdorfer.' I said, 'I was indeed talking to Don but not a word about anything to do with this. I never interpreted your injunction to mean we couldn't talk to the press about anything. Had I understood that, I would have honored it.'" Shultz let Perle off the hook with a stern warning. He knew the assistant secretary would have to be kept under close watch, given his reputation for making up his own rules and wandering off the reservation. But before his first sit-down with Gromyko, Shultz came to understand why Richard Perle was so important to have on one's side when dealing with the Soviets. This was January of 1985, the tail end of the so-called Brezhnev stagnation. Yuri Andropov had come and gone, and now Konstantin Chernenko was playing out the string of old men the Soviets would spotlight in the May Day parades. Gromyko was one of those old men, a lion in winter; there was no reason to believe his attitude and demeanor at this meeting would be any different than it had been for at least the past twenty-five years. So, each member of the American delegation was asked to give Shultz his views on what to look out for with the cagey Gromyko, and how to keep the talks on the U.S. agenda and not on the Russians'. When it came to Perle's turn, he calmly told Shultz, "It is highly likely that at some point in the discussions, Gromyko will threaten to walk out. My advice is: let him walk. He almost certainly will be bluffing. He doesn't want a failed meeting. He'll take a very tough position, but he doesn't want a failed meeting."

As though scripted, Gromyko indeed threatened to walk and Shultz threatened to let him. "I'm prepared to sit here until we reach a solution," the secretary told the foreign minister. Gromyko sat back down. On the plane ride back, Shultz summoned Perle to his cabin. According to Perle, the secretary told him, "I'd heard a lot about you before this mission and none of it was complimentary. And we got off to a rocky start. But I want you to know I think you did a terrific job." Perle replied that he was immensely flattered. Shultz also admitted that he and others believed Perle was the source of an embarrassing leak about strategy Shultz might employ for the Gromyko meeting. But, Shultz added, he had since discovered the source and knew that Perle was innocent.

The secretary added, "You were a team player and my door is always open to you. I want to know what you're thinking." Back in Washington about a week later, Perle's secretary buzzed to say the secretary of state was on the line. "So I get on and Shultz says, 'I'm waiting and you haven't come to see me.' So I guess he really meant it." Indeed in his autobiography, *Turmoil and Triumph*, Shultz writes of Perle, "The air had been cleared and our relations proceeded amicably. Increasingly, I found Perle one of the most creative and reliable thinkers on arms control matters."

Those matters would soon take a surreal turn in March of 1985 with the ascension of Mikhail Gorbachev; for the first time in history the leaders of both the United States and the Soviet Union publicly declared a goal of a nonnuclear world and claimed to mean it. The notion was at once thrilling and troubling as its implications spread to matters far beyond the scope of national security. When Ronald Reagan would speak of his dream, those around him would usually nod in solemn approval while thinking that the old man was still back in Hollywood. Richard Perle thought the idea was lunacy but was too deferential to characterize it as such in public. In private, such as during the meetings of the Senior Arms Control Group, an interagency free-for-all where Perle was always at his tactical best, he would describe it as "a disaster, a total delusion." After one such contentious meeting, Paul Nitze sidled up to Shultz and told him, "The idea of a nonnuclear world has to be ventilated, but I don't know whether we can keep Richard Perle in line. It's good to talk to him; it's good to have him on our side, but it's just as important to stand up to him at times." When Reagan received a letter from Gorbachev calling for the elimination of nuclear missiles, Perle told Shultz, "We must not discuss this as though it was serious. The worst thing in the world would be to eliminate nuclear weapons." Shultz laughed and replied, "You've got a problem. The president thinks it's a *good* idea."

When the returns are all finally in, Ronald Reagan probably will be the most dissected and deconstructed president since Abraham Lincoln. Most of the biographies written so far have wrestled with the question, How much did he know and when did he know it? The shorthand, never stated publicly, being, Was he as lazy and ill informed as he often appeared to be, or was he a kind of homespun savant who relied on an internal pendulum that swung at the mention of any issue the American people favored or opposed? In the end, it might not have mattered; Ronald Reagan was determined to do what Ronald Reagan wanted to do. His motives remain fodder for the historians.

In the context of confronting the Soviet Union, these questions took on a particular urgency. Gorbachev's arrival triggered a deluge of press stories speculating that the more youthful and better-educated Soviet leader, unbound from the ideology of Stalin, Khrushchev, and Brezhnev, would be too nimble and too sophisticated for Reagan. But for Perle, all the handwringing was both irritating and amusing: Meet the new boss…same as the old boss. He had seen this setup before, just a few years earlier with the KGB-produced campaign to promote Andropov as a new, urbane, cosmopolitan, and therefore friendlier communist leader, even if he was the former head of the KGB. "Andropov was sold as a scotch-drinking, Western-oriented liberal," Perle said. "He was nothing of the sort. Whether he liked jazz or not I don't know and don't care. But there was a deliberate campaign by the KGB to humanize Andropov because they understood perfectly well that it was not a good thing to have someone who was feared as the successor to Beria as head of the country. No one who was in a senior position at that institution was likely to be friendly."

If Richard Perle was concerned about Reagan's ability to deal with the Soviets, he kept it to himself. "Reagan was very sophisticated," he told me. "He wasn't stupid. I think he saw things more clearly than I did." Whether this remark is Perle showing respect for a much-beloved president, or genuine awe at Reagan's prescience, is difficult to judge, especially considering Perle's frequent characterization of Reagan's no-nuke vision as "a total delusion." As for Gorbachev, Perle saw an adversary who had spent a goodly amount of time pondering great questions only to come up with the wrong answers. "He believed in communism and thought he could fix it. He wanted to fix the shortcomings of the communist vision, which is why he was focused on technical things like decentralizing. But the unspoken part was, How do you decentralize and still maintain control? He was out to save a system, not dismantle it."

But the particular concern for Perle and the players on his side was not Gorbachev's public pronouncements of a new, peace-seeking Soviet Union but Ronald Reagan's vision of a world free of nuclear weapons. Part of the Reagan legend was his 1979 visit to the NORAD missile warning facility in Cheyenne Mountain, Colorado. The trip had been arranged by a Hollywood screenwriter friend of Reagan's, and Reagan had invited another friend, economist Martin Anderson, to join him. Anderson, an unabashed Reagan worshipper, described the visit as an epiphany for the California governor. When their tour guide, air force general James Hill, explained to Reagan that because the facility had been designed in the 1960s, the current Soviet ICBMs could not be stopped if launched, "a look of disbelief came over Reagan's face." Apparently, this was the first time it had occurred to the president-to-be that there was no reliable defense for incoming missiles. Anderson then claims that it was his memorandum to candidate Reagan proposing development of a missile defense shield that set in motion the Strategic Development Initiative, or Star Wars, program that became the centerpiece of Reagan's overall foreign policy. As author Frances Fitzgerald points out, why Reagan would listen to what an economist had to say about nuclear missile defense is a mystery, especially since his memo is filled with so many mistakes regarding terminology and plausible systems design that he was "clearly talking through his hat."

Nevertheless, the very idea of a missile shield guarding the "shining city on a hill" had obvious appeal to Reagan; it was a simple idea he could sell. Aiding and abetting the exercise were former B-Teamers Edward Teller and Dan Graham, who were busy flooding the Defense Department with proposals for fantastic weapons that would require billions of dollars with very little chance of a meaningful return. Teller's rhetoric was especially preposterous; he warned Reagan in one memo that the Soviets were ready to deploy "powerful directed energy weapons to militarily dominate both space and the earth." Despite Teller's fantasies, his opinions carried great weight in political circles, especially among those whose knowledge of science was minimal at best. Teller and his followers would be joined by Perle acolyte Frank Gaffney, from the old Scoop Jackson team, who became such a relentless advocate for the missile shield idea that even some of his friends and colleagues consider him "out there."

"I'm not a rocket scientist," Gaffney told me. "I'm not an engineer or a physicist. I don't know the answer to the question of what exotic technologies might be brought to bear. But my sense of technology and the extraordinary capability of this country is that it will be." Gaffney remains a believer despite more than two decades and $100 billion of research that has produced no significant results. Even with the benefit of hindsight, Gaffney refuses to concede that Reagan's infatuation with SDI was misguided or that the long list of skeptical scientists was correct after all.

Wolfgang Panofsky was on that list. He was the father of the Stanford Linear Accelerator, one of the major nuclear facilities in the world. The German-born physicist had moved to the United States with his family in the 1930s, and later made his reputation as a researcher and professor at Caltech. During the McCarthy era, Panofsky resigned from the faculty at Berkeley after refusing to sign a loyalty oath. He settled at Stanford and was the driving force behind the funding and building of the accelerator. When the idea of a missile shield, created by orbiting weapons systems capable of firing beams of energy at missiles in flight, first appeared in the press, reporters, including this author, sought the opinion of the elfish scientist known affectionately as "Pief."

"I do not believe in it," he had told me back then. "The weapons must have sensors to track the missiles and it is too easy to spoof them, to trick them. Simple aerosols can do it. And you cannot use laser. Laser cannot see through clouds…the beam is dispersed." While not responding specifically about Panofsky, Perle once told me he mistrusted both intellectuals and scientists because, in his view, they lived in "a dream world." "Physicists are notorious. Einstein? Einstein was a wild man when it came to practical politics. He didn't have a clue. Carl Sagan, who I clashed with on several occasions…these guys were not dealing with the same world I was dealing with. I was dealing with some very tough, aggressive Soviets who had objectives that were not good for us and were prepared to use whatever it took to accomplish those goals."

For reasons still debated, Reagan decided to announce his plan for the shield that would make nuclear missiles obsolete as an insert to an otherwise routine speech. This momentous announcement was never cleared by the Pentagon. In fact, one of Perle's close friends recalls that Perle and Weinberger were at a NATO meeting in Portugal when the defense secretary received a copy of the speech the night before it was to be delivered. "Cap handed it to Richard and said, 'What the hell do we do about this?' And Richard and Weinberger agreed that it was extraordinary lunacy." Although Weinberger and Perle were advocates for the program, they knew that Reagan's sudden announcement, without prior warning to NATO's defense ministers and foreign ministers, would be a diplomatic disaster, engendering opposition needlessly. They needed more time to brief the allies and assure them that SDI would be a stabilizing force. Perle telephoned Shultz's deputy, Lawrence Eagleburger, who also weighed in for a delay, but neither State nor Defense was successful in postponing the announcement. America's allies would hear about Star Wars when the rest of the world did.

"Even the *New York Times* believed it," Fitzgerald said. "I took it seriously too, because I would wade through those press accounts and congressional hearings where senators appeared to be taking it seriously. I mean if anybody had said, 'This king has no clothes....' it might have been different." But few, except for those crazy scientists and the Joint Chiefs, were saying that at the time. Indeed, Admiral James Watkins, the chief of naval operations and a member of the JCS, said, "We never believed in the umbrella. What we said was that if you could confuse the Soviets there would never be a first strike." Of course, the military brass would oppose a system like SDI, because it would detract from the gold-plated weapons systems that each service branch wanted. Spending billions on a "maybe" system was not as appealing as buying more fighters, bombers, tanks, and aircraft carriers. But Richard Perle soon saw SDI as the Soviets' worst nightmare. He knew they were in awe of American technology, of the America that had sent a man to the moon. And so what if the system didn't work quite the way the president envisioned it, or maybe didn't work at all? In the time it would take for the Soviets to figure that out, they just might conclude that their huge ICBM arsenal had been rendered useless and just might agree to dismantle it in exchange for the best deal it could get. This, of course, was a penultimate-case scenario.

"The Reagan conception of SDI was protection for the country as a whole," Perle said. "I knew that was a very long way away. In order to defend the whole country, you need a degree of reliability that seemed far from achievable to me. What was technically feasible, in my view, was a more modest defense of our ballistic missiles. What you need to do is put up a barrier so that the number of weapons it would take to destroy our retaliatory capability would be so large the Soviets wouldn't be able to do it."

But selling Congress and the public on an expensive high-risk system that might protect only missile silos was a political improbability, even for a president as popular as Reagan. No, the more extravagant vision was the one to push, except for a nettlesome detail: the ABM Treaty, signed by Nixon and Brezhnev in May of 1972, and ratified by the Senate three months later. The conventional interpretation of the treaty was that it banned both sides from constructing any missile defense system beyond the one conventional site already permitted, the argument being that, in theory, a powerful and effective defense might allow one side to attack the other without fear of reprisal. Negotiations had taken place in great secrecy with little or no consultation with the Departments of State or Defense, or of Congress. In that, it was fairly typical of the manner in which Nixon and Kissinger preferred to do business.

Richard Perle hated the ABM Treaty. Not only did it place suffocating limits on U.S. technology, but it was also sure to be violated by the Soviets. That, Perle believed, was their modus operandi: agree only to deals that handcuff the other guy while proceeding with whatever strategy they chose. They would find many ways to cheat, such as introducing a new weapons system while claiming there was nothing new about it, just an upgrade of what was permitted by whatever treaty was in place at that time. As Perle saw it, the United States had only three options in dealing with the ABM Treaty: (1) abide by its terms, knowing the Soviets would not; (2) find some new way of interpreting the restrictions; or (3) simply walk away from it, announcing that because of Soviet noncompliance, the United States was no longer legally obligated. Naturally, Perle favored this third option, brushing aside objections that such an abrogation would seriously damage American credibility in future treaty negotiations with any friend or foe. But he was astute enough to know this was a step Ronald Reagan was not yet prepared to take. The president wanted to be known for creating something, not tearing something down and walking away. Since the first option was unacceptable to Perle, he knew he had to concentrate on the second: finding a way to parse the treaty's terms so that SDI could survive, if not as a real, nuts-and-bolts system, then as a kind of mirage the Soviets could see but not touch. His task was given a major push when Shultz's State Department brought in a former U.S. District Court judge named Abraham Sofaer to review the now thirteen-year-old treaty and rule on what it said. Sofaer had no practical experience whatsoever in international law, arms treaties, or weapons systems. Nevertheless, he divined that the treaty probably allowed research and development of SDI, but not deployment, making the entire endeavor pointless.

Undaunted, Perle and Fred Ikle, director of the Arms Control Agency, decided to bring in a lawyer of their own. They chose Philip Kunsberg, a sharp, former assistant district attorney in New York who had made his bones prosecuting mafia types, drug dealers, and pornographers. Kunsberg had worked his way up the ladder at the Defense Department and was working as counsel to Ikle. Perle told Kunsberg to take a week off and study both the treaty and the background notes of the negotiations and report back with his interpretation. Of course, Kunsberg had as little practical experience with arms control treaties and international law as Sofaer had, so at least it was a fair fight.

To Perle's astonishment, Kunsberg came back with a verdict that it was the Soviets, not the Americans, who wanted no restrictions placed on the development of space-based defensive systems. Apparently, Moscow had wanted to keep its options open, so no decision on the subject had been written into the treaty. Research, development, and deployment of exotic laser or particle-beam weapons, which did not exist at the time but which were envisioned at the time the treaty was drafted, would be permitted, at least as Kunsberg saw it. Perle was ecstatic. "You could have knocked me over when he finished that report. What it certainly did not say, as the State Department was saying, was that systems based on other physical principles were banned. Paul Nitze saw it and even he agreed with it." This was the kind of ace in the hole that Perle could really operate with. But unfortunately, it did not remain in the hole for very long. On a peaceful Sunday morning while all this was being thrashed about, the unpredictable, thrill-a-minute National Security Advisor Bud McFarlane appeared on *Meet the Press* and, in a response to a simple question about SDI and the ABM Treaty, proceeded to give a lengthy, highly detailed answer that said, in essence, that it was the position of the U.S. government that SDI could go forward toward deployment while staying within the boundaries of the ABM Treaty.

Perle, sitting calmly at home, was blown away. "He blurts this out? He says, 'Yeah, it's all right under the Treaty'? All hell broke loose. A NATO group was meeting in San Francisco and this headline comes across saying the U.S. says it can do whatever the hell it wants, and suddenly you've got a big international crisis." Indeed, Congress, the allies, even the negotiators had been blindsided. It was left to George Shultz to put a temporary lid on the erupting volcano by publicly announcing that although the United States recognized the "broad" interpretation of the treaty, it would continue, for now, to abide by its traditional letter and spirit.

But the SDI/ABM dilemma was only part of what Perle was confronting in the weeks and months before the first major summit meeting between Reagan and Gorbachev, scheduled to start in just a few weeks in Geneva in November of 1985. The other pressing issue that would end up being linked to SDI was the defense of NATO. As the Soviets continued to deploy their large SS-20 intermediate-range missiles targeted at Europe, the United States was ready with a response in the form of the Pershing II; more than one hundred of them were scheduled to be installed throughout Western Europe, over the protest of no-nuke marchers and the Soviets themselves. Moscow insisted that a balance of intermediate-range nuclear forces (INF) existed between NATO and the Soviet Union, and that deploying the Pershings would not only upset the balance but cause Moscow to escalate its SS-20 deployment.

Not long after joining the Reagan team in 1981, Perle was assigned to draft a response to the Soviet intermediate-range missiles aimed at Europe that would not further rouse the antinuke movement, which was having an effect on governments in Bonn, Paris, and London. The Europeans were in a bind, politically sensitive to the mounting call for disarmament but frightened of bolting from beneath the American defense umbrella. The origin of the famous proposal that resulted is in some dispute. Some historians point to a West German peace group as having first outlined it; others say that Fred Ikle was its father. In any event, after examining how many nuclear weapons the Soviets actually needed to destroy critical installations in Western Europe and realizing that the number was far lower than either he or anyone else had expected, Perle extrapolated until the lightbulb went off in his head: zero.

While the idea may have been spawned elsewhere, it was Perle who proposed what came to be known as the INF zero option, which would eliminate all Soviet intermediate-range ballistic missiles in Europe in exchange for the United States not deploying its Pershing IIs. After all, the Soviets had publicly said they were in favor of arms reductions, and the ban on Pershing deployment would erase their claim of imbalance. The Europeans would be off the hook with the peace movement and would still retain their own missiles for deterrence. And the United States not only would save the cost of having to deploy their new missiles but would come off as the peacemakers in the bargain.

Predictably, the zero option was ridiculed as utopian and unrealistic by the buttoned-down Council on Foreign Relations and, privately, by more than a few naysayers from the State Department. Naturally, they included Richard Burt, who declared that the Soviets would never buy into the deal unless the United States showed some flexibility. Burt, anxious to get his side into the game, came back with a proposal he called "zero plus," in which both sides would be permitted to keep a small number of missiles in Europe, some number less than 100 but greater than zero. So, once again the Kabuki of the Two Richards would become the backstory behind the official posturing. And once again, as Burt proposed, Perle disposed, with Reagan siding with zero and announcing it at a speech to the National Press Club that was beamed to Western Europe. The response in Bonn and London was mostly positive; the response from Moscow was the Russian equivalent of a Bronx cheer. Still, Rick Burt managed to leak zero-plus to the press, making it seem as though the U.S. position had more than a little give to it.

"I'm not sure that there was any arms control agreement that he could have lived with," Burt said of Perle. "What he really disliked was not so much the technical differences—whether they had more of this or we had more of that—but the political symbolism that would have grown out of these agreements, the idea that, hey, maybe these Russians aren't so bad after all. Maybe we can do business with them. That's what he couldn't stand." Complicating matters further was Perle's one-time mentor and now part-time meddler Paul Nitze, who had a tendency to wander off on his own during negotiations with the Soviets, trying to broker deals like a freelancer. Nitze's "walks in the woods" with his

Soviet counterparts were seen as dangerously arrogant on Nitze's part, regardless of how well-intentioned they might have been. Whenever Nitze felt his own people, particularly Perle, were being unreasonable, his ego would overrun his authority. When news that he and Soviet negotiator Yuli Kvitsinsky had agreed on an Intermediate Nuclear Force deal written on a scrap of paper during a walk in Switzerland's Jura Mountains in 1982, a deal neither man had any authority to make, the blowback was fierce and included a reprimand from the president. To associates, Perle described Nitze's proposed deal and the way he had gone about it as "an act that signaled premature retreat and of political and intellectual cowardice." After listening to Nitze's arguments and explanations, Reagan decided to stick with Perle's zero option even though the Soviets already had rejected it.

So there they all sat...INF, SDI, and ABM, the trifecta that would frame the first negotiation between Reagan and Gorbachev. It would also be Perle's first summit, and he knew he had to heed Scoop Jackson's warning to stay focused and not get caught up in the frenetic back-and-forth. "There is a tendency as people go into negotiations to lose sight of what they were trying to achieve," he told me, "because they want an agreement. Sir Samuel Hoar served in the British government and was with Chamberlain in Munich. In his diary he wrote, 'We got caught up in the negotiations and after a time the objective became an agreement.' If your objective is an agreement, you will get one, because in the immediate aftermath of an agreement, there's a kind of euphoria. And that was something Scoop and I thought we needed to be scrupulous in avoiding. The problem exists all the time. But in a summit, it's on stilts."

VI.
AT THE SUMMIT

BY TRADITION AND protocol, summits are State Department shows; they plan them and they run them, with theoretical input from other departments and agencies. This input is aired in interagency meetings in which participants attempt to browbeat one another into arranging not only the issues to be raised by the president but also who goes on the trip and what role they are supposed to play once there. In the weeks prior to the Geneva summit of November 1985, there was more than the usual push-me-pull-you among the administration's capos regarding the agenda, the manifest, and the positions to be taken and held. The presumptuous freelancing by McFarlane and Nitze already had created an impression in the press that Reagan's people were not in sync, and that the more nimble wits of Gorbachev and his foreign minister, Eduard Shevardnadze, would prevail.

Secretary Schultz traveled to Moscow shortly before the summit to take the temperatures of both Shevardnadze and Gorbachev. As described in his memoir, Shultz found the foreign minister to be thoughtful and deferential but difficult to read. Gorbachev, on the other hand, was an in-your-face competitor, greeting Shultz with a copy of a think tank compendium of conservative politics called *The United States in the 1980s* and proudly declaring, "I know all about your ideas." Shultz made the mistake of saying that in Ronald Reagan, Gorbachev would be dealing with a president who could deliver on his promises. Apparently, that set Gorbachev off on a rant about the agreed-upon but still unratified SALT II Treaty, which Reagan had nothing to do with. When Shultz pointed out that the treaty effectively died when the Soviets invaded Afghanistan, Gorbachev shot back, "Leave arguments like that for the press. Don't use arguments like Afghanistan. It shows you don't respect us. The U.S. got out of SALT because it didn't want to be constrained by it." As if that were not sufficiently blunt, Gorbachev responded to Shultz's attempt to link arms control and regional issues with "You ought to put that one in mothballs. It's old hat."

But as the conversation progressed, the new-old Bolshevik displayed both his charm and his restless intellect, telling Shultz that the world had left the industrial age and that new countries, new technologies, and new ways of seeing the future would force everyone to reform to ensure that people would be free to express their ideas and challenge the status quo. And, remarkably, he ended with a kind of job pitch to Shultz: "The next time you come to Moscow, you should forget about your government duties and come as a businessman or an economist." Shultz doesn't say whether he called his agent or his broker.

Meanwhile, back at the Pentagon, Richard Perle was busy pushing his charges to come up with galvanizing position papers that Weinberger could present to Reagan as talking points for the summit, all designed to ensure that the Pentagon would have its say. Of course, his opposite in the Bizarro World game between State and Defense, Rick Burt, was busy as well, making sure that the summit would reveal to the world that Ronald Reagan was not a trigger-happy cowboy intent on vaporizing Moscow and that the United States was a reasonable and flexible negotiating partner. But the memo Perle was drafting for Weinberger was not so much advice as it was a warning—in fact, a series of warnings, a litany of don'ts that included such caveats as "Don't commit to any communiqué or other language that enables the Soviets to appear equally committed to full compliance—even as they continue to enlarge their pattern of violations." The message, pounded home from the typewriter of Richard Perle, was: Stick to your guns, don't let them set the agenda, don't make concessions just because they're making concessions; sometimes the best deals are the ones you walk away from. The letter also included a list of alleged Soviet treaty breaches as a lesson in why not to give in on SDI. No matter what you do, say, or agree to, Gorbachev will cheat.

It was vintage Perle, and it would probably have been lost in the shilly-shally of summit planning had it not been leaked to the *Washington*

Post just before the president was preparing to depart. The Weinberger memo set off an inferno, and naturally Richard Perle was suspected as the torch. It was known he didn't want this summit, so this seemed an obvious attempt by him to scuttle the trip. But Perle insisted that the leak could only have come from a recipient in the State Department, someone who objected to the points being made in the letter and who wanted to ensure that Weinberger was portrayed in the press as Rasputin while Shultz came off looking like Disraeli. No one was ever flagged for that violation, but, in keeping with the general theme of grown-ups behaving badly, Perle discovered to his horror that *someone* had switched the president's agreed-upon talking points for the summit away from the issues of concern to Defense and onto those of prime interest to State. Unfortunately, he discovered this while on the backup plane on the way to Geneva, knowing that the president, the secretary of state, and his nemesis, Rick Burt, were comfortably ensconced on Air Force One reviewing the briefing book. Straightening that one out would have to wait until the delegation arrived in the Swiss city.

At the hotel, Perle met with Shultz and reviewed the support role the assistant secretary would play; it wasn't all that Perle wanted, but it was enough. Both men knew that eventually any serious talks would have to come down to SDI, and Shultz made no secret of his belief that the Pentagon had oversold the program, even given the broad interpretation of the ABM Treaty. But Perle insisted that limiting SDI would kill it, and that would be giving the Soviets exactly what they wanted. He felt out-manned and outgunned on the trip, but, as part of the working group that would draft any communiqués, he knew he could not be steam-rolled by State.

Nancy Reagan accompanied the president, and before the talks began, the couple took a tour of the facilities with Shultz, looking for some quiet place where Reagan could work his one-on-one charm on Gorbachev. They found a pool house near the main building that would be perfect, and the fireplace was kept going to provide an intimate venue for a spontaneous-but-planned chat. While Reagan and Gorbachev seemed comfortable with each other, it was Gorbachev who took the gloves off first, countering Reagan's complaints about human rights violations in the Soviet Union with a blistering attack on the human rights record of the United States, beginning, of course, with slavery. It was standard thrust and parry, but once the subject turned to arms control, Gorbachev came right to the point: There could be no arms reduction if the United States went ahead with SDI.

While Gorbachev stayed on the offensive, Reagan scribbled some notes on a scrap of paper, passed it to Shultz, and said, "Have a look at this and see if it makes sense." Shultz passed the paper to Perle, who studied it quickly. It was the president's attempt at a compromise but not, in Perle's judgment, an acceptable one. Fortunately, Reagan did not take the paper back. The session broke up a few minutes later, with both sides retreating to their corners to figure out if there were any areas of agreement that could be exploited. Gorbachev wanted a communiqué, so the delegations stayed up all night arguing over every word, every nuance.

All-nighters were all too familiar to Perle. "In NATO," he told me, "they had a term for this: They called them 'white nights'...*nuits blanches*. At two, three, or four in the morning, as they were making concessions, there were people on our side who wanted to reciprocate with concessions. So I asked for a break," he laughed, "and I said, 'They're making concessions now. There's no reason for you to make concessions.' That kind of pulled us back, and we ended up doing very well."

While Gorbachev had agreed to consider "human rights" issues, his staff refused to put the term in the communiqué, claiming there was no such phrase in the Russian language. They insisted on the phrase "resolving humanitarian causes," which was not acceptable to Perle. "I told the chief negotiator that if you don't have a word for human rights that's your problem. But it won't stop us from dealing with a concept that is understood all over the world." Perle then proposed two versions of the statement, one containing the Russian spin and the other the literal English. This, Perle felt, would be a big victory since the Soviets had never before acknowledged "human rights" as an issue. They agreed to the two versions, but somehow, back in the United States, the State Department's official version was sanitized and did not include the "human rights" phrase. Had Rick Burt struck again?

"God bless him," Perle said sarcastically. The memory had faded somewhat, but it still hurt. "It just shows you the ability of the State Department to snatch defeat from the jaws of victory. I certainly was pissed off, having won the point only to have it thrown back."

But language aside, the summit could be read only one way: Gorbachev did not get what he wanted. He had tacitly, but not formally, agreed to a 50 percent cut in offensive weapons and indicated a willingness to close an INF deal. But he had not won an American pledge linking those concessions to limits on SDI. Perle, of course, was elated. Any doubts he may have had about Reagan's vitality and, most of all, his resolve were put to rest after Geneva. During the farewells, Gorbachev moved down the line, shaking hands with the members of the U.S. delegation. He stopped in front of Richard Perle and just stared at him. This was the man who was "running U.S. foreign policy," along with Cap Weinberger, Gorbachev had once told Margaret Thatcher. Perle extended his hand, but Gorbachev didn't move. "He wouldn't shake my hand," Perle recalled. "He just kind of looked past me so as not to make a scene and so I took my hand back." Before his departure, Perle received a small package, a Russian trinket of sorts, with a pro forma thank-you card signed by Gorbachev. Perle's staff found it so amusing they had the card framed and mounted in his office.

Perle received another warm note from Shultz, praising him for his performance during the all-nighter. The next summit wasn't scheduled for another ten months, so everyone could relax for a while, content in the knowledge that they had gotten through the torturous exercise with no regrets or apologies. In Moscow, Gorbachev's performance was viewed with dismay by many in the Politburo and in the military. With falling oil prices further battering the Soviet economy, and growing unrest in Eastern Europe, Gorbachev desperately needed a win, something he could trumpet to the beleaguered population, something that would ease the economic pressures that were threatening his leadership. He needed to stop the Americans' phantom missile defense program while it was still on the drawing board, so he could justify further reductions in military spending and fund his vision of modern factories and decentralized commerce.

To Perle, Gorbachev's dilemma was exquisite; in the tit-for-tat arms race, any American initiative had to be countered by the Soviets, missile for missile, warhead for warhead. But Gorbachev knew he could not counter SDI, even though he took every opportunity to claim that he could. During one rant at Bud McFarlane, Gorbachev not only challenged reports of a new U.S. interpretation of the ABM Treaty but proved he knew more than the Americans thought he did. "I'm amazed that you would base your judgment on the advice of a lawyer who had previously only had experience prosecuting drug and pornography cases. [How did he know about Kunsberg?] You think you're ahead of us in technology and that you can use these things to gain superiority over the Soviet Union. But this is an illusion!" It was a hollow bluff and Perle knew it. Of course, he also knew it was a bluff against a bluff, which made it all the better. In the weeks before the summit, he had lunch with a friendly reporter from the *National Review* and made his point with a parable of sorts, which he told with great relish:

"Farmer Jones finds he has mice. He tells his wife and they agree to get a cat. The mice overhear this conversation and become alarmed. They form a negotiating team, and the chief negotiating mouse requests an opening round of talks with Farmer Jones. 'There is a need for dialogue,' says the mouse. Finally, the mouse puts his negotiating position on the table: 'If you don't get a cat, we won't get a cat.'"

As the winter of 1986 moved into the spring, it became increasingly clear to the Americans that Gorbachev was not inclined to wait for the next summit set for Washington sometime before the year's end. He sent a letter to Reagan proposing the elimination of all nuclear weapons, starting with the intermediate-range missiles in Europe, tacitly accepting Perle's "zero option." But once again, all the promises were contingent on limiting SDI and adhering to the traditional definition of the ABM Treaty. It smelled to Perle like the usual Soviet grandstanding, making headlines with a dramatic but insincere proposal. Nevertheless, Reagan was heartened by the offer and said he would give it "serious study." What had happened, it turned out, was that Gorbachev was essentially repeating an offer Reagan had made to him in the pool house in Geneva; if we eliminate nuclear weapons, we won't need defenses. Reagan did not recall having made that suggestion, but Shultz found that indeed he had when the interpreter's notes were reviewed.

In August, the Soviets asked for a meeting of "experts" to try to light a fire under the negotiators in Geneva. For Perle, it would mean his first trip to Moscow. While the talks went nowhere, Perle was surprised to find that he was being treated with considerable deference, almost as though the Russians believed that he, and not Paul Nitze, was the go-to guy on the American team. When not on call, Perle would wander the streets by himself, Alice in Neverland. He liked to look into open windows, not out of voyeurism, but for a small picture of the larger society he had never before seen in its habitat. What he saw magnified what he already knew.

"It was clear that this was a poor country. You could see how shabby the furnishings were—bare light bulbs, filthy hallways. It was like a tenement section in the South Bronx. And this was Moscow! This was the best the country had to offer." In Red Square, Perle watched Russian tourists lining up to have their photos taken. For a ruble, the photographer would mail them their picture. It dawned on Perle that the tourists had no cameras because they couldn't afford them. Then he saw a crowd standing in front of a vendor, pushing and shoving to get at whatever he was selling. As Perle moved closer, he saw that the commotion was over frozen pineapple. "And it wasn't high-quality frozen pineapple," he recalled. "It was the leavings from a pineapple processor. They were fighting for an opportunity to buy this stuff that nobody would buy in the U.S."

For Perle, the images reinforced the theory, never publicly stated by the administration, that the United States could simply spend the Soviet Union into oblivion. But he does not believe that strategy was in Ronald Reagan's playbook. "I don't think we ever set out to spend them into oblivion. We were accused of that. Reagan was accused of that. But my view at the time was that Reagan was doing what needed to be done given the fact that he had inherited a strategic capability that was approaching obsolescence. We had old missiles, old aircraft, old submarines, and we were on the verge of the next generation, which was going to be expensive." The capper of his long stroll was his first contact with Russian ice cream, which he had been led to believe was a many-splendored thing. "Believe me," he said, "if you've been to Vivoli in Florence you would not have regarded this as fabulous ice cream." Perhaps to ease his pain, the farewell gift Perle was given by his hosts was four tins of Beluga caviar, his favorite.

In response to Gorbachev's proposed phased elimination of nuclear weapons, which would include removing bombs from bombers, Perle's colleague Fred Ikle resurrected his idea of eliminating just ballistic missiles, whose speed made them the most dangerous part of the nuclear arsenal. This way, the Russians couldn't claim that SDI would make a first strike by the United States viable. Ikle had actually framed that proposal in an article he had written a decade earlier during the Nixon administration. Perle and Ikle recruited their Geneva negotiator Max Kampelman, who had angered just about everyone by trying to free-lance, a la Nitze, with his Soviet counterpart. The trio sold Weinberger on the "zero-zero," bypassing the usual intramural process, and Weinberger brought it to the president. When even Shultz said he thought it was an idea worth pursuing, Perle's team went about refining it. Gorbachev's proffer called for strict adherence to the ABM Treaty for the next fifteen to twenty years. The American counter would be five years, with a sweetener that if either side was ready to deploy a missile defense system after that, it would have to submit a plan to share the technology with the other side. Why the Americans felt the Soviets would believe this is a mystery. And, in fact, they did not. When Gorbachev received Reagan's proposal, he fired off a mostly angry response, accusing Reagan of destroying what progress the two had made in Geneva. But what made Gorbachev's letter strange was its final paragraph, in which he called for a meeting in advance of the scheduled summit in either London or Iceland.

"I thought it was a stupid idea," Ken Adelman told me. "Poindexter [NSC advisor John Poindexter] showed it to me before he shut his door. He was always shutting doors; that was his problem. Anyway, the last paragraph is like, 'Therefore, let's meet in October in either London or Reykjavik.' And I said, 'That last paragraph sounds like it comes from a different letter, like someone cut and pasted it in.' It didn't fit with the whole screechy rude tone of the rest of it. And I said, 'Is he going to do it?' And Poindexter said, 'Yup.' I was surprised because the atmosphere was so bad."

In fact, the atmosphere could hardly have been worse. The Soviets were hopelessly bogged down in Afghanistan; the Chernobyl nuclear plant had ruptured, exposing, among other things, Moscow's pathetic, even criminal attempt to keep it quiet; the United States had bombed the Libyans for an attack that killed several Americans in Europe; the Iran-Contra scandal was percolating below the surface; the Russians had arrested an American journalist, Nicholas Daniloff, on specious charges of espionage (he was eventually exchanged for a KGB recruiter being held in the United States); and the United States had announced it would no longer abide by the still unratified SALT II Treaty. Of course, Perle considered this a victory and was singled out in the press as being the bogeyman behind the move. He insisted it was Reagan being hard-nosed and realistic. When he got wind of this impromptu meeting, he hoped the president would turn it down. "My guess is that Shultz and the State Department generally were eager to impart some momentum to the talks that were still floundering in Geneva," Perle recalled. "Now, this was billed as a preparation for a summit. Normally these are done by people other than the summit participants—Sherpas as they're sometimes called. And normally, there have been things that have been negotiated by teams at lower levels that get announced at the summit. But there was nothing in this case."

The decision was made to hold the meeting in Reykjavik because Gorbachev's other choice, London, would complicate matters even further. In London, the Americans would have to figure out some role for Margaret Thatcher to play, as well as the NATO ministers, not to mention the crush of the international press. Reykjavik was cold and damp, but at least it was a more controlled environment. With only ten days to prepare, the scramble for places on the team began, with the State Department taking a hard line on whom it would allow to come to "its" show. When the first list was passed around, Perle realized that he would be the Defense Department's only representative; he would be severely outmanned and isolated again by State's posse. He phoned Weinberger and said he had to have Frank Gaffney with him, at the very least, to relay details of the meeting to Weinberger. Weinberger leaned on Shultz, and the State Department relented—almost. Gaffney could come, but he might have to sleep on the street since hotel rooms were no longer available. Perle told his aide he could sleep on the floor of his hotel room. Another Perle aide at the time, Bruce Jackson, remembers it more dramatically. "I think both Perle and Gaffney, out of suspicion that Reykjavik was a setup, had to struggle to get on the plane. I think Gaffney was a stowaway; he just threw himself on the plane and refused to get off. But I don't think we at Defense were surprised. We were feverishly writing talking points because there was always the suspicion that—whether it be a walk in the woods or some other initiative—we would cave."

Despite rumblings in the press that the U.S. delegation would not have time to prepare, Perle insists that his people went into overdrive in planning for every conceivable hybrid proposal that Gorbachev could possibly put on the table. They were taking the exercise seriously while reassuring Congress, the press, and the American people that the two-day meeting, which would include no ceremonies of any kind, would be a planning session for the main event to be held in just two months in Washington.

To no one's surprise, it was cold and rainy on October 11, 1986, when the summiteers arrived in Iceland. The site for the meeting was Hofdi House, a small but quaint cottagelike home assembled in Norway from a catalog and shipped to Iceland at the turn of the century by the

French government to house its consul. That the entrance still bore the markings of the French Republic was no doubt a minor irritant to some members of the American delegation, to whom the French had long been a major irritant. Hofdi House was also said to be haunted by a female ghost who had driven out the British ambassador in 1952.

The president and the general secretary arrived in their limousines and walked up the few stairs to the front door shielded from the rain by umbrellas carried by their aides. In the tiny foyer, photographers jostled one another amid the antique furniture, prompting Gorbachev to warn in Russian, "Be careful now. We don't want to damage the property of the Icelandic government."

With the photographs taken, Reagan and Gorbachev moved to an equally tiny sitting room, accompanied only by Shultz and Shevardnadze (then Soviet prime minister) and their interpreters. A small table had been placed between the chairs, and Gorbachev parked his attaché case on top, snapped it open, and began removing stacks of paper. Reagan, who had only a legal pad and pen in front of him, eyed the growing stack of documents with alarm.

"Looks like you've got a lot of papers with you," he said.

"That's because I have a lot of suggestions to make," Gorbachev replied.

Indeed he had. As Reagan and Shultz sat silently, Gorbachev laid out his sweeping three-tiered plan to sharply and dramatically reduce the nuclear arsenals of both nations. The details came so quickly that Shultz had to scribble them at breakneck speed on his own pad. For the most part, Reagan stared at his counterpart with a mixture of confusion and fear; this was not supposed to be a summit.

Although there was a press blackout, word began to circulate that this was no photo op, that the two leaders were going nose to nose on the panoply of nuclear weapons issues. From his perch as the new U.S. ambassador to Germany, Richard Burt watched events unfold with astonishment. "I remember that I just couldn't believe that somebody in the administration didn't say to themselves, 'Gee, what happens if we get there and Gorbachev wants a deal? We better have a plan.' It's a little bit like going into Iraq not knowing what you were going to do. These guys were thrown off balance by Gorbachev's proposals."

That was simply not true, as Perle is quick to point out. "Rick Burt wasn't there. The materials that were prepared for that meeting dealt with every issue. There were no surprises in the sense that nothing we heard from Gorbachev was new, except he was prepared to go further in terms of U.S. proposals than he had ever gone."

After laying out his proposals, Gorbachev explained that all would be possible, including the removal of intermediate-range missiles in Europe, if the United States agreed to not only honor the letter of the ABM Treaty but extend it.

"But I promised SDI to the American people," Reagan protested.

Both Gorbachev and Shevardnadze explained they were not proposing that all research be halted, only that any system created by that research not be deployed for at least ten more years, at which point the treaty could be renegotiated in light of new threats and new technologies. "Just honor the treaty," Gorbachev said.

Reagan and Shultz returned to their nearby hotel, where senior members of the delegation were waiting for them in a portable security structure known as "the Bubble." The soundproof and spy-proof enclosure, manned by an armed guard, resembles a small Winnebago and can seat about ten people.

The Gorbachev proposals had been typed up and copied, and each member of the delegation began reading. As they studied the details, Reagan said to no one in particular, "He went on and on about the ABM Treaty. That's his code word for killing SDI." Seated across from Reagan, Paul Nitze looked up from his paper, removed his glasses, and spoke directly to the President. "In my 25 years as an arms negotiator, I've never seen a Soviet proposal as good as this one. They accept *our* definition of strategic weapons. That means they're serious about a 50 percent cut! Mr. President, I'm excited."

But whatever euphoria that may have been building inside the Bubble was quickly burst by Richard Perle. "Wait a minute," he said. "This isn't as good as it looks. The Soviets say they accept the zero option in Europe and they're trying to pass that off as some big concession. But by keeping their missiles in Asia they keep open the option of moving them right back to Europe on short notice." Perle then looked directly as Nitze. "So what's so good about that?"

In fact, the Soviet missiles in Asia, numbering more than one hundred, were highly mobile and could be moved into Eastern Europe in a matter of days. When the issue had come up once before, Moscow had proposed allowing the United States to base an equal number of Pershings in Asia. But the Americans had no place to put them and the idea had died. George Shultz did not jump in at that point, but he had made no secret of his belief that agreeing not to deploy Star Wars for five or ten years was giving up nothing, since the mythical system would not be ready for prime time for at least that long. As he once explained to the president, "We should give them the sleeves from our vest and let them think they got our overcoat." The average development time for a weapons system is nineteen years, and for one as complex and theoretical as SDI, who knew? It did not seem to matter to Reagan.

"Reagan didn't care whether Star Wars was real or not," Frances Fitzgerald told me. "He was never going to make a decision on arms reduction and everybody knew that. Reagan just saw all this as something he had to do for the public, to project this image of being a powerful negotiator and of making decisions. But that was fantasy." Of course, Perle did not see it that way. He joined the main negotiating team which included Nitze, Adelman, Colonel Robert Linhard from the NSC, General Rowny, and about a half dozen others seated across a long table occupied on the other side by the Soviets. Their leader was a surprise: Marshall Sergei Akhromeyev, the Russian's top military officer and the last active commander to have fought the Germans in World War II. To the Americans, he introduced himself as "the last of the Mohicans." Akhromeyev was known as a precise negotiator and a shrewd tactician, but he was pleasantly free of the grim and dour personality that had been typical of Soviet negotiators in the past. Nitze described him as "a good man in a bad system."

After some initial back-and-forth, Akhromeyev proposed a 50 percent cut in each category of nuclear weapons, which, because of the asymmetry of the two forces, would leave the Soviets with more than the United States in every category in which they already had an advantage. The Americans decided to repair to their quarters and awaken Shultz in his hotel room to spell out the pros and cons of the Soviet proposal. Perle and Rowny voiced the strongest objections, with Nitze arguing the need for flexibility. Shultz cautioned the group not to shut the door on any proposals at this stage and told Nitze that he [Nitze] was in charge. After the group reported back to the table, Nitze explained the problem of agreeing to any proposal that would leave the Soviets with an edge. And then Perle piped up and informed the Russians that such a proposal would be against U.S. law, referring to the Fred Ikle–inspired Jackson amendment that Perle knew was an advisory to the president and without force of law. But the Soviets' American "expert," Georgi Arbatov, pointed his finger at Perle and fairly shouted, "Yes, and *you're the man who wrote it!*" proving that he was not quite as expert as he should have been.

However, to the Americans' surprise, the Russians agreed to the 50 percent calibrated in such a way as to leave neither side with an advantage. Akhromeyev also agreed that each strategic bomber would count as one for each side, regardless of whether it was carrying bombs or attack missiles. This thorny issue had been vexing negotiators for years and had now been put to rest. Perle returned to his hotel at around 7 a.m., briefed his exiled roommate, Gaffney, and tried to sleep for a bit. Yes, the game was going his way, but he knew this was too early to feel much beyond fatigue. There would be a price for all this giving, and it would come sooner rather than later.

The endgame to this bizarre episode would go down in summit lore, embellished perhaps in the retelling, but still awesome in its implications. The proposals and counters were coming fast and furious; at one point, Perle and Linhard, hunting for a private place to quickly draft a proposal, found themselves in the bathroom. With no flat surface on which to write, the men placed a piece of plywood across an ancient bathtub and knelt on the floor, scribbling furiously. Perle smiled broadly, recalling the weekend. "There was a sense, of course, that we were on a roller coaster. There was somebody down there pulling the levers, but it sure wasn't us. We were just riding, and it was wild. And you knew that history was being made. You just didn't know how it was going to come out."

On INF, Gorbachev agreed to dismantle his SS-20s if the United States did not deploy its Pershings. He would keep his hundred or so intermediate-range missiles in Asia, while the Americans would be allowed to deploy an equal number in Alaska aimed at Soviet Asia. Perle realized immediately that Gorbachev was scrapping the Russians' long-held position that missiles in Europe were already in balance without the Pershings. It was a telling moment. Like the Azerbaijani-born Soviet grandmaster and world chess champion Garry Kasparov, who would pick up his wristwatch from the table next to the board and snap it on when he absolutely *knew* his opponent was finished, Richard Perle knew that for Gorbachev, the game was over.

"I knew they could never take back the concessions they made," he told me. "Yes, this was one meeting. There was an historic process under way and this was one episode in it. But having said yes to 50 percent reductions and essentially yes to the zero option, I knew that when we would sit down and discuss it further they would have abandoned the key elements of their position."

Of course, the other shoe dropped shortly: What were the Americans prepared to give in return? Perle and Linhard then scribbled out the ban-ballistic-missiles proposal that both Weinberger and Shultz had signed on to back in Washington. The proffer was a 50 percent cut in nuclear arsenals over five years with no deployment of SDI but testing "as permitted under the ABM Treaty," the meaning of which was still not agreed upon. Then, over the next five years, the total elimination of all ballistic missiles with either side permitted to deploy defenses at the end of this second stage, meaning the Russians would get only a decade's respite from having to deal with a working missile defense system.

Both Shevardnadze and Gorbachev wondered why, after the elimination of all ballistic missiles, the United States would need a missile shield. Reagan's response was weak: "Who knows when the world will see another Hitler? We need to be able to defend ourselves." The Soviets, having suffered so horribly at the hands of the Germans, could have made the exact same argument for their side. No, Gorbachev insisted—SDI research and testing must be confined to the "laboratory" for the ten-year period, and then defensive systems could be *negotiated*. As Frances Fitzgerald reported in *Way Out There in the Blue*, Max Kampelman asked Ken Adelman, "Why do we do this? Why propose something he'd never accept, something even we might not want?" According to Fitzgerald, Adelman just shrugged. But if Kampelman had asked Perle the same question, he would have received a tutorial on the art of the deal. "It's entirely justified to make a proposal that you know will not be accepted," he told me, "because it isn't the last proposal. It's to take their temperature and set up a situation for a compromise that comes closer to the minimum you're prepared to accept. If you walk in there and say 'Just tell me what you want and I'll give it to you,' you won't get a very good deal."

Reagan stretched that tactic to the extreme when he repeated his lame proposal of sharing SDI technology (of which there was little to share at the time) with Moscow so that both could have the shield. Gorbachev batted away that volley with a wave of his hand, pointing out that the Americans were not even willing to share technology for milk production.

Had Perle been in the room while this was going on, he probably would have gritted his teeth. The president of the United States was offering to get rid of the entire ballistic missile arsenal in order to continue research and development of a system few believed would ever work. Folly was an inadequate description, and it was folly for both sides. The notion of the United States and the Soviet Union ceding their superpower status to the British, the French, and the Chinese was preposterous. But it was indicative of how desperately Gorbachev wanted an agreement, and how guileless Reagan was in the complex field of strategic warfare. Word of this would come out, and when it did the reaction was both incredulity and considerable anger.

Reagan and Gorbachev played out the string, grappling over the single word "laboratory."

"Just one word," Reagan pleaded.

"My conscience is clear," Gorbachev replied. "It's 'laboratory' or good-bye." At that moment, according to Shultz, Reagan passed a note to him that read, "Am I wrong?" Shultz whispered, "No, you are right." The empty-handed leaders walked grimly out of Hofdi House and into the cold night. The oncoming winter was in the air, and to Richard Perle it had the smell of victory. Had Reagan known he was bluffing with an empty hand, he might have savored the moment. But Reagan wanted to believe the Star Wars fantasy, and to Richard Perle the president's ignorance was bliss. There was nothing up their sleeves, no sleeves on the vest, and hence no arms control deal that the Russians would have violated anyway. As Paul Newman's Cool Hand Luke once said, "Sometimes havin' nothin' is a real cool hand."

Reykjavik would become a kind of *Rashomon* moment for historians, with each player and observer recalling the events in his own way and often quite differently from his colleagues and counterparts. The wild weekend would be preserved, after a fashion, on videotape as a reenactment that would withstand the scrutiny of the participants. Perle's friend from his days at the London School of Economics, British filmmaker Brian Lapping, had already produced what he called "cabinet reconstructions," in which journalists who had received thorough briefings of British cabinet meetings would re-create them as closely as possible to the substance and tone of the actual meeting. Of course, using the same method to re-create a summit would be a stretch. But, on the last day of Reykjavik, Gorbachev did something unprecedented in summit history: He held a news conference in which he quoted himself and Reagan from the interpreter's notes. Lapping read this in the London *Times* and was flabbergasted. He found two American journalists to play Reagan and Shultz, and hoped to find two Russian journalists to play Gorbachev and Shevardnadze. But when he tried to recruit some in Moscow, not a single journalist would agree to play the Soviet leaders.

"To them, it was just unthinkable," Lapping told me. "But while we were there, we went to see Jack Matlock, the U.S. ambassador, and told him what we were trying to do. And he said, 'Well, you're in luck. The complete transcripts have just been declassified.' He said, 'If you want to come to see me at my home in New England, I will let you sit down and use the transcript. I will not give it to you, but I will let you copy it.'"

With a script already written for him, Lapping hired actors to play not only the four principles but also the entire working groups. He and his people interviewed the participants to get the tone and the body language right. The result, *Breakthrough at Reykjavik*, produced for Britain's Granada TV and broadcast by PBS in 1988, was a strange and fascinating interpretation of just what had happened in and around Hofdi House, including the middle-of-the night meeting in Shultz's hotel room, and Perle improvising a writing table over the Hofdi bathtub. Some of the participants, including the Soviets, met for a panel discussion after the show was aired in the United States, and to a man agreed that what Lapping had put together was as close to reality as one could reasonably have gotten. Perle had reviewed the film before its broadcast and offered suggestions, but according to Lapping had nothing to do with the original idea or with the production itself.

"Reagan's beliefs were so amazing," Lapping said, "as was his conduct at Reykjavik. I mean, one of the things he did there was to say, in effect, to Gorbachev, 'Look, we both agree that we'd like to get rid of all them, wouldn't we?' And Richard was just horrified!" Concerned? Yes. Horrified? Not quite. In Perle's mind, the dramatic dance between Reagan and Gorbachev made for great theater but, like the SDI that played a central role, was not grounded in reality. Perle understood this process better than Reagan, and he knew that all this shilly-shally about eliminating all nuclear weapons could never possibly happen. He knew that agreeing on a concept, an abstraction, was quite different from seeing it etched in stone on a treaty. Ideas are reduced to drafts and drafts are reduced to articles and paragraphs, and then, line by line, they are dissected and poked and prodded in the hope that they will reveal meanings and implications agreeable to all parties. "It's a very long way from a remark in the midst of a summit to a provision in a treaty," he said. "I did not believe we were that close to an agreement. The thing that was taken as a sign by many that we had been very close was when Gorbachev said something like, 'Then let's get rid of all of them.' And Reagan said, 'That's fine with me.' Now, there are people who took that to mean that we were on the cusp of total disarmament."

There were people indeed. In the weeks that followed, virtually all the usual suspects of the foreign policy world weighed in with their views of what they thought Ronald Reagan had almost done, and the verdict wasn't pretty. Senator Sam Nunn said the final deal on the table "would have been the most painfully embarrassing example of American ineptitude this century." Jim Schlesinger called it "a near disaster from which we were fortunate to escape." Of course both Richard Nixon and Henry Kissinger expressed their alarm, especially over the INF plan, which, in their view, would damage the Western alliance. Mrs. Thatcher said it was "like an earthquake." None of what had been discussed at Reykjavik had been run by Congress or by most of the defense and intelligence establishments. They found out about it when the public did. Conservatives mostly praised Reagan for refusing to give up SDI, but moderates and liberals were incredulous that Reagan walked away from what might have been significant reductions over what Schlesinger called, "a collection of technical experiments and distant hopes." And he noted with irony that SDI, as a hollow threat, probably did more to protect America than it ever would as an actual defensive system. A review by the House Armed Services Committee of who said what at the summit concluded that no one in the U.S. delegation dared to even suggest some compromise on SDI that would have led to an actual breakthrough.

Predictably, Frank Gaffney read Reykjavik differently from everyone else, believing it was the Soviets who almost pulled off a big-time hustle, not the Americans. In Gaffney's view, Gorbachev would have agreed to anything to kill SDI, and then would have cheated on his end of the deal. "The idea of ridding the Soviet Union and the United States of all nuclear weapons was preposterous. It was not a serious proposal. The fact that Shultz and Adelman and Nitze thought there was a pony around there that we needed to keep chasing notwithstanding, there was no 'there' there. The irony was that these clever guys who thought we were about to pull the wool over the Soviets' eyes didn't appreciate that it was the Soviets who were going to give us nothing in exchange for strangling SDI in its crib. I see it completely the other way."

For his part, Ken Adelman believed that the INF part of the deal, the zero option, would have been historic enough if that had been the only agreement the two sides had reached. "It was such an enormous step that when Reagan told us about that, we put in calls to the U.S. ambassadors in London, Bonn, Paris, and throughout Europe to give them a heads-up that the zero option was going to happen in Europe. It's interesting that a lot of people like Haig and Scowcroft didn't want it because it would break the link between the U.S. and Europe. But it was a perfectly safe, perfectly wonderful deal, and we didn't need another weapons system [the Pershings] to link our security to Europe's."

I asked Adelman, who has known Perle for more than thirty years, if it was fair to state that despite all of his behind-the-scenes machinations and impromptu proposals, Perle did not want a deal of any kind. Adelman laughed. "Richard had the attitude that no arms control treaty could be good. I thought the Non-Proliferation Treaty was pretty good. I came to believe that the Comprehensive Test-Ban Treaty was probably good. I never had the hate-all-arms-control-treaties attitude that Richard did." And it was that attitude that made the Prince of Darkness moniker fit, the Novak mistaken-identity story notwithstanding.

Ironically, it would take a true Russian patriot, Nobel Prize–winning physicist Andrey Sakharov, to talk some sense into Gorbachev about arms control in general and SDI in particular. Just two months after Reykjavik, and two days before Christmas 1986, the dissident was allowed to return to Moscow from his seven-year exile in Gorky, his release personally ordered by Gorbachev. On December 28, he held a press conference in which he criticized Gorbachev for linking reductions in offensive weapons to restrictions on SDI, essentially explaining that SDI was not only theoretical but bad theory to boot. He said no shield could ever stop a heavily armed opponent and that it was appalling that so much time and money were being wasted on such efforts. He assured his listeners, and, by extension, Gorbachev himself, that in time SDI would "simply die on its own, quietly and peacefully." Some of his colleagues, who secretly agreed with him, criticized Sakharov for engaging in "politics," but Gorbachev was listening. Months later, the General Secretary resurrected the INF deal without linkage of any kind to SDI. As Francis Fitzgerald put it, Sakharov's revelation was "like finding something hidden in plain sight." Sakharov's colleagues, realizing it was now safe to jump on the bandwagon, began telling reporters they had made a big fuss over nothing, that SDI "is nothing but a bluff." Apparently, Andrey Sakharov was not among those scientists who according to Richard Perle "live in a dream world."

In December, Perle was not only invited to a state dinner at the White House for Mr. and Mrs. Gorbachev but was also seated at the main table, with Nancy Reagan bracketed by Gorbachev and Perle. The occasion was the signing of the INF deal that would eliminate U.S. and Soviet nuclear weapons from Europe. Other guests included Kissinger, Joe DiMaggio, David Rockefeller, Georgi Arbatov, and Representative Dick Cheney. Democratic Party chairman Bob Strauss said he was struck by how much the evening's festivities moved him. "I've only felt it once before," he said, "at the dinner for Sadat and Begin." When Van Cliburn played "Moscow Nights," Strauss believed he saw tears in the eyes of the Gorbachevs. Days later, George Will, in a curmudgeonly mood, wrote in his column that the evening would be remembered as the night the United States lost the cold war.

At first, Gorbachev teased Perle about the fact that the actor whom Brian Lapping had cast to play Perle in his TV reenactment was noticeably trimmer than the man he was playing. But at some point, Perle decided to poke a bit at the guest of honor. "I remember asking him how much the Soviets spent on the military," Perle told me. "And he said, 'That's a secret.' And I said...and I think that this was a bit impertinent upon reflection…, 'Are you sure that you know?' And he said, 'I'm the chairman of the Defense Council and I know everything.' But the way he said it, there was a subliminal message that, hey, maybe I don't know everything."

Gorbachev was eager to talk about General Motors and decentralized manufacturing. He had come to realize that many large American companies buy many of the parts they use from suppliers, giving others a piece of the action, whereas Soviet state-run companies were expected to do everything by themselves. As a result, they would produce an inferior product at a greater cost. Even Perle recognized that Gorbachev was sincere in his desire to rid the system of the intractable and corrupt bureaucrats who stymied every effort at reform and modernization. He knew that hopelessly entrenched institutions would try to sabotage any initiative that would change the status quo. But Perle also saw Gorbachev's fatal flaw: In the end, he still believed that his reforms could proceed within the context of the Communist Party. In documents released after the collapse of the Soviet Union, transcripts of Politburo meetings reveal just how ugly the atmosphere became for Gorbachev as the empire began to fall apart. This statement from Uzbekistan's party leader Islam Karimov to Gorbachev on the floor of the Politburo in January of 1991 is a case in point: "It was possible, Mikhail Sergeevich, not to begin perestroika in 1985. It was possible to live quietly and in the period of stagnation reform slowly. It might not have been necessary to stir up enormous masses of people. All would have gone on as it had, and you would have prospered, and we would have prospered. And there would not have taken place any kind of catastrophes."

In August of 1991, while on a seaside vacation, Gorbachev was arrested and temporarily removed from power. The poorly conceived coup attempt failed miserably when the military refused to join. One of the plotters, Marshall Sergei Akhromeyev, the "last of the Mohicans," and the "good man in a bad system," committed suicide.

When a frightened, disheveled Gorbachev returned to Moscow, he came down the steps from his plane and walked unsteadily to a microphone. He told the throng of reporters that reform would continue, but only within the context of the Communist Party. Right after that statement, a longtime friend of Gorbachev's reportedly grabbed him by his lapels and told him, "You cannot reform the unreformable!" That attempt would be his legacy.

"He was a Communist to the end," Perle said. "He may still be a Communist today, I don't know. In living and working in the West so much, maybe his views have evolved. If he knew beforehand that going down his path would lead to the collapse of the empire, he would have turned back. But things careened out of control. He couldn't turn back." On December 31, 1991, the flag of the Soviet Union was lowered over the Kremlin for the last time.

By then, Richard Perle had been out of government and ensconced in his new life as a speaker, writer, advisor, and businessman. Before leaving the Pentagon in 1987, he was invited for a private farewell in the Oval Office with President Reagan, and he used that opportunity to reiterate his view that a world free of all nuclear weapons was neither possible nor desirable.

In an open letter to Reagan published in *U.S. News and World Report*, Perle urged the president not to use the INF Treaty as some sort of "new beginning" in U.S.-Soviet relations, as many were urging him to. He implored Reagan to not fall victim to the "dangerous and unwarranted euphoria" that generally follows summits and treaty signings. He closed with a paraphrase of Robert Frost: "Summits are wonderful salves, but they are something that ought to be done by halves."

And, as he watched the domino theory actually work for the first time, in Poland, Czechoslovakia, Hungary, Romania, Latvia, Lithuania, and the rest of what had been caged humanity, he thought of Scoop Jackson and Dickie Fosdick, and of Peter Fechter bleeding to death beneath the Berlin Wall, and of Solzhenitsyn coming down the stairs with Scoop at his side, and of Walter and his family at the last train from East Germany. He felt exhilaration, fatigue, and vindication. "There was a sense that it was right to fight that fight, even though there were people who would have given up a long time ago or done deals with the

Soviets that would have made it more likely that they could have remained in charge. That was all very gratifying. But now I was in a different place. I was no longer professionally involved in all that stuff. I was thinking about what I was going to do next."

VII.
CITIZEN PERLE (1)

AS THE REAGAN presidency drew to a close in 1988, so did Richard Perle's appetite for working in government. Over the next dozen years, he would move into the private sector, first as a commentator and lecturer and then as a consultant to multinational businesses in the fields of global strategy, technology exporting, homeland security, and communications. It was the traditional and accepted reward for low-paying government service, and, with young Jonathan now in private school, payments on their share of a vacation home in Provence, and Leslie strongly opposed to her husband remaining at the Pentagon, Perle did not balk at the transition. He had a monthly column for *U.S. News*, lecture gigs at $15,000 a pop, plus a $300,000 advance on his forthcoming novel, *Hard Line*. Perle knew that a roman à clef was the most convenient way he could write about many of the sensitive issues with which he had dealt while at the Pentagon, while settling more than a few old scores in the process. Neverthless, the announcement of the novel did trigger a mild admonishment from Senator Sam Nunn (D-Ga.) who chided Perle for profiting from his government service. Perle felt that if he could add some consulting business to what he already had, it would make for a pretty good life. Years of battling the State Department, the CIA, the arms control lobby, and occasionally the White House had taken a toll, but he would leave with few regrets and no desire to return.

Besides, Reagan's successor, George H.W. Bush, was not Perle's kind of man. He was too much the reed bending in the wind, too much the insider without an inside. He famously lacked "the vision thing." Perle much preferred leaders who he felt had core beliefs, even beliefs he might not always agree with. To his mind, not only was this Bush coreless, he was also, apparently, spineless. As the Iran-Contra scandal began to eat away at the Reagan presidency, rolling up some of Perle's protégés in the process, the then vice president clung like grim death to the absurd position that he had been "out of the loop" while all the skullduggery had been going on.

It was not until 1993, a year after Bush had completed his one and only term, that independent counsel Judge Lawrence Walsh got his hands on Bush's diary and concluded that had he not been elected president in 1988, he would have likely been indicted for perjury. Perle contends that the operation, run out of the White House basement, came as a complete surprise to him. He believed in supporting the Contras, but he found absurd the notion of dealing with the Iranians as some sort of honest brokers, and laughed at the image of Ollie North and Robert McFarlane trying to deliver a birthday cake to Ayatollah Khomeini. "Who did they think they were dealing with?" Perle said. "They were kidding themselves. They didn't understand the Iranians. This ludicrous idea of going over there with a cake! The Ayatollahs were not Americans whose culture and value structure were like ours. They weren't going to be impressed by a birthday cake."

Two of his friends, Elliott Abrams and Michael Ledeen, were caught up in the scandal, with Abrams avoiding prison only via a pardon from the outgoing Bush. Perle is still not convinced that the Boland Amendment, which banned aid to the Contras, extended to actions by the NSC that hatched the arms-for-hostages scheme in the first place. Nor does he believe that Abrams should have plea-bargained to two counts of lying to Congress. "I'm not convinced he committed a crime." Relying upon a now familiar defense, Perle added, "There's a terrible tendency, and its gotten worse, to criminalize policy differences, to use the law in what I think is a really abusive way."

Although Perle had no involvement in Iran-Contra, it did form the backdrop for what was billed as an epic debate between Perle and the darling of the liberal/Left intellectuals, Noam Chomsky. The date was April 12, 1988, and the venue was Ohio State University. Chomsky, the MIT linguist and tireless critic of capitalism and American foreign policy, was considered a master debater and showman, a man who could strut while sitting down. He spoke not in sentences or even in paragraphs, but in entire chapters, barely pausing for air. In Perle's view, Chomsky was a polished phony, carefully constructing arguments built on specious research but delivering his message with a crowd-grabbing flair. He was particularly effective before a college audience, and the auditorium for this event would be packed with Buckeye students and faculty. The fact that the crowd would be against him from the get-go appealed to Perle, whose ego and self-confidence allow him to believe he can always win over at least some of his detractors. For the next two decades he would willingly enter the lion's den, be it a talk show, a documentary, or a speaker's forum and calmly articulate his views, infuriating most but stimulating at least some to reconsider their views about the issues of the day. "I suppose I could just sit home and not say another word," he said when asked why he agrees to debates like the Ohio State affair. If sitting at home and saying nothing was his only alternative, Perle would always opt for a walk on the wild side, such was the certainty of his positions. And so what if some hecklers made the debate unpleasant? There just might be a few in the silent minority whose feelings he might buttress. He mentioned an e-mail he had received from a recent appearance in which the audience hissed and booed. "The gist of it was 'you made some good points,'" he said with a smile. "Now, that's a step forward." Having a forum, a hearing, was better than not having one, and this, no doubt, was his reason for agreeing to see me in the first place.

The subjects for the Chomsky debate would be Latin America and the Middle East, with each guest allowed an opening statement and then alternating remarks. If the plan was to allow both guests equal time, it was not understood by the moderator. From the opening, Chomsky simply controlled the microphone, unleashing a lengthy stream of "facts" and "figures" in what sounded to Perle like the world's longest run-on sentence. His thesis was that in planning the post–World War II world, a small group of powerful elites in the United States plotted an empire, an unchallenged world power that would contrive and exploit a new world order in the interest of big business. Chomsky continually referred to State Department documents "now declassified" as evidence for his case, specifically citing newly unearthed memos by George Kennan which allegedly stated, "We have 50 percent of the world's wealth but only 6 percent of its population...we must maintain this disparity to the extent possible by force if necessary, putting aside vague and idealistic slogans such as human rights, the raising of living standards and democratization, preferring police states if needed over democracies that might be too liberal." As if to drive home the point, Chomsky added, "These are all quotes, incidentally. The declassified documents on U.S. foreign policy in Latin America applied these points in detail."

After some ten minutes of this "brief" opening statement, followed by enthusiastic applause, the stage was turned over to Perle. He began by questioning the source of Chomsky's premise. "He keeps referring to these documents...he keeps coming back to these policy planners of the Department of State. I've served in government for a good many years and I've yet to see a policy planning document that interested anyone except the authors." Perle then framed the vision he would champion throughout his career, the vision of a good, decent, and freehearted superpower unafraid to use its might to ensure freedom for those who seek it and ruin for those who would deny it. "There are mistakes to be sure," he told the audience. "There's a lot of idealism in the process on the part of those who believe the United States ought to make sacrifices of various kinds in order to assist the expansion of democracy around the world. And we've gotten ourselves into trouble from time to time in an effort to accomplish that. But if you listen to Mr. Chomsky, we are moti-vated entirely by a kind of rapacious elite looking after their own interests. And I think this is complete nonsense."

As the session wore on and it became clear to Perle that the modera-tor had no intention of stopping Chomsky's filibuster, Perle seemed to lose interest. As Chomsky recited a litany of America's crimes and shameful conduct with hyperbole that would make any self-respecting radical blush (e.g., "the Reagan administration has been responsible for atrocities com-parable to those of Pol Pot"), Perle apparently concluded that this exercise would not generate any meaningful exchange. When Chomsky concluded one particularly dense recital with, "We [the United States] are ranked rather high in the definition of major terrorist states," the moderator said, "Mr. Perle?"

"I have nothing to add to that," Perle replied. Finally, the audience laughed and applauded. Through the Contra war in Nicaragua to the endless struggle between Israelis and Palestinians, Chomsky bloviated and Perle remonstrated until the moderator mercifully called for a halt.

"I now ask Mr. Chomsky to make a concluding remark of about five minutes.

Said Perle, "That should be sometime around breakfast." The audience again laughed and applauded. Perle's summation may or may not have converted many in the audience, but at the very least it left no one confused about where he stood. Perhaps few noted the incongruity of the Prince of Darkness deriding his opponent for having such a dark, disconsolate perspective, but it was not lost on Perle:

> I have sat tonight and listened, probably at greater length than I would have liked, to a vision of a world that I have not seen in my years in government. It is a vision of a world in which a small number of men, in order to enrich themselves, are prepared to inflict suffering and cruelty throughout the world....
> It is a deeply cynical view of the world...a view that recognizes no decency in the making of American policy and its implementation. If you believe that that is what this country is all about, if you believe that we are organized principally to serve the selfish interest of a few, that the historical experience of this country since the war has been dedicated and devoted to that, then I think you will have a lot of difficulty explaining the enormous prosperity that this country has managed to bring to much of the world through the benefits of democracy.

In a sense, Perle sees no difference between defending America and defending himself; the country's interests are his interests, or so he believes. He will do business for profit when he can justify the outcome as being as good for America as it is for himself. As a private citizen, he operates in the quasi-governmental twilight zone where former cabinet members, deposed committee chairmen, and retired military brass are hired for their influence and knowledge of how the system works. Yes, some will sign onto anything for the right price, regardless of conse-quences or policy implications. Despite numerous allegations to the contrary, Perle contends he has never been a part of any business deal or arrangement that ran counter to the policy of the United States, even a policy with which he might disagree.

Among the first offers Perle received after leaving the Pentagon came from his friend Turkish president Turgut Özal. While assistant secretary of defense in 1987, Perle had negotiated a deal that made Turkey the third largest recipient of U.S. military aid after Egypt and Israel. Subsequently, over objections from the State Department, Perle had set up a high-level defense liaison panel between the Pentagon and the Turkish high com-mand, which he co-chaired. The State Department was so concerned about Perle's cheerleading for Turkey that when he traveled there on one occasion, State dispatched the future counterterrorism director Richard Clarke to go along as a spy. In his book, *Against All Enemies: Inside America's War on Terror,* Clarke wrote of Perle that he was "charmed by his manner and persuaded by his logic about the strategic importance of Turkey." Perle's consuming interest in Turkey was rooted in strategic the-ory he had learned from Albert Wohlstetter. Conventional NATO defenses during the cold war had been built on the assumption that if the Soviets did attack, the main thrust would come through the center of Europe, the Fulda Gap in Germany. This was a so-called design scenario; you assume an action by the other side and then fashion a defense.

Perle, influenced by both Scoop Jackson and Wohlstetter in this real-life gaming, insisted that the United States and its allies were leaving themselves exposed to the north and south, Norway and Turkey, respec-tively. So Perle lobbied hard and successfully for increased military aid to both countries. Norway was not a tough sell, but helping to arm the Turks was a significant and controversial step. First, there was the fact that Turkey's longtime enemy Greece was also a NATO ally. Second,

Turkey was and remains the principle transshipping and processing point for opium from Afghanistan into Europe and then the United States, leading to persistent corruption within the Turkish government, the military, and the police. Third, the Turks had never been called to account for the massacre of more than a million ethnic Armenians just after World War I, an event that met every known standard for genocide. And finally, there was Turkey's image in the popular American media, fostered by such films as *Midnight Express*, which portrayed Turks as barbarous, cruel, and anti-American. It was this last reality that Perle recognized as the major obstacle to building Turkey as a major ally with U.S. money.

Perle says President Özal asked him to come to Turkey to reorganize and rebuild the country's military. "I think he had doubts about whether he had the people with the background and experience to develop this independently," Perle told me. "And he said, 'Come and do this for me. You can have anything you need. If you need thirty people you can have thirty people, if you need ninety you can have ninety, but I think it's best if you keep it small.' He said, 'We'll pay you very well.' And I turned it down because that wasn't my area of expertise."

Perle put the Turks together with FMC Technologies of San Jose, California, the prime contractor for the U.S. Army's Bradley Fighting Vehicle. Through a coproduction deal Perle put together, he and former army chief of staff General Edward C. Meyer directed the new entity that would produce almost seventeen hundred Bradleys in Turkey for the Turkish army. Of course, all the money that went into designing and building the Bradley came from the U.S. taxpayers, so the new company would be selling the know-how of a product without having invested a dime. Perle's stock options on the deal netted a reported $250,000. The revolving door on the Bradley was classic Washington: Meyer went from top kick in the army to a seat on FMC's board, and his chief spokesman, Colonel William Hylander, became FMC's chief spokesman.

But Perle didn't think coproduction arrangements were good for Turkey and countries like it, because the product, be it a rifle or a tank, usually ended up costing the host country far more than it would if the country simply bought the product outright because the host country would have to set up factories and a distribution system for spare parts. Besides, the defense business wasn't really Perle's forte; defense policy was. He says he told Özal, "There's something else you really need that you don't have. You're not well represented in Washington. You send over ambassadors who are trained in the old school, probably unchanged since Ottoman times, and their narrow focus is on government-to-government relations. They don't communicate well with the American people. And Americans are largely ignorant of Turkey. You need people who can explain Turkey a lot better than your ambassador. And it's not just the current ambassador; it's going to be every ambassador. They're not change oriented." Perle's enmity for ambassadors and foreign-office types did not end at the U.S. borders. He also advised Özal not to hire a large, impersonal public relations firm; they're not effective and they will bill you a lot for very little work. Obviously, Perle was pitching himself as Turkey's man in Washington, and Özal jumped at the idea.

Perle then recruited Doug Feith, his onetime summer intern and a lawyer, to form International Advisors, Inc., a lobbying concern with only one client: Turkey. Feith's interest in Turkey was widely believed to have much more to do with Israel's security than with America's. As a secular Muslim country, Turkey might well have common cause with Israel as a counterweight to radical fundamentalist neighbors such as Iran. Israel also possessed technology that Turkey could use to bolster its defense force. It seemed like a good fit, since Israel could use any friend in the region it could find. As a registered agent of Turkey, International Advisors took in between $600,000 and $800,000 per year from 1989 to 1994, with Perle's consultancy fee a reported $48,000 per year. Perle says he told the Turks he would not lobby, meaning he would not court senators and congressmen, and technically there is no evidence that he did. But, as with the FMC deal, he put parties in touch with one another, reprising the godfather role he had played so effectively on the Hill and in the Pentagon.

This was just the start of a get-down-with-Turkey bandwagon that in time would include a long list of former top U.S. officials, including former Senator William Cohen (who later served as Bill Clinton's Secretary of Defense from 1997 until 2001), former national security advisor Brent Scowcroft, and a half dozen former ambassadors, under-secretaries, and congressmen. The stated reason for all this attention to Istanbul was the claim that both the Armenian and Greek lobbies in Washington were far better organized and significantly more effective than whatever Turkey had in place throughout the 1980s, and therefore it was in the overall interest of the United States to make sure the circles of power paid attention to the Turks.

But the backstory was that there was plenty of money to be made in pushing Turkish interests. The more aid the United States sent to Turkey in various packages, the more money came right back to the consultants, lobbyists, and defense contractors, some of whom could slink through loopholes in the laws governing the registration of foreign agents, mak-ing full disclosure unnecessary. The suspicion that at least some of the money Ankara was flashing around Washington came from the opium trade was buttressed by periodic exposés in the Western press about offi-cial corruption involving Turkish government officials and members of the military and police.

The Turks and their enthusiastic American supporters gradually con-structed a web of interlocking relationships so dizzying in its intricacy that it is often difficult to distinguish client from service provider. Foreign governments can lobby in Washington provided their surrogates register with the Justice Department as either foreign agents or lobbyists. The distinction is important because lobbyists are required to disclose far less about their activities and their finances than foreign agents. If a group can successfully argue that its acitivites are not directly controlled by a foreign government and that their funding does not come directly from that government, it can operate under the more liberal disclosure rules of the lobbyist. One of many examples is the Cohen Group, a pow-erful Washington "consulting" firm headed by William Cohen. The Cohen Group sits on the board of the American Turkish Council (ATC), a lobbying operation, and is also a paying client of the ATC. Lockheed Martin is a client of the Cohen Group. Retired air force general Joseph

Ralston sits on the board of Lockheed Martin, for whom he is also a registered lobbyist. Ralston is also a vice chairman of the Cohen Group. Lockheed is also a paying client of the ATC. Lockheed sells F-16 fighters to Turkey, the most recent purchase a $1.78 billion deal, and everyone goes home happy.

Everyone, perhaps, except the Greeks, the Armenians, and especially the Kurds—those proud, stateless people repeatedly victimized by both Saddam Hussein and the Turks, who have denied them their independence and against whom those F-16s could be turned. Here the moral relativism of both America's War on Terror and its messianic vision of a benevolent hegemony is apparent. While the money Feith and Perle received from the Turks over the years is small potatoes compared to fees collected by others, there remains the question of how a man like Perle, who is rhetorically so staunchly committed to the oppressed, a man who would frequently provide housing and food for dissidents, a man whose heroes include the Sakharovs, Solzhenitsyns, and Sharanskys, could rationalize the continued oppression of the Kurds for the "greater good" of arming the Turks.

"Well, I knew Mustafa Barzani [the legendary Kurdish nationalist leader who died in 1979] and I have a lot of sympathy for the Kurds. In fact, I met Barzani because I wanted to help him. I was working for Scoop at the time and I introduced him to Bill Safire and Bill's been a strong defender of the Kurds ever since. This was at a dinner party I organized. I have a lot of sympathy for the Kurds in Iraq and in Iran. The treatment of the Kurds in Turkey flows from a fear that the separatist movement that the PKK represents could become more general, although I'm not all that convinced that's true."

The PKK, the Kurdish Workers Party, is a violent branch of the Kurdish independence movement. It is listed by the State Department as a terrorist group. Perle and other supporters of Turkey make a sharp distinction between the PKK and the Kurds in general to justify their efforts on behalf of the Turks. But even here, the hairs are split. Perle believes the United States should help the Turks to wipe out the PKK to protect the Turkish government but finds a similar group, the MEK, a violent guerrilla band dedicated to the overthrow of the Iranian regime and also listed officially as a terrorist organization, not quite so bad. In fact, Perle was once a paid speaker at an event at the Washington, D.C., convention center that turned out to be an MEK rally. He insists he was told the event was a fund-raiser for Iranian earthquake relief.

"They had a list of all the sponsors, and it was the northern Virginia Iranian community and the Phoenix Iranian American Society, and so forth. It was only partway through the program when they put up a video clip of the woman who runs the MEK that I began to get a little uncomfortable, because her rhetoric was pretty extreme and the response from this crowd, which had otherwise been a family crowd, was wildly enthusiastic. Some speakers were talking about the earthquake, but some were talking about freeing and liberating Iran. It made me a little uncomfortable."

But why? Isn't regime change in Tehran part of the Perle game plan? "They're on the terrorist list," Perle replied. "I would not appear under their sponsorship, and had I known they were a sponsor I would not have come. But there is a debate about whether they should be on the list. I'm told the last act of terror the U.S. has attributed to them happened some twenty-five years ago." Actually, the MEK, the Mujahideen-e-Khalq, was responsible for the assassination of the deputy chief of the Armed Forces General Staff of Iran in April of 1999, and was involved in mortar and hit-and-run attacks on Iranian government and military targets throughout 2000 and 2001. More important, the MEK helped Saddam Hussein's brutal repression of the Kurds following the Gulf War of 1991 and worked for Hussein thereafter as part of his internal security force. MEK military camps surrendered to U.S. forces following the invasion of Iraq in 2003. Terrorist group or not, there were persistent press reports that anti-Iranian neocons saw in the MEK a useful tool that could be employed against the mullahs in Tehran.

"Absolutely false," Douglas Feith insisted to me. "Completely false from beginning to end. There's not even a kernel of truth to it. If you tell me that once upon a time Richard talked to an MEK group, that would be news to me. Our position in the administration when I was undersecretary was we can't say there are terrorist groups that we like and there are terrorist groups we don't like. My position was we don't like the Iranian regime, but a terrorist group that is antiregime is still a terrorist group. And yet there are stories out there that have accused me and Richard and others [of supporting the MEK], and they're completely false."

Perhaps, but there is no ambiguity on the subject of pressure on the U.S. Congress not to acknowledge the Armenian genocide by the Turks despite overwhelming evidence that the massacre took place. House Speaker Dennis Hastert was accused—but never formally charged with—accepting a payoff from Turkish agents to squelch debate on a bill recognizing the systematic murders as genocide. Hastert denied the charge. But each year the issue comes up again before the Congress, and each year Turkey's lobbying allies, the Israelis, add their considerable clout to squelch a debate. Israel has officially maintained that the question of the Armenian deaths is a matter for historians, not politicians; this despite congressional testimony by Elie Wisel and other prominent holocaust scholars in support of a congressional resolution recognizing the genocide. In September of 2005, Brent Scowcroft, as head of the American Turkish Council, sent a letter to Hastert saying, "Even discussion of the Armenian genocide on the floor of the U.S. House of Representatives would be counterproductive to the interests of the United States....The genocide resolutions encourage those who would pull Turkey from the West. The careless use of genocide language provides an excuse to do so, delivering a direct blow to American interests in the region. I strongly urge you to oppose floor deliberation of this sensitive issue."

Nor is there much doubt about Turkey's continuing role in the international drug trade. A 2005 report by the British Foreign Office states that as much as 80 percent of all heroin used in Great Britain has come through Turkey.

Perle dismisses both arguments. "Well, the drug thing has largely been eliminated, or at least brought under control. That's a success story for the Turks. As for the Armenian issue, I don't believe that what happened is akin to Hitler's extermination of the Jews. It was not a final solution and to the best of my knowledge there was never an occasion in which the Turkish government sat down and said, 'Here's a plan for the destruction of the Armenians.' "

While there may not have been a Wannsee Conference outside Ankara, it is difficult to call the murder of more than a million people in a five-year period anything other than genocide. It is also difficult to accept that Turkey has gotten its "drug thing" under control when mountains of heroin continue to appear throughout Europe and the United States. More likely, these rationalizations and self-delusions are a holdover from the cold war, when a bloody dictator, whether named Pinochet or Mohammed Reza Pahlavi, could be prettied up by his American supporters as long as he was anticommunist. At least Perle concedes the general point. "We aligned ourselves with some pretty awful regimes, no doubt about it. The historical record is clear. I don't think we were happy about it. But it was always with the question, What are the alternatives? We supported Battista, who was obviously rotten and corrupt, and it was shameful that we supported that regime. But what was the alternative? Castro? That's been pretty horrible too from a human rights perspective. There was the shah versus Khomeini. These things are not always so easy."

Evidently the choice was easier between Iran and Iraq during their savage war in the 1980s. Although the United States was officially neutral, it provided Saddam Hussein with everything from intelligence officers to training for Iraqi nuclear weapons scientists and a long list of chemical and biological agents whose export was officially banned, but which, with a wink and a nod, were listed as "dual use." Not only was the United States aware that Iraq was using chemical weapons against the Iranians, it was helping their efforts. Iraq employed U.S. military intelligence to "calibrate attacks with mustard gas on Iranian ground troops," and used some sixty U.S. officers of the Defense Intelligence Agency to help plan battles and airstrikes and to assess bomb damage. Washington also gave Saddam intelligence gathered by Saudi-owned AWACS aircraft operated by U.S. personnel, plus huge loans from the Export-Import Bank.

Once again, the moral relativism of foreign policy makers allowed them to justify backing Iraq for the sake of oil, for the sake of the Arab-Israeli balance, and as payback to Iran for taking and holding American hostages. Daniel Pipes, son of the old Team B captain, and Laurie Mylroie, a Harvard professor and one-time apologist for Saddam, wrote a *New Republic* essay unambiguously titled "Back Iraq," in which they stated not only that the dictator was a more desirable winner compared with Khomeini, but also that his regime had actually mellowed: "The Iranian revolution and seven years of bloody and inconclusive warfare have changed Iraq's view of its Arab neighbors, the United States, and even Israel....Its leaders no longer consider the Palestinian issue their problem. Its allies have forced a degree of moderation on Iraq....Iraq is now the de facto protector of the regional status quo."

To his credit, Richard Perle never bought that argument. As assistant secretary of defense and overseer of export licenses, he opposed the Iraq tilt and the transfer of so much material, money, and know-how to Saddam Hussein. But he admits that during this time, his primary focus was on keeping technology from the Soviet Union; Iraq was a sideshow. "It just didn't make sense to be helping the Iraqis," Perle said.

"We sold them an awful lot of Bell helicopters," I said.

"I was against that. The record will show that that part of the Defense Department that I was responsible for recommended against it."

"So who was pushing it?"

"It was well above my pay grade, for sure. It was a State Department and administration policy. That's the way they think over there."

Of course, Saddam Hussein repaid the American favors by invading Kuwait in 1991, some four years after Perle had left the Pentagon. He says he was not surprised in the least by the invasion, although many of his former colleagues argued that it was just an exercise, an opening gambit by Saddam to force negotiations with the Kuwaitis on the Iraqi debt they would not forgive. When that proved false and the United States assembled its coalition, Perle urged the administration from the sidelines to finish the job by ensuring Saddam's ouster. He no longer had the Soviet Union to joust with, he was keenly aware of how much dangerous matériel the Iraqis had received from the United States, and he believed that the anti-Saddam Iraqis were strong enough to take him down with a little help from their American friends.

"We didn't have to go to Baghdad," Perle said. "We had the remaining Republican Guard units surrounded in the desert. And we just let them return to Baghdad! If we had forced them to walk home, that is, to leave their armor and their weapons in the desert, I don't think Saddam would have survived that. And if he had survived it, the subsequent uprising in the north and south, which he brutally put down, might well have succeeded."

Perle's version of events is accurate. On February 27, 1991, corps commanders Lieutenant General Frederick Franks and Lieutenant General Gary Luck had major elements of the Republican Guard boxed in just south and west of Basra. They paused to regroup and awaited word from General Norman Schwarzkopf, who had phoned JCS chairman Colin Powell to tell him he was prepared to drive to the sea and "totally destroy everything in our path." According to the army's official historian, "offensive military operations came unraveled in the early morning hours." For reasons unclear, Schwarzkopf held a live news conference at 9 p.m. local time, 1 p.m. in Washington, to say the Republican Guard was trapped. "We have accomplished our mission." Powell, watching back in Washington, immediately advised Bush to stop the attack.

Bush agreed and announced that a cease-fire would take effect at 5 a.m. Iraq time, giving U.S. forces about six hours to do as much damage as they could. The 1st Armored Division destroyed about 100 tanks and personnel carriers, and the 24th Mechanized Infantry knocked out 185 more. But most of the Guard made it safely back to Baghdad, where they regrouped and were later used to crush the Shia and Kurdish uprising President Bush publicly encouraged. Perle is convinced that this was the genesis of Iraqi mistrust of Americans that undermined the effort to transform Iraq in 2003. "From the very beginning, one of the problems we had to face was our betrayal in urging an uprising and then standing by. So from 1991, a lot of Iraqis didn't like us."

For Perle, Bush's acquiescence to Powell was yet another example of the president's shallowness and lack of vision. He enjoyed the highest job approval rating in the history of that statistic at the Gulf War's end, and promptly squandered it, aided and abetted by men such as James Baker and Brent Scowcroft, who, to Perle's mind, were the worst kind of realists, the kind who rejected the notion that a superpower should act like one. The capper was Bush's August 1, 1991, speech in Kiev as tens of thousands of Ukrainians waved signs reading "The Evil Empire Lives" and "53 Million Ukrainians Demand Independence." However, instead of playing to their dream, Bush played to the Kremlin, warning Ukrainians to beware of "suicidal nationalism."

It took columnist William Safire about seven seconds to dub Bush's address the "Chicken Kiev" speech, and to Perle and his friends the put-down was well deserved. "He was clearly opposed to the breakup of the Soviet Union and so if it had been up to Bush the Ukrainians probably would never have gotten their independence. The rest of his record is pretty undistinguished. A great deal has been made about the skill of him and Baker and Scowcroft in putting together the coalition to fight the Gulf War. But it would be hard to imagine an easier case. You had a blatant act of aggression across national borders. Maggie Thatcher had to push him very hard into going, and when she said, 'George, don't go wobbly on me,' it's because George *was* going wobbly. She didn't just say that out of the blue. And if you listen to what Scowcroft and others in the administration were saying, they were ready for reconciliation with Saddam Hussein. Talk about moral insensitivity! And you could no longer claim that we were choosing the lesser of the evils, because essentially that war was over. And Bush and Scowcroft and Richard Haas and others couldn't wait to put the relationship with Baghdad on a friendly basis."

For his part, Scowcroft insists the speech should be seen in the context of events unfolding in the Balkans, where less than two months earlier Slovenia and Croatia declared their independence from Yugoslavia, setting off a tribal war among ethnic groups whose grievances had been simmering for ages. "What the president was saying was

'Don't you Ukrainians split up between East Ukraine and West Ukraine over the issue of nationalism,'" Scowcroft told me, "because Yugoslavia was in trouble at that time. 'Don't let nationalism break up your union.' But nobody thought of that. And having lived in Yugoslavia, it was just in my bones even in the first Gulf War." On the Iraq War, "I said, 'Don't do it.' We don't understand that country. It's not a country any more than Yugoslavia was. It's an artificial entity. Deep down the Iraqis weren't even as cosmopolitan as the Yugoslavs were. It's tribalism. Once you start killing each other, all civilization fades away."

Scowcroft, the consummate Kissinger protégé, shakes his head when asked what he thinks motivates Richard Perle, a man he has wrestled with for more than thirty years. "I really don't understand Perle," he says with a sigh. "If you talk about the two real neocons, there's Richard Perle and Paul Wolfowitz, and they're very different. Paul Wolfowitz is an idealist, but he's prepared to impose democracy by the sword. Perle's not about that. I don't think Perle gives a shit about democracy. Fundamentally, it's all a means to an end."

But to what end? As Citizen Perle he is simultaneously businessman, essayist, pundit, lecturer, policy advisor, quasi government official, and unofficial spokesman for an entire foreign policy movement. As he told a reporter, "There is no main gig. It's all those things and it changes from one day to the next." It is this multitasking that has frequently placed Citizen Perle in hot water and raised questions about his ethics and the sincerity of his views. For example, right after the Gulf War, Perle contacted the ambassadors of Kuwait and Saudi Arabia on behalf of Vikonics Inc., a New Jersey company that marketed computer security systems for the U.S. armed forces, and for whom Perle was both board member and salesman. Vikonics' president, John L. Kaufman, traveled with Perle to Kuwait and marveled at the reception Perle received. "The minister of this or the secretary of that—no matter who it was, everyone wanted to meet him."

For Perle's critics, trying to sell security systems to the Kuwaitis made him a war profiteer, and contacting the Saudis' flamboyant ambassador to the United States, Prince Bandar bin Sultan, made him a hypocrite, given his frequent outspoken criticism of the Saudi regime as one of the principal sponsors of terrorist groups. "This company did part of the security system for the White House," Perle told me. "I didn't see a particular problem with selling those things. In the case of the Saudis, all I did was ask the ambassador if they would receive someone from the company. I never went to Saudi Arabia to talk to anybody. That was the extent of my involvement."

Perle insists that when he is approached by any company or entity willing to pay for his contacts and his entrée, he makes it clear that he does not and will not do that. What you are buying, he claims, are his insights and advice. "It's about how the process works, how to make a better presentation, how to understand and develop a strategy for achieving a result. I know a lot of senators and congressmen. I don't go to them and say, 'Could you please do this in connection with some business interest.' I just don't do that." Of course, he did precisely that during his first interregnum when he tried to intercede with the army on behalf of the Zabludowiczes and the mortar they wanted to sell, and he would do the same years later with a phone call to the State Department on behalf of a high-tech company involved in a dubious deal with the Chinese. "They were trying to make a settlement with State and I made one phone call just to see where the case stood. I make no apologies for that. I was not trying to pressure anybody to come out a certain way, but just to find out where the case stood."

Former government officials—particularly those whose expertise in sensitive areas like defense and technology—always have and always will attract the attention of various parties for various reasons. But with Citizen Perle, the action was, as he would put it, "on stilts." Not only would he find himself still involved in foreign policy disputes, but his roles would be consequential, not incidental. On at least one occasion, it was the unintended consequences to the world community—the effort to stop the ethnic cleansing in the former Yugoslavia—that placed Perle in the spotlight again. The 1991 UN Security Council Resolution 713 sought to stop the violence among Serbs, Croats, and Bosnians by placing the region under an arms embargo. But that left the heavily armed Serbs, led by the maniacal Slobodan Milosevic, effectively free to continue the carnage against the virtually defenseless Croats and Bosnian Muslims. Although Perle understood the resolution's lofty goal, he saw the embargo as "one of the most despicable acts of diplomacy in my lifetime" and blamed the Clinton administration for promising to defend the Muslims and then abandoning them.

In fact, the administration had been providing covert aid to the Croats and Bosnian Muslims through unmanned reconnaissance flights from a CIA base set up on the island of Krk, as well as airdrops of military supplies. When the Croatian defense minister came calling in Washington for more help, he was referred to a private company called Military Professional Resources Incorporated (MPRI), despite the fact that the UN embargo also extended to private entities. MPRI, lead by retired army chief of staff Carl Vuono, is a testament to the free enterprise system, a perfect meld of business and warfare. As MPRI executive Ed Soyster once bragged, "We've got more generals per square foot here than in the Pentagon." Colonels, majors, sergeants, and generals make up the thousand-employee firm, based in Alexandria, Virginia. It acts as a private-sector extension of the Pentagon, going places and doing things the Defense Department may be barred from, either by international law or by official government policy. In 1994, it took on a contract called "Drina River" which sent forty-five border monitors to Serbia to enforce the economic blockade against the Serbs in Bosnia and Krajina. In September of that year, MPRI and Croatia signed an agreement for the company to train Croatian officers, a deal known as the "Democracy Transition Assistance Program."

This in turn led to Operation Storm, a massive attack in August of 1995 by the Croatian army against the Krajina Serbs, which resulted in the displacement of an estimated 200,000 civilians. According to Croatia's intelligence chief, electronic, real-time intelligence was sent back to the Pentagon and the National Security Agency in Washington in what he described as "a partnership." Soyster denied his operatives had anything to do with ethnic cleansing, insisting "We went over and taught democracy transition because that is what the Croatians wanted."

Seeing and hearing of this development, the leadership of the Bosnian Muslims in Washington pressed for the same deal for their beleaguered troops. When the U.S. special envoy Richard Holbrooke announced that peace talks would be held in Dayton, Ohio, in November of 1995, Perle received an urgent phone call from the Bosnian foreign minister, Muhamed "Mo" Sacirbey, asking for his personal help in counseling the Bosnian Muslims at the negotiations. Knowing the clock was ticking, Perle told Sacirbey he'd get back to him in a few minutes. His phone rang again, but this time it was Holbrooke telling Perle the United States would be grateful if he accepted Sacirbey's invitation and came to Dayton to help the Bosnian Muslims negotiate how to spend the $100 million allocated by the United States for military assistance. Perle said he provided his services pro bono, hence neither he nor his partner Doug Feith filed papers with the State Department that they were acting as agents for a foreign government. After sitting through presentations from various companies, Perle and Feith chose Vuono and MPRI, unaware that the company had already been working for the Croats.

As far as Perle was concerned, the United States should have overtly broken the embargo, because that is what a superpower is supposed to do when faced with an injustice. "You don't want to do that every day because you pay a certain price. It's bound to be portrayed as arrogant. It doesn't win you points on the diplomatic circuit, but this was a matter that made it justified. The embargo was never intended to put a whole people in danger of annihilation." He blames special envoy Holbrooke for gaining a cease-fire just as the Serbian forces were being pushed back, leaving a circumstance in which Bosnia was carved up and tens of thousands could not return to their homes. "That was a mistake. We should have allowed them to go a little longer until the Serbs were driven out of Bosnia. Instead, we stopped it in a way that left three entities. I understand the pressures to end the war at that time, but the settlement reflected, as these always do, the reality on the ground. You show me one settlement that doesn't reflect whose troops are where. I know of only one example and I wrote a paper about it: the Treaty of

Ghent in 1814. We lost that war but we won the peace. It's almost always the other way around."

The mental picture of the Treaty of Ghent is a source of delight for Perle: an all-star cast of Americans suing for peace against a lackluster team of Britons who had the upper hand in what had become the stale-mated war of 1812. "We had an unbelievable negotiating team," Perle gushed. "John Quincy Adams, Albert Gallatin, who later became the first secretary of the treasury and was a brilliant man, Jonathan Russell, who had been our ambassador to the UK, and Henry Clay! Because the British had essentially won the war and were arrogant, they sent a retired admiral whose claim to fame was the shelling of Copenhagen during the Napoleonic Wars! So they sent a second-rate team and we just ate 'em!"

The concatenation of events in the Balkans could have been read as a cautionary tale of what transpires once a totalitarian regime falls and ethnic loyalties and warlords rush to fill the vacuum. It is cautionary also as a demonstration of unintended consequences: the UN embargo, meant to starve warring parties of matériel, made matters worse. Many in the foreign policy establishment read it exactly that way and advised that the America of the twenty-first century, the America without the countervailing Soviet Union, should use its power sotto voce, mindful of the repressed rage that had built up over centuries of subjugation and the tragically human desire for revenge and retribution.

But, in the context of Iraq and Saddam Hussein, Perle did not see the tragedy of the Balkans as a harbinger. He studied the disparate views of Cambridge historian Noel Malcolm and American journalist Robert D. Kaplan. In the breakup of Yugoslavia, Kaplan saw the future: a world of collapsing nation-states and warring tribes and jihadists of all stripes, a world of unbridled fury and carnage flowing through the cracks of the crumbling world powers like molten lava down a volcanic mountain. Noel Malcolm saw nothing of the sort; he saw Slobodan Milosevic, one more in a long list of messianic murderers. It was Malcolm's view that Perle adopted.

"Malcolm said, 'This is a man-made war. There is no spontaneous com-bustion. This is just Milosevic making a landgrab.' Tito had maintained equilibrium by being a very shrewd politician and parceling out authority among different ethnic groups, making sure everyone was a little bit happy. Milosevic threw all that out the door. He didn't want everyone to be a little bit happy. He wanted the Serbs to be very happy at the expense of everyone else. So he launched a war of aggression to do it."

Perle visited Bosnia after the war and was taken on a tour of Sarajevo by a young Bosnian Muslim. As they walked past the Serbian gun emplacements from which the Bosnians below had been shelled, Perle asked the man to point out the Serb neighborhoods and the Muslim neighborhoods and Croat neighborhoods. The young man told him there were no neighborhoods; they were completely integrated. "Sarajevo was more integrated than Washington, D.C.," Perle said. "They shared the same cafés, listened to the same music, and went to the same restaurants, the same schools. Any distinctions were based on income and education and so forth. Not on ethnic lines." Of course, that was the view from Sarajevo, which, like Baghdad, did not conform to the reality in the rest of the country.

In Perle's view, the carnage in the Balkans was the result not of tribalism but of the bloodthirsty ambitions of a handful of men. And if those men were removed, the newly liberated populace would live and prosper together in harmony. Saddam Hussein was a true mass murderer, and while the minority Sunni had it better than the majority Shia, the two shared a common fear of the dictator and lived in an integrated, albeit repressed society. Remove the menace, this theory held, and you remove the common fear. But nothing good could happen, in Perle's view, as long as Hussein remained in power.

Those holding Kaplan's view of a future in which centuries-old blood feuds and religious hatreds would eclipse the desire for freedom for all also saw in the U.S. intervention in the Balkans a more cynical motive: an American military presence in an area in which it had never been a presence before, and an opportunity to integrate Turkey and Israel into the region's defensive profile. To counter the Serbs, the United States already had backed the Croats, and used the MPRI to assist the Bosnian Muslims.

In January of 1996, following the peace agreement in Bosnia, Richard Perle told a Turkish newspaper not only that the arming and training of Bosnian Muslims was of "vital interest" to the United States, but that Turkey "is the number one candidate for the job." Six months later, the first phase of this policy was unveiled when Croatian officials met with the Turkish defense and foreign ministers in Ankara and agreed on a broad defense pact that allowed for joint military exercises and an exchange of officers for training. This in turn triggered an opening for Israel, which, under a defense agreement with Turkey, is mandated to upgrade and modify any equipment an ally might acquire. Their work included modernizing Croatia's MIG-21 aircraft and T-55 tanks, as well as a joint production deal for the Tabor assault rifle. The upgrading of the MIGs included all-new avionics either manufactured in Israel or taken from its inventory of American-made gear intended for Israel. At least one Israeli opposition member declared in the Knesset that allying with the Croats was "like selling our souls for a hundred million dollars." Nevertheless, Israel, with its new hard-line prime minister, Benjamin Netanyahu, elected as the Turks and Croats were meeting, had now become a player in the region, raising anew questions about who was zooming whom in U.S.-Israeli relations. These questions would shape much of the debate about the motives and allegiances of the ubiquitous neocons, especially those of Richard Perle.

VIII.
PERLE AND THE JEWS

IN AUGUST OF 2006, an Australian comedian at the Fringe Festival, a three-week carnival in Edinburgh, Scotland, where anyone can stage just about anything one wants, railed against the Bush administration and the Iraq War. By itself this was not unusual and may not have been even noteworthy, until he said, "I want to bash Condoleezza Rice's brain to bits and kill that fucking Jew Richard Perle!" The festival's organizers, invoking the mantra of free speech, solemnly declared that although many in the audience may have found the comic's remarks offensive, most would defend his right to make them. There was no public comment from Perle and he may not even have been aware of the incident.

But four months earlier, when the *London Review of Books* published a lengthy essay by two professors, one from the University of Chicago and the other from Harvard, Perle was well aware of what had been written and how it would affect him. The essay, simply titled, "The Israel Lobby," by John Mearscheimer and Stephen Walt, was a rare, open-field tackle of a subject that had long been out of bounds in American political discussion: the role of American Jews in shaping U.S. foreign policy. Among the paper's conclusions were (1) the pro-Israel lobbies in Washington, recently joined by Christian Zionists, have no serious opponents and therefore wield inordinate influence on government policy; (2) American politicians, sensitive to campaign contributions and other forms of pressure, see advantages in being sympathetic to Israel; (3) the effectiveness of the lobby has made the United States "the de facto enabler of Israeli expansion in the Occupied Territories, making it complicit in the crimes perpetrated against the Palestinians"; and (4) the lobby's attempts to quash debate about Israel is unhealthy for democracy—"silencing skeptics by organizing blacklists and boycotts, or by suggesting that critics are anti-Semites violates the principle of open debate on which democracy depends."

Predictably, Mearscheimer and Walt were themselves branded anti-Semites and their paper held up as a modern equivalent of *Mein Kampf*. The Anti-Defamation League called the paper, "a classical conspiratorial anti-Semitic analysis invoking the canards of Jewish political power and Jewish control." The University of Chicago's Daniel Drezner, managing to be vulgar and recondite in a single phrase, called it "piss-poor, mono-causal social science." Much of the criticism of the thesis came from the Left and its usual suspect, Noam Chomsky, who argued that American foreign policy since World War II has been driven by its own imperial interests with only occasional concern for its "junior partners," including Israel. Perhaps the wittiest critique came from Lieutenant Colonel Lawrence Wilkerson, Colin Powell's longtime chief of staff, who said the report conveyed "blinding flashes of the obvious." Indeed, the debate over Jewish-Israeli influence is starkly framed when one considers that Jews make up only about 2 percent of the American electorate, while Israel takes in by far more U.S. aid than any other country in the world.

There are now thirty members of the House who are Jewish and thirteen senators (the *Economist* notes with some amazement that there are now more Jews in Congress than Episcopalians). To be sure, there are no laws against one group being better funded and better organized than other groups, but because the Israel lobby is concerned mainly with how the United States uses its power in the Middle East and throughout the world, questions about true allegiances and loyalties are inevitable, as are suspicions of darker activity such as espionage.

For Richard Perle, this stirring up of old resentments about Jewish power in American society was problematical simply because he is a Jew, albeit nominally, and because he is clearly a man of influence. Yes, his education on Middle Eastern affairs and the importance of Israel as a strategic ally had come from Scoop Jackson and Dickie Fosdick, not from some inner heartbeat that made him yearn for the land of milk and honey (Perle clearly prefers a land of sauvignon blanc and raclette). And yes, the Jackson-Vanik amendment was of primary benefit to Soviet

Jews, among whom Perle considered Natan Sharansky a hero. But that was a freedom issue, a stick-it-to-Moscow issue, not strictly an Israel issue. The record shows that Perle became a target for the anti-Jewish, anti-Israelites because he put his face in the bull's-eye. Intentionally or not, Perle has become a symbol of unchecked and unwarranted Jewish meddling in U.S. foreign policy because of who his friends are and because of the position papers he has agreed to sign. And Exhibit A makes a convincing case.

In 1996, a report by the so-called Study Group on a New Israeli Strategy Toward 2000 was published in the United States and circulated internationally. The paper was strangely titled *A Clean Break: A New Strategy for Securing the Realm*. It purported to be a position paper for incoming Israeli prime minister Benjamin Netanyahu, the Likud Party leader whose tough rhetoric did not bode well for the Palestinians or for those Israelis in the peace movement. The paper bore the names of the study group members: Charles Fairbanks, Jr., of Johns Hopkins University; Robert Loewenberg, president of the Institute for Advanced Strategic and Political Studies (IASPS); Jonathan Torop of the Washington Institute for Near East Policy; David and Meyrav Wurmser of the IASPS and Johns Hopkins, respectively; and Douglas Feith of the law firm of Feith and Zell, based in Israel. The study group leader was Richard Norman Perle.

The six-page tract was partly a list of policy recommendations and partly a draft speech, or speeches, the authors proposed for Netanyahu. They marked what they considered key passages with the word "TEXT" in bold capital letters to underscore the "clean break" on policy the authors urged the new administration to adopt, and to neatly frame each position as a speech Netanyahu could deliver in either bite-sized portions or in toto.

Essentially, *A Clean Break* was a blueprint for Israeli dominance in the region, a paean to Zionist aspirations and biblical claims of divinely ordained destiny. It was a Jew-hater's delight, a gift that kept on giving, and lit up like a menorah on the radar screen of the millions who believe Israelis and American Jews run the world, economically, politically, and militarily. Even a cursory reading of the manifesto reveals not a single attempt at nuance or subtlety; this is a put-up-or-shut-up, in-your-face, use-it-or-lose-it litany that urged, among other things, "an *entirely new intellectual foundation* [emphasis theirs], one that restores strategic initiative and provides the nation the room to engage every possible energy on rebuilding Zionism." The authors proceed to recommend that Israel attack Syria and remove the ruling Ba'athist regime of Hafiz al-Assad, and, perhaps on the way back, attack Iraq and remove Saddam Hussein from power, replacing him with a Jordanian with a claim to the Iraqi throne. As for dealing with the Palestinians, the message was: Don't waste your time. There is no one with credibility to negotiate with, so put aside all pretense of the "peace process" and "uphold *the right of hot pursuit* [emphasis theirs] for self defense into all Palestinian areas and nurturing alternatives to Arafat's exclusive grip on Palestinian society."

Needless to say, *A Clean Break* caused what the British might describe as "a bit of a hash." Here were eight American citizens, led by a former assistant secretary of defense, publicly advising the leader of a foreign government to attack two sovereign neighboring states and to break off peace talks with its indigenous population. Had the authors not gone out of their way to generate publicity, this missive might have been ignored or dismissed as the usual rantings of American Zionists with far too much time on their hands. But because the intended recipient of the paper was already well-known as a man not favorably disposed to diplomacy as long as his military was dominant, and because he had come to power in the wake of an extremist Israeli Jew's murder of Yitzhak Rabin, and because the most prominent name among the signatories was that of the Prince of Darkness himself, *A Clean Break* moved from who-cares position paper to prima facie evidence in the can-you-believe-the-chutzpah-of-these-people dossier of Jewish influence in foreign policy.

Just count up the names and the argument appears to have merit: Leo Strauss, Albert Wohlstetter, Herman Kahn, Edward Teller, Bernard Lewis, Hans Morgenthau, Irving Howe, Allan Bloom, Irving Kristol, Daniel Bell, Nathan Glazer, Norman Podhoretz—philosophers, strategists, nuclear weapons experts, economists, social scientists, essayists, and journalists. All of them are Jewish and all of them, in one manner or another, exponents of America as an exceptional power on an exceptional mission: to prevail in a world of evil as a moral imperative. They were powerless against the pharaohs, powerless against the Cossacks and the czars, powerless against the Nazis, powerless behind the Iron Curtain. But an America with a strong government and the strongest military needn't fear any man, nation, or ideology. At some point the United States had to stop apologizing for its prosperity and take center stage as the world's leader; if not America, then who?

"What makes America powerful?" one of the the creators of *A Clean Break,* David Wurmser, asked me. "The answer you get from the rest of the world is: You Americans are lucky. It's a wealthy country. You're rich. And you're powerful because you're rich. But most Americans know we started out as a besieged country with not a lot of resources and we defeated the greatest empire on the planet. Our power comes from our ideas. America doesn't love underdogs; what they love is the story of principle overpowering people who may be technically more powerful. Is it just military resources, or is it a set of ideas and principles that make you great?"

Wurmser, now a special advisor to Vice President Dick Cheney, was born in Switzerland and raised in Baltimore. He was the only Jew in his high school in the 1970s. It seemed to him that the adults in his life saw in Israel everything that America had once been but was no longer, mainly strong. Not only had America failed in Vietnam, but it was also being humiliated on the world stage by having its embassy personnel in Tehran blindfolded, mocked, and paraded about. In contrast, the Israelis rescued their hostages at Entebbe, and their air force had flown hundreds of miles through hostile air space to destroy Iraq's nuclear reactor. Of the Iranian hostage crisis, all of Wurmser's friends kept saying, "Why don't we let the Israelis handle it?" In the 1970s, he made his first visit to Israel and was impressed and surprised by the fervor of the nation's citizen army and their sense of empowerment, a feeling Wurmser had never had as a youth in America. Feeding his inferiority was his mother's anger toward the regime in her native Czechoslovakia, which she fled in 1948, a regime that would black out large portions of letters she received from her family, and would confiscate photos meant to keep the family connected. Wurmser concluded that the Soviet Union was not a misguided and misunderstood power as so many of his friends believed. It was evil, and its surrogates were evil.

Wurmser spent twelve years as a naval intelligence officer in the Pentagon before joining the IASPS, a right-wing Jerusalem-based think tank with an office in Washington, which spawned the study group that led to *A Clean Break*, He had met Richard Perle several times at the American Enterprise Institute, which Perle had joined after leaving the Pentagon in 1987, but doubts that such a major player even knew his name then. Like Perle, Wurmser had been influenced by Hans Morgenthau's *A Realistic Theory of International Politics*, but drew somewhat different conclusions from it than Perle. Yes, power is the coin of the realm in international affairs, but meaningful power must have a moral underpinning exemplified by democracy and self-rule, concepts that, as far as Wurmser could see, were an anathema to Islamists.

"They think we have no soul," he told me. "They're not attacking us because we're Christians and Jews. They think we're not even Christians and Jews. And they see things that confirm that over and over, culturally with our music and movies and so forth, and theologically. We believe the individual has sovereignty because for us sovereignty is a human attribute. For the Muslim, sovereignty is a divine attribute. As a result, what we see as the culture of a nation, they see as polytheism. So the miscommunication leads them to believe we have no soul, no religion…we're not even Christians and we're not even Jews. We're heretics, or worse, apostates. We're not even infidels, because infidels have the option of converting. An apostate is someone who is supposed to be part of the three main religions but turns against it. There's no forgiveness for the apostate. You can't recant. He may be forgiven, but he still must be executed."

At the IASPS, Wurmser and his Israel-born wife Meyrav were the driving force behind the study group, but they believed they needed someone with a bit more gravitas to generate the publicity they sought. So Wurmser asked a friend to ask Perle if he would join the group and help promote their paper. Although Perle's name on the paper did attract attention at the time, *A Clean Break* would attain significant status five years later, when, in the aftermath of 9/11, it was seen as a blueprint for America's War on Terror.

In account after account by critics of the war, *A Clean Break* is mentioned prominently as hard evidence that a U.S. attack on Iraq and its saber rattling toward Iran and Syria were inspired by American Zionists promoting not only U.S. hegemony but also an Israel that is dominant in its region...hence the subtitle's reference to "securing the realm."

"The whole context is different from what people say," Wurmser insists. "Israel was becoming a burden. We were afraid they would so weaken what we considered the cornerstone of American strategy in the region that they were becoming a burden. And what we were trying to say was if they could move in the right direction they could then reposition themselves as a major asset and a useful ally rather than as an albatross. People think this was initiated from the Israelis, telling us what to say, using the power of the United States to execute an Israeli agenda. And the truth of it was exactly the reverse. We were a group of conservative Americans concerned about the course that both Israeli and American policy had been taking."

In fact, they were a group of mostly *Jewish* conservative Americans attempting to foment another war in the Middle East. Their affiliations are a cross section of the Israeli-Jewish lobbying complex, including the American Israel Public Affairs Committee (AIPAC), the Jewish Institute for National Security Affairs (JINSA) and the Washington Institute for Near East Policy (WINEP). While Richard Perle has appeared at all of those institutions, and is a board member of both JINSA and WINEP, his reputation as a fervent Zionist is not nearly as clear or as deserved as that of Doug Feith and the Wurmsers. In fact, Wurmser admits that Israel has never been high on Perle's list of causes.

"He has some ambivalent feelings about Israel," he said. "I think he was turned off a lot by the cynicism of Israeli politics, the cynicism of

Israeli leadership. I don't think he particularly trusts their judgments. He has had as many run-ins with Israeli elites as he's had positive relationships. On the Iraq issue, he tried desperately to make the Israelis understand that this may be in their interest. And it was the Israelis who were very cynical. They were very dismissive of everything, and I think Richard was put off by that."

But Arabs were not dismissive. When Perle served as foreign policy advisor to candidate George W. Bush in 2000, the Arab American Institute sent out a press release commending the candidate for his positive remarks about the peace talks going on then between Yasir Arafat and Ehud Barak, but called on Bush to fire Perle. It seems Perle was advising Barak to walk away from the talks if a comprehensive deal was not reached. The press release brought up *A Clean Break*, which had advised Benjamin Netanyahu to walk away from the talks, and concluded, "Perle should decide whether advising Israel how not to make peace is more important than advising potential U.S. presidents on how to make peace. While he is deciding, the Bush campaign should consider putting Perle under a news blackout."

But the mention of *A Clean Break* elicits barely a shrug from Perle, who is surprised to learn that he is listed as the study group's leader. "A friend of mine asked me to join. In fact, I was busy. I never went to any session of the study group. Not one. A report got produced and I didn't write a word of it. At the last minute, in order to give it more publicity, they decided to call it a memorandum for Netanyahu. Now, I never signed up to prepare a memo for Netanyahu, but I didn't have a problem with the substance of it."

"Why is it subtitled *A New Strategy for Securing the Realm*?" I asked.

Perle smiled and said, "Yes, a terrible title. I didn't pay much attention to it." Perle admits he did give some advice to Netanyahu directly, and it was to tell the U.S. Congress that Israel would no longer accept economic assistance from the United States. He says he told the new prime minister, "Look, your economy has been very successful. Stand on your own. You would be in a much stronger position if you were not receiving welfare from the United States." Although U.S. aid to Israel represents only a small percentage of the Israeli economy, Perle knew that the perception of Israel with its hand out was a negative image that Tel Aviv needed to address.

Netanyahu told Perle he was intrigued by the idea but, like the recommendations in *A Clean Break*, ultimately he ignored it. As for Wurmser's feeling that Perle is less than enamored of Israeli leaders past and present, Perle nods in agreement. "I think the country is badly governed. I think Israeli politicians more than in most countries are self-centered and put their own narrow interests ahead of the national interest. They can't seem to pull themselves together even on urgent matters. The last Israeli government that I really admired was Golda Meir's. I thought she was terrific and she was on the Left." Yet Perle's most virulent critics label him a Likudnik and a staunch supporter of the infamous prime minister Ariel Sharon. "A guy from the *Telegraph* came to interview me and asked about my relationship with Sharon. I said 'I never met him.' And he was stunned. He had done his homework and seen dozens and dozens of references to my relationship with Sharon. How do these people say I'm a Likudnik? What is that based on?"

More than likely it is based not only on Perle's reputation as a rejectionist, but on a series of incidents involving Israel in which Perle or his friends were accused or suspected of compromising U.S. security for the sake of the Jewish state. The first was the previously detailed FBI wiretap that Seymour Hersh claimed revealed Perle disclosing classified information to the Israeli embassy in Washington. The second was Perle's unwavering support for Stephen Bryen despite Bryen's alleged attempts to hand classified data over to the Mossad's Washington station chief at the Madison Hotel. A third involved Perle's lobbying on behalf of the Zabludowiczes' Israeli arms firm. And a fourth involved Bryen again, who had been placed in a sensitive post at the Pentagon by Perle. In 1988, when Israel was close to completing a prototype of its Arrow ballistic missile, Bryen allegedly attempted to hasten the export to Israel of a key piece of technology the Israelis needed for the missile, a component that was highly restricted and closely guarded by the DOD. When Bryen's supervisor told him the component could not be exported, Bryen tried to do an end around the system but was stopped by then assistant secretary of defense Richard Armitage.

Bryen resigned his DOD post in late 1988 but reemerged in the George W. Bush administration in 2001 as a member of a high-level commission to monitor so-called backdoor transfers of U.S. military technology to China from other parties, particularly Israel. Both Israel and Turkey had a long history of receiving U.S. matériel, through both sales and grants, changing the end-user licenses, and selling the matériel to China and other countries. Israel had previously been caught providing state-of-the-art U.S. electronics to the Chinese for their F-10 fighter and Python air combat missile.

Bryen was chosen for the commission by two important supporters of Turkey and Israel, House Speaker Dennis Hastert and Deputy Defense Secretary Paul Wolfowitz. What raised eyebrows within the intelligence community was the fact that as a commission member, Bryen would be granted a "Q" security clearance, which gave him access to nuclear weapons technology. Given the previous accusations against Bryen for allegedly passing classified information to the Israelis and attempting to export a banned component to Tel Aviv, the appointment seemed preposterous to those in the technology-transfer business. Bryen and his wife, Shoshana, are also wired in to the pro-Israel political action groups in Washington as directors of JINSA, perhaps the most aggressive of the Israeli lobbies, which Perle has supported since its inception.

"I supported JINSA because its initial mission was to try to explain to American Jews that if you think you're for Israel you can't be hostile to the American defense effort," Perle told me. "JINSA was founded by people who were damned annoyed at those American Jews who wanted the U.S. to defend Israel but didn't want the defense budget that would permit us to do it....That's basically the liberal Jewish community. It just drove me crazy to hear those guys say, 'You've got to get in there to fight for Israel, and, oh, by the way, you should be cutting the defense budget.'"

As its first executive director, JINSA chose Michael Ledeen, another Perle friend with a dubious background. Even by Washington standards, Ledeen is considered an oddball, a self-described "democratic revolutionary" and admirer of Machiavelli; his education was in modern European studies at the University of Wisconsin–Madison, and he is considered a world-class bridge player. While working as an advisor to the NSC during the Reagan administration, Ledeen was the contact between the Oliver North–McFarlane–Poindexter–Iran-Contra-arms-for-hostages scheme and Iranian arms dealer Manucher Ghorbanifar. He also met with Israeli prime minister Shimon Peres to facilitate the transfer of U.S. arms to Iran through Israel. In the succeeding investigation, Ledeen swore that his contact with Peres had been approved by his superiors, a claim denied by NSC chairman McFarlane.

Ledeen was also the man who negotiated a deal to sell TOW antitank missiles to Israel at a price far below normal. Because the deal was practically a giveaway, Ledeen's superiors renegotiated the contract and removed him from the process. Ledeen has long been suspected of having an ongoing relationship with Israeli intelligence and with SISMI, the Italian intelligence service—claims he describes as nonsense. Ledeen, who once lived and worked in Rome as a visiting professor, has had numerous contacts with SISMI, most recently during the run-up to the invasion of Iraq. When I asked Ledeen about reports that his security clearance had been downgraded during the Iran-Contra planning because of suspicions about his loyalty, and that Oliver North had recommended to incoming NSC chairman John Poindexter that Ledeen be given regular polygraph tests, Ledeen ordered me to leave his office, but not before delivering this volley: "What is the most potent lobby in Washington? Hands down it's Saudi Arabia. Saudi Arabia *owns* more former secretaries of defense and secretaries of state than anyone else. Anyone who thinks the Israeli lobby is a defining force in American foreign policy just doesn't understand Washington."

"Michael is absolutely not a Mossad agent," Perle told me, although how he would know is unclear. "I was one of the very first people Michael met when he came to Washington. We've been friends for a long time. I would bet my life that not only is Michael not a Mossad agent, but has never done anything for the Mossad. I don't know where it comes from."

Then there is Harold Rhode, a PhD in Ottoman Studies who speaks Hebrew, Arabic, Turkish, and Farsi, and who served as Hebrew instructor to Perle's son, Jonathan, prior to the boy's bar mitzvah. He first met Perle in 1982, introduced by Defense Department undersecretary Bill Luti, who told Perle, "You should hire this guy." Perle hired Rhode to serve as his advisor on how the Arabs think, a kind of interpreter of Arab DNA. Rhode, a small, stocky fellow who speaks in a high-pitched voice, describes himself as "a son who wishes to remember what my parents wish to forget." An ardent Zionist, Rhode was grateful for the chance to contribute to what he felt was a revolution in U.S. foreign policy during the Reagan administration and is fulsome in his praise for Perle.

"My mother came to one of Richard's picnics [an annual ritual at the Perle house in Maryland] and she went up to him and said, 'Thank you for employing my son.' And Richard put his arm around her and said, 'Your son is a national treasure.' I would kill for him…although I don't really mean kill." Rhode generally refuses reporters' requests for interviews, telling one, "Those who speak, pay," but he sat with me on several occasions at the Mayflower Hotel as the blowback from both the Iraq War and a potentially explosive espionage case unfolded in Washington. Rhode had traveled to Rome with Ledeen and a Pentagon analyst named Lawrence Franklin for meetings that would have a volatile impact once revealed in the various investigations of the decision to invade Iraq.

The proverbial fly on the wall would have found Ledeen and Rhode provocative conversationalists. Among Ledeen's more quotable remarks: "Every ten years or so, the US needs to take some crappy little country and throw it against a wall, just to show we mean business." Among Harold Rhode's zingers is this fusillade directed at a visiting Arab diplomat: "No more bartering in the bazaar anymore! You're going to have to sit up and pay attention when we say so!" CIA personnel monitoring Rhode reportedly observed him "constantly on his cell phone to Israel, discussing U.S. plans, military deployments, political projects and Iraqi assets."

As the Bush administration sought to make a case for war in Iraq and perhaps with Iran as well, the trio came together in Rome with Ledeen's old friend Manucher Ghorbanifar and the head of SISMI, Nicolo Pollari, as well as Italian defense minister Antonio Martino. The government of right-wing billionaire Silvio Berlusconi has long been suspected of having fabricated the infamous Niger document, which purported to show that Saddam Hussein was attempting to purchase yellowcake uranium from Niger to be used for a nuclear weapon, and which also implicated Iran as part of the conspiracy.

The purpose of the meeting has been the subject of much debate. The speculation is that the subject was either American plans to attack Iran or a deal being pushed by some in the State Department and the CIA that the attendees wanted to kill, a deal in which the Iranians would turn over five captured Al-Qaeda operatives in return for Washington's ending covert support for the MEK, the terrorist group trying to overthrow the Iranian government. Asked about the MEK, Rhode would only tell me, "I hate them," and about his mission in general, "If there were any secret meetings, nobody told me about them." He claims to have never heard the acronym SISMI. The CIA was not alerted about the Rome meeting, but when they learned that Ghorbanifar was involved they made sure to steer clear of it. The agency had gotten sucked into Ghorbanifar's bait-and-switch games during Iran-Contra and had gone over the cliff with him.

This time, Ghorbanifar had brought with him a man he claimed was a former top official of Iran's Revolutionary Guard. Apparently Rhode and Franklin bought the routine and cabled the Pentagon that they had "made contact with Iranian intelligence officers who anticipate possible regime change in Iran and want to establish contact with the United States government....A sizeable financial interest is required." There is no evidence that any money was paid, but Rhode did go on to another meeting with Ghorbanifar in Paris, a meeting even the Pentagon later admitted was "unplanned."

Perle doesn't recall whether he knew about the Rome meeting before or after the fact, but saw nothing wrong with it in any case. "Michael tells me that Ghorbanifar has been over the years a consistently reliable source of information about the regime in Iran, that he's very well connected there; people talk to him and he knows a lot. So if there was a chance that useful information could be obtained by meeting with him, why not?"

Not long after these sessions, Larry Franklin, a Catholic with a PhD in East Asian studies, was seen walking into a Washington restaurant in the company of an lobbyist for the American Israel Public Affairs Committee and an official of the Israeli embassy. That got the FBI's attention, and they were watching and listening when Franklin discussed classified information about U.S. plans for Iran with two officials of AIPAC, Steve Rosen and Keith Weissman, and Israeli diplomat Naor Gilon at a restaurant in the Washington area. The FBI had long suspected AIPAC of being a conduit for secret information to the Israelis, and had been watching Franklin, Rosen, and Weissman for months. The information Franklin disclosed was a draft national security presidential directive on Iran, a summary of the deliberations going on within the White House regarding the Iranian threat. Franklin eventually plea-bargained his way to a twelve-year sentence and agreed to work with the FBI, who kept the case under cover.

In June of 2004, Perle received a phone call from Franklin at his home in Maryland and immediately became suspicious. He had known Franklin only slightly, and now the Pentagon analyst was asking Perle to relay a message to Ahmed Chalabi, the controversial head of the Iraqi National Congress whom Perle had been pushing as Iraq's interim leader. Perle thought the call was "weird," declined to relay the message, and got off the phone in a hurry. He later learned the FBI had been listening. For reasons that are not clear, the trial of Rosen and Weissman has been repeatedly delayed to the point where some believe it might never take place at all. In April of 2007, the government lost its bid to bar the press from covering large portions of testimony at the eventual trial on national security grounds, as Judge Thomas Ellis ruled such a ban would infringe on the defendants' constitutional rights. Still, no trial date was set. In the meantime, Franklin tried to make a living as a park-

Another day at the office: Perle at a policy forum in Madrid, circa 2004.
Spanish delegate Ramón Pérez Simarro appears underwhelmed by the testimony.

(top) Former president Gerald Ford, with Leslie and Richard Perle. To Perle, Ford was a creature of his secretary of state, Henry Kissinger, and his continuing promotions of détente in dealing with the Soviet Union.

(bottom) Perle and Kurdish leader Mustafa Barzani, who died in 1979. "I wanted to help Barzani," Perle said. "I introduced him to [*New York Times* columnist] Bill Safire who's been a strong defender of the Kurds. I have a lot of sympathy for the Kurds in Iraq and Iran." But Perle's work on behalf of Turkey made his Kurdish sympathies suspect.

Perle and Vice President Dan Quayle. Perle stayed out of government during the
Bush 41 administration, but remained an influential player among those, like Quayle,
who were more hawkish than the president and his top foreign policy advisors.

Jack Kemp, Perle, Ehud Olmert, Helen Jackson, Douglas Feith, and Natan Sharansky at the dedication of the Henry M. Jackson Square in Jerusalem in 1994.

(left page: top) Henry M. "Scoop" Jackson, Jack Perle, and Perle in 1972. Of Jackson, Perle said, "He was my father when I still had a father." Of Jack Perle, his real father, he said, "I am eternally grateful that I came to appreciate him while he was still alive. As I got older, I realized he was really a terrific person."

(left page: bottom) Israeli prime minister Yitzhak Rabin and Perle. While not referring to Rabin specifically, Perle has never been enamored of Israeli leaders. "I think the country is badly governed. Israeli politicians more than in most countries put their own narrow interests ahead of the national interest. The last Israeli government I really admired was Golda Meir's."

Perle, President George H.W. Bush, and British prime minister Margaret Thatcher, circa 1991. When the president demurred about rolling back Saddam Hussein's invasion of Kuwait, Thatcher reportedly said, "Don't go wobbly on me, George." Perle insists, "She said that because he was going wobbly on her."

Paul Wolfowitz and Perle before Wolfowitz's departure from the Pentagon to
head the World Bank. Although friendly since the late 1960s, Perle says he
hasn't spoken to Wolfowitz in years, believing Wolfowitz wanted a new start and
a new set of friends at the bank. Wolfowitz was forced to resign from the bank
in July 2007 amid scandal.

Perle and Colin Powell during the Reagan years. Their friendship ended during the Bush 43 administration over the war in Iraq. "He's a very smart man, very capable," Perle said of Powell. "But I don't know why he's apologizing; he used the intelligence he was given, just like everybody else."

(right page: top) Perle's final meeting with President Reagan in the Oval Office, 1987. Perle used the opportunity to reiterate his view that "nuclear weapons are here to stay. You can't uninvent them. A world without nuclear weapons isn't credible and I wouldn't want it even if we could."

(right page: bottom) Perle and President Reagan at the White House in 1987. "He wasn't stupid," Perle said of Reagan. "He saw things more clearly than I did." But Reagan's yearning for a world free of nuclear weapons was, to Perle, dangerously naive.

Prince Bandar bin Sultan bin Abdul Aziz, then Saudi Arabian ambassador to the United States, at a committee hearing with Perle in the 1980s. After 9/11, Bandar all but accused Perle of attempting to extort an investment from a Saudi businessman in exchange for Perle's easing up on his criticisms of the Saudi regime and its sponsorship of terror groups. Perle denied any such conduct.

Perle at a policy forum, date uncertain. "He is for sure a godfather," says former aide Doug Feith. "He would work to help anybody he liked and admired and who he thought was useful to the cause of U.S. national security. He would exert himself . . . and he had a tremendous number of people who felt grateful to him."

Perle and Gen. Wesley Clark (ret.) at a congressional hearing in 2005. A year earlier, Perle had ridiculed Clark's warning about the dangers of invading Iraq, calling the general "hopelessly confused."

Perle and his boss at Colin Powell's home in March 1986. In Perle, Defense
Secretary Caspar Weinberger knew he had someone who would protect
the Pentagon's interests in the never-ending policy battles with the State
Department during the Reagan years.

Perle being sworn in as assistant secretary of defense by Defense Department counsel Will Taft, 1981. Leslie Perle is to Richard's left. Perle designed the job for himself after turning down an offer to work for Alexander Haig in the State Department.

(left page: top) Colin Powell, Caspar Weinberger, and Leslie Perle at a dinner at Powell's home in March 1986. As Weinberger's military deputy, Powell was responsible for keeping Perle from "wandering off the reservation" by speaking his mind to the press. It was a habit Perle refused to break.

(left page: bottom) Albert Wohlstetter, Perle's intellectual godfather, congratulates his pupil and Leslie Perle at Richard's swearing-in as assistant secretary of defense for international policy in 1981.

Perle, Douglas Feith, Harold Rhode, and Helen Jackson in Israel. As one Jewish-American lobbyist said of Perle, "He hangs with a pro-Israel crowd, but that's not the main thing with him. He's not Doug Feith. He's not a right-wing lunatic on Israel."

ing lot attendant at a West Virginia racetrack, while Rosen and Weissman remained free on bail.

The federal prosecutor hinted that he was considering a review of all contacts among U.S. government employees, lobbyists, and Israeli government officials going back at least to the mid-nineties, a prospect that clearly made Harold Rhode uncomfortable. He seemed fidgety during our last meeting when I asked about the Franklin case, and admitted it worried him. As for Perle, he shook his head when Franklin was mentioned, perhaps thinking about Franklin's wheelchair-bound wife and five children. He knew that Franklin had been taking a much harder line on Iran than many of his colleagues at the Pentagon and apparently became frustrated that things weren't moving fast enough. "I'm told by Larry that he never gave documents of any kind to anybody. So, if he took stuff home it was a technical violation because lots of people take stuff home. The working day isn't long enough. People break those security rules all the time. I had a safe here in my home when I was assistant secretary. I was authorized to bring things home up to the top secret level. I'm not going to tell you that I never brought home material that was classified higher than that. But you're careful about them. You don't leave them on the kitchen table."

While Franklin was arguably motivated by a genuine concern for national security, Rhode and his boss, Doug Feith, were known as unabashed supporters of Israel and were believed around Washington to have no qualms about putting Tel Aviv's interests ahead of everything else. Their association with and support for JINSA and AIPAC are prime examples to critics of American policy in the Middle East who insist that Israeli influence in Washington is insidious and out of control. A top official of a moderate Jewish lobbying organization, who once worked for AIPAC, believes Perle's involvement with Feith, Ledeen, Franklin, and Rhode and their ilk is more a result of his loyalty to friends rather than some burning allegiance to Israel. "Perle hangs with a pro-Israel crowd, but that's not the main thing with him. He's not Doug Feith. He's not a right-wing lunatic on Israel. Most of those guys are so far right they're beyond Israel…they're into 'Greater Israel.' I mean, what did they call their paper? 'A strategy for securing *the realm*?' Feith is beyond an Israeli-firster. There is nothing that matters to Feith except Israel. Perle's not part of that."

As for Larry Franklin's involvement, the man believes he was a fall guy manipulated by Steven Rosen. Rosen, who once wrote in a memo that a lobby "is like a night flower…it thrives in the dark and dies in the sun," was fired by AIPAC in 2004 for conduct unbecoming. "That's how Rosen operated," he said.

> I was at AIPAC the same time he was and the only guy who would show up at senior staff meetings with secret stuff was Steve Rosen. But nobody ever said, "We don't want to hear it." The thing is that before Rosen got there, AIPAC didn't do executive branch lobbying. There was no such thing. When you worked the legislature you talked to people who didn't have classified stuff and you'd say, "So what do you hear?" But as soon as you start trolling the Pentagon or Foggy Bottom, it changes. You're talking to people with high security clearances who shouldn't be talking to you. So Rosen created that position for himself, and AIPAC let him do it. But I don't think Richard Perle had anything to do with that.

Indeed, there is no evidence that he did. When I asked Perle a second time the what-would-you-do hypothetical about learning that a friend or colleague was passing classified material even to a friendly government, he paused for some time. "I certainly would not shelter him," he said finally. "If he was not reporting to me in government, would I get on a hotline and inform? I'd have to think about that. It would depend on the circumstances. If they reported to me, I would take appropriate action. I don't approve of violating those rules…not at all."

There was no overt mention of the Franklin-Rosen-Weissman case at AIPAC's annual convention in Washington in the spring of 2007, an affair that has grown in size and political importance over the years. AIPAC itself came into its own as a response to Ronald Reagan's decision to sell AWACS early-warning aircraft to Saudi Arabia in 1981. Reagan saw the deal as part of an effort to forge an Arab-Israeli union to counter Soviet influence in the region, and also as a test of his own prestige. Now AIPAC's literature quotes the *New York Times*, describing it as "the most important organization affecting America's relationship with Israel," and its members boast of jamming more than a hundred pieces of pro-Israel legislation through Congress each year. A cross section of the U.S. defense industry either sits on the AIPAC board or faithfully attends its meetings and conferences. This three-day extravaganza drew six thousand people, including most congressional leaders and presidential candidates Hillary Clinton, Barack Obama, and Joe Biden. According to former Israeli cabinet speechwriter Gregory Levey, who was in attendance, Biden "kept repeating 'Hi, I'm Joe Biden....I've been hanging out with AIPAC for years!' " Evangelical Christians also showed up because they believe that without Israel there can be no Second Coming. Pastor John Hagee roared at the crowd at the opening reception, "The sleeping giant of Christian Zionism has awoken!" After equating the Palestinians with the Taliban, he led the crowd in a chant of "Israel lives!" prompting one delegate to mutter, "I'm going to vote for him instead of McCain." Vice President Cheney appeared to thunderous applause, perhaps the only thunderous applause he will hear for the foreseeable future. Israeli prime minister Ehud Olmert appeared via teleconference from Jerusalem, more popular among the convention audience than he is in his own country. These and other moments reinforced the otherworldly atmosphere of the conference, the sense that the attendees were living in a parallel universe blissfully dismissive of the ugly realities facing both the United States and Israel. Of course, no one spoke of these things because any deviation from dogma is met with fearsome rebuke. And if AIPAC is about anything, it is about fear. A letter from a high school senior that appeared on the Internet offers the view of one impressionable adolescent:

> The first thing I noticed, besides the sheer volume of participants, was the carefully manufactured atmosphere of fear and urgency. The cavernous hall that hosted all our meals and plenary sessions was always filled with dramatic classical music,

red lighting and gigantic signs reading, "Now Is the Time." That, combined with montages of terrorism footage projected onto six giant screens, whipped the audience into a "Save Israel" fervor that most found inspiring....I returned from the conference, however, feeling manipulated, disturbed and disgusted with a great deal of what I had witnessed there.

As I read the letter to David Wurmser, he frowned, stared down at his shoes, and nodded. "There's no doubt that fear is part of the manipulation of people. But fear is the easier argument to make. The harder argument is to outline the positive things you are for. Intellectually, it's a lot easier to fall back on a negative argument, the most common of which is fear. But it doesn't get much done. It's a very good Washington tradition, but I don't think it gets a lot done."

Actually, it gets quite a bit done and always has. In the mid-1920s, the U.S. chemical industry teamed up with the federal Chemical Warfare Service (CWS) in a shameless propaganda campaign to help secure protective tariffs, an embargo on chemical imports and rejection of the Geneva protocol banning chemical warfare. Along with such groups as the American Legion and the Veterans of Foreign Wars, the CWS and the chemical industry flooded Washington with pamphlets asserting that the Geneva protocol was part of a communist plot to leave America unprotected in the event of a gas attack, asserting that "the very safety of civilization" would depend on its rejection. Even the *Washington Post* climbed on board, commending the Senate's rejection of the protocol and dismissing the view that gas warfare was inhumane as "arrant humbug." Clearly the policy fight, regardless of its merits, had been carried by the effective use of fear. Likewise this comment from John Foster Dulles in 1939 regarding America's ambivalence about entering a world war: "The creation of a vast armament in itself calls for a condition midway between war and peace. Mass emotion on a substantial scale is prerequisite. The willingness to sacrifice must be engendered. A sense of peril from abroad must be cultivated."

Of course, in that instance, the peril from abroad did not require the creation of a "sense," except perhaps to the senseless. Hitler was a clear, imminent, and identifiable threat, a slam dunk. But when Perle made a similar comment almost forty-five years later in the chill of the cold war, the circumstances were not quite so clear. "Democracies will not sacrifice to protect their security in the absence of a sense of danger. And every time we create the impression that we and the Soviets are cooperating and moderating our competition, we diminish that sense of apprehension." Hence, the anathema not only on treaties and cooperative agreements, but even on discussion about them, lest such discussion lead to increased hope for peace and decreased apprehension.

This was the AIPAC strategy as well. It rejected the Oslo Accords, and talks of any kind with the Palestinians and their state supporters, and pounded home the Iranian threat to Israel. At the 2005 conference, Perle stirred the faithful with a call for "decisive action" against Iran, while a multimedia show, *Iran's Path to the Bomb*, played on a loop in the convention center's basement. As the *Washington Post*'s Dana Milbank described it, "In a succession of rooms, visitors see flashing lights and hear rumbling sounds as Dr. Seuss–like contraptions make yellowcake uranium, reprocess plutonium, and pop out nuclear warheads like so many gallons of hummus." The 2007 event was not quite as bombastic, and there was certainly no mention of yellowcake uranium. Perle attended, of course, but did not speak. This was not the time for cheap theatrics. Things were falling apart all around him, and his friends and acolytes had become piñatas in the court of public opinion. Although he did not now nor had he ever considered himself a toady for Israel, that's how Perle was perceived. Right or wrong, former CIA deputy director Bobby Inman spoke for many when he told a reporter, "Iraq is not about oil. Iraq is about, on the one side, weapons of mass destruction, the UN and disarmament. And on the other one, [it] goes back to '96 and Richard Perle's study [*A Clean Break*] and the absolute dedication that Wolfowitz, Perle, Feith, Rumsfeld, Wurmser, Bolton, others have had ever since '96 on regime change. And that was the way you guarantee

Israel's security.... Zealots often carry the day. They are USA loyalists. But their vision of the Mideast is shaped by concern for Israel's long-term security. Myself, I don't think you will ever get security in the Mideast until you have what on the surface appears to be fair to both sides.... One side can't impose a solution."

It can't? Perle would see about that.

IX.
THE BAYEAUX TAPESTRY

PERLE ISN'T SURE just who introduced him to Ahmed Chalabi; it might have been Bernard Lewis, but it probably was Albert Wohlstetter. He remembers it was in London in 1985, when Perle was working for Cap Weinberger, and the Soviet Union and Gorbachev were still very much on the front burner. But off to the side was the Iran-Iraq War, which had implications that overlapped U.S.-Soviet relations. Not only was the United States shipping out matériel and advisors to help Saddam Hussein, but it had dispatched special envoy Donald Rumsfeld, at the time CEO of the GD Searle pharmaceutical company, to obtain Saddam's approval for construction of a new pipeline that would run Iraqi oil through to Aqaba in Jordan, the Iranians and Syrians having cut off the flow of Iraqi oil through its territories.

The now infamous photo of Rumsfeld and Saddam shaking hands at their meeting in Baghdad has since become an Internet icon, a symbol of the moral relativism of American foreign policy. Saddam Hussein was every bit the murderous tyrant in 1983 that he was in 2003, but, according to an Iraqi intelligence officer present at the meetings, "All [Rumsfeld] wanted to talk about were business deals." It is a testament to both Rumsfeld's impudence and his ignorance that his secret plan was to run a tap off that pipeline into Israel, a scheme he hoped to sell to Jordan's King Hussein. When Rumsfeld told U.S. ambassador to Jordan Richard Viets about the idea, Viets replied, "Proposing that is a terrible idea. I will not support it, and in any case, the King will never under any circumstances agree to it." Undeterred, Rumsfeld told Viets, "You may be looking for another job soon." But when King Hussein immediately rejected the idea, Rumsfeld grudgingly admitted that Viets had been right.

When Perle was recalling with pleasure how Ronald Reagan refused to be photographed clinking champagne glasses with Gorbachev lest it convey the wrong message, I mentioned the Rumsfeld-Saddam photo. "I don't remember the circumstances around that," he said. "I need to look into that. It was certainly overblown. I think it was a simple visit. I don't remember what the occasion was."

But he does remember being solidly impressed by Ahmed Chalabi, the scion of a prominent Iraqi Shia family, born into a culture of wealth and influence in 1944. The Chalabis fled Iraq in 1958 after the coup that toppled Iraq's King Faisal II and spent their lives hopscotching the world's capitals, setting up bases in the United States, Lebanon, and London. Chalabi received his BS in mathematics from MIT in 1965, and his doctorate four years later from the University of Chicago. He taught for a time at the American University in Beirut.

In 1977, Chalabi opened the Petra Bank in Jordan and within two years made it the second largest in the country. He is the man who brought the Visa card and ATMs to Jordan, an achievement for which he was never formally recognized. He was the first to open bank branches in the Israeli-occupied West Bank. Accounts of the bank's brief history indicate that Chalabi used his family's connections to move money through the international banking network without pausing to abide by Jordan's currency controls. Among the beneficiaries of Petra's liberal lending policy was Jordan's Prince Hassan to the tune of $30 million.

When Jordan's central bank governor became concerned about liquidity ratios and the flow of currency out of the country, he ordered twenty banks to deposit 30 percent of their foreign exchange holdings with the central bank. Petra was the only bank unable to comply, a crisis that triggered an investigation that led first to the ouster of the bank's board of directors and then to the bank's closing in 1989. By this point, Chalabi had fled Jordan, with Prince Hassan reportedly driving him to the border to make his escape. All that he left behind turned out to be worthless. An audit found that some $200 million of depositors' money had been transferred to other holdings of the Chalabi family in Switzerland, Lebanon, and the U.K., which included a gold-dealing company, an investment firm, and another bank, Mebco, in Geneva and Beirut.

Jordan's central bank governor was astonished by what the auditors found. "The scale of fraud at Petra Bank was enormous," he said. "It was like a tiny Enron." The breakdown of the audit included $80 million in bad loans (most of them to Chalabi-owned companies), $20 million in money owed other banks, and $60 million unaccounted for. A five-hundred-page, 106-chapter report detailing every questionable transaction was filed with Jordan's military attorney general in 1990, and concluded that Chalabi was the man most responsible for "fictitious deposits and entries" designed to inflate the bank's paper income, as well as bad debts and investments. He was tried and convicted in absentia in 1992 and sentenced to twenty-two years in prison.

At the time of his conviction, Chalabi was living in a sumptuous flat off London's Park Lane, where his bonhomie and globe-trotting style would earn him the derisive nickname "The Jay Gatsby of the Iraq War." As a graduate of the neoconservative factory, the University of Chicago, Chalabi had cultivated and seduced many of the movers and shakers who would come together as a shadow Iraqi government during the Clinton years, and he used those contacts in an attempt to polish his tarnished image. Chalabi's daughter Tamara wrote an op-ed piece in the *Wall Street Journal* in August of 2003 asserting her father had been a victim of his attempts to block Saddam Hussein's influence in Jordan. London's *Daily Telegraph* published a valentine to Chalabi, calling him "the de Gaulle of Iraq." At the time, the *Telegraph* was owned by Conrad Black, a man with whom Richard Perle would be closely identified in the years to come. Chalabi posted a convoluted explanation of the bank's failure on a Web site, an explanation that refers to "Dr." Chalabi's success in thwarting a grain sales scheme that was allegedly a cover for prohibited arms sales to Saddam Hussein, and claiming that Jordan's central bank was involved in the scheme.

At the end of the Gulf War in 1991, President George H.W. Bush signed an order directing the CIA to foment an overthrow of Saddam Hussein by his own military. According to at least one estimate, $100 million was set aside for the project. Not having enough operatives in place to make that happen, the CIA hired the Rendon Group, a public relations company, to set up radio and television operations to produce anti-Hussein propaganda. The company's president, John Rendon, was a lifelong Democrat who had been executive director of the Democratic National Committee and managed Jimmy Carter's 1980 nominating convention in New York. Under somewhat obscure circumstances, he was in Panama during the 1989 U.S. invasion that removed Manuel Noriega and was asked to help broker the transition of power to a new government. Rendon's contacts with the CIA continued into the 1990s, when his clients included Kuwait's government in exile, which needed a tub-thumper for their efforts to oust Hussein's occupying army.

The destabilize-Iraq account was so large that Rendon had trouble spending the money fast enough. As one employee put it, "We tried to burn through $40 million in a year. It was a very nice job." The Rendon propaganda machine would churn out phony stories about Saddam in the British press and watch how each would be picked up and embellished by the American press. In its first year on the Iraq account, Rendon claims not only to have formed the Iraqi National Congress (INC) but also to have given the organization its name. The INC, a coalition of Iraqi and Kurdish groups dedicated to the overthrow of Saddam, became the vehicle for the CIA's propaganda efforts. In the summer of 1991, CIA agent Whitney Bruner contacted Ahmed Chalabi in London and asked him to take the lead in organizing Iraqi opposition groups. Little did Bruner or his bosses realize that this would be the start of not a beautiful friendship, but rather a marriage made in hell. In January of 1992, the Rendon Group set up the Iraqi Broadcasting Corporation as well as Radio Hurriah, which began beaming bunk from a U.S.-controlled transmitter in Kuwait. Months later, it convened a meeting in Vienna of major Iraqi opposition groups and named the umbrella organization the Iraqi National Congress.

For the next several years, Chalabi spent much of his time in Kurdish-controlled northern Iraq, riding around with a fleet of six Land Rovers, and acting for all to see as Washington's guy in Iraq. As the

CIA's money continued to flow, the agency became increasingly concerned that nothing was flowing back. "He was reporting no intel," said the CIA's Robert Baer. "It was total trash. Their intelligence was so bad we weren't even sending it in." Of course, there was concern about where all the money was going, especially since Chalabi refused to share his books with others members of the INC, claiming it would compromise his group's operations. Meanwhile, the Rendon Group was taking in $326,000 per month from the U.S. government, including $22,000 per month paid to a single employee. In March of 1995, Chalabi rounded up about a thousand fighters in the Kurdish-controlled city of Mosul for an attack on Saddam. He paid tribal leaders to guarantee their men, and brought in Iranian intelligence officials who promised their forces would hit Saddam from the south when Chalabi's militia struck from the north.

Back in the United States, Chalabi's main booster and patron, Richard Perle, out of government but never out of the game, urged the CIA to provide logistical support including air cover for the coup attempt. But the agency learned that Saddam's political operatives knew all about the plot, and Chalabi was informed that he and his men would be on their own if he gave the signal. The operation fell apart quickly as many of Chalabi's men deserted and the Iranians stood by and watched. Perle was told that his recommendation for U.S. air support would have led to a "Bay of Goats."

In August of 1996, a clash between rival Kurdish factions within the INC led to intervention by Iraqi troops, who stormed the city of Irbil with forty thousand soldiers and three hundred tanks. All but twelve of one hundred Iraqi Broadcasting Company employees were executed as well as some one hundred INC supporters. The Clinton administration arranged to evacuate some seven thousand Iraqis in an operation that received scant attention in the American press.

With Clinton hobbled by the Lewinsky scandal and the rush to impeachment, several opposing forces came together to wrest foreign policy from the Madeleine Albrights, Strobe Talbotts, Sandy Bergers, and Richard Holbrookes. While the Clinton administration applied

American power in places such as Haiti, Somalia, Bosnia, and Kosovo and had in fact made at least an effort to capture or kill a terrorist named Osama bin Laden, its foreign policy seemed shapeless and formless to those critics anxious for America to cash in on the investment made during the Reagan years. To many neocons, Clinton seemed as uninterested in foreign undertakings as they believed his predecessor had been.

Following the refusal of the Israelis to act on the recommendations of *A Clean Break*, and with Saddam's position appearing to grow stronger despite UN-imposed sanctions, a cadre of mostly neoconservatives announced the formation of the Project for the New American Century (PNAC). It was another chapter in the playbook used so much more effectively by conservatives than liberals, whose policy initiatives generally broke down over what font style to use. From the Committee on the Present Danger (in its many incarnations), through the Committee for a Free Chechnya, the policy manifesto signed by the usual suspects places the recipients clearly on the defensive and forces them to either effect a policy change or respond with a defense of their position.

PNAC's "Statement of Principles," published on June 3, 1997, opened with the affirmation "American foreign and defense policy is adrift." Having asserted that, the authors declare, "We aim to change this. We aim to make the case and rally support for American global leadership." How? The answer is a harbinger: "The history of the 20th century should have taught us that it is important to shape circumstances *before* crises emerge [emphasis added], and to meet threats before they become dire." The authors close with a call to increase the defense budget, to "challenge" hostile regimes, promote political and economic freedom abroad, and—the big one—"to accept responsibility for America's unique role in preserving and defending an international order friendly to our security, our prosperity and our principles." It is signed by most of the neocon capos, including Elliott Abrams, William Bennett, Fred Ikle, Frank Gaffney, and Donald Kagan, and also such Beltway Brahmins as Donald Rumsfeld, Dick Cheney, Paul Wolfowitz, and Dan Quayle. AIPAC's Steve Rosen signed, but curiously Perle did not. Contrary to press reports, he was not a founder of PNAC and either was not reachable when the "Statement of Principals" was circulated or was never asked to sign (an improbable scenario). Perle did sign other PNAC manifestoes, including the open letter to Bill Clinton, but dismissed the organization as a straw man constructed by conspiracy theorists. "I never went to a PNAC meeting," he e-mailed me, "if indeed there were any, which I doubt. I don't believe it ever consisted of more than three people doing the same things they would do on their day jobs, writing and researching."

Meanwhile, Chalabi concluded that his best bet to gain U.S. support for his plan was with the neoconservatives and their lobbying groups. When he told JINSA that Saddam Hussein was just a jostle away from being replaced by a government friendly to Israel, Paul Wolfowitz and Douglas Feith took notice. When he showed up at social events with Richard Perle and Haliburton CEO Dick Cheney, Washington took notice. To his Jewish audiences, he vowed that as the new president of Iraq he would build an oil pipeline from Mosul to Haifa, but he reportedly told a Jordanian friend, the managing director of an international investment group, a different story. "He just needs the Jews in order to get what he wants from Washington, and then he will turn on them after that." Chalabi denied the story, but there is no denying the fact that he, David Wurmser, and Perle turned to the Israelis to pressure the U.S. Congress into coming up with more money for the INC, with Perle telling a Jewish American magazine, "Israel has not devoted the political or rhetorical time or energy to Saddam that they have to the Iranians. The case for the Iraqi opposition in Congress would be a lot more favorable with Israeli support."

At this point, the Clinton administration was fighting a holding action against the neocons on at least three fronts and was losing them all. One was a doomsday scenario laid out by a so-called bipartisan commission tasked with dredging up that old chestnut: ballistic missile defense. Thanks to an amendment to a defense authorization bill sponsored by House Republican and missile shield fan Curt Wheldon, the commission was funded, staffed, and in true Team B tradition, stacked with flag wavers for more missile defense R&D. Its chairman, Donald Rumsfeld, was surrounded by the familiar faces of Paul Wolfowitz, former undersecretary of state William Schneider, and another Perle fellow traveler, onetime CIA director Jim Woolsey. Predictably, the Rumsfeld commission concluded that the not-yet-christened axis of evil—Iraq, Iran, and North Korea—could deploy nuclear ballistic missiles within five years, directly contradicting the CIA's estimate of ten to twenty years. Wearing other hats, Rumsfeld, Wolfowitz, Woolsey, Schneider, and this time, Perle, also signed a PNAC open letter to President Clinton flatly calling for the forceful removal of Saddam Hussein from power and an end to the administration's policy of containment.

Finally, under intense pressure from Congress, Clinton signed the Iraq Liberation Act. The legislation, reportedly ghostwritten by Chalabi, requires the United States to "support efforts to remove Saddam Hussein from power in Iraq and to promote the emergence of a democratic government to replace the regime." To that end, the act directed the president to decide how the various Iraqi opposition groups would spend the $97 million set aside for them, plus another $43 million for propaganda activities. But Clinton dragged his feet disbursing the funds, and George W. Bush did as well, perhaps impressed by the argument from both State and CIA that Chalabi was not only untrustworthy but might in fact have been a front man for the Iranians. Perle dismissed all of the arguments against his friend, no matter how compelling the evidence.

"He's been vilified and the stories by now are repetitive," he said. "The former crown prince, now Prince Hassan [who allegedly borrowed $30 million from the Petra Bank and then helped Chalabi flee Jordan] told me years ago that the legal action against Ahmed was 100 percent political. I've heard different theories expressed, and one is that the relationship between Saddam and the king was such that King Hussein would be receptive to Saddam's complaints about an enemy of his doing business in the king's country."

But what of the reports that tens of millions of dollars earmarked for the INC were either wasted or unaccounted for?

"The INC never got $97 million. That was the amount in the Iraq Liberation Act, but that money never went to the INC. The administration refused to disburse most of the funds because they didn't like the Iraq Liberation Act...both Clinton and Bush. I believe most of the money went to the Rendon Group.

The issue of whether Ahmed Chalabi was a godsend or a goniff would have been of only passing interest had it not been for 9/11. From the moment the hijacked planes hit their targets, all the position papers, speeches, op-ed columns, forums, seminars, and weighty tomes lost their theoretical character and assumed a grave urgency. In an extraordinarily ironic passage from their voluminous case for a massive defense buildup, PNAC's *Rebuilding America's Defenses*, published in 2000, concluded that "the process of transformation [of the U.S. military] is likely to be a long one, absent some catastrophic and catalyzing event—like a new Pearl Harbor."

And now they had one.

Richard Perle was at his vacation home in the South of France when the first plane struck the World Trade Center. It was 8:45 a.m. in New York, 2:45 p.m. in Provence. He was on the telephone with a lawyer friend named Les Goldman who was in New York at the time. In the middle of the conversation, Goldman said to Perle, "Oh, my God...an airplane has just hit the World Trade Center." Perle could hear a television set in the background from where Goldman was speaking, and then the lawyer repeated "a plane has just crashed into the World Trade Center." Perle isn't sure whether the thought of a terrorist attack came to him at that moment or after the second plane hit some eighteen minutes later. He then received a call from Bush speechwriter David Frum, who had been evacuated from the White House and was sitting in Perle's office at the American Enterprise Institute (AEI). Frum, a Canadian national, had met Perle at AEI; they would later collaborate on *An End to Evil*. The two men compared notes about what President Bush should say about the attack.

"The only point I really recall," Perle told me, "was saying that the president should say he will not distinguish between the individual terrorists and the countries that support them. I didn't identify the attack with a specific group since there are multiple groups that would cheerfully have done this. But I had felt for a long time that chasing individual terrorists was a losing proposition. Terrorists could hide, but countries that accommodated them couldn't." With all flights grounded, Perle could not leave France until September 14, having to travel from Marseilles to London and then London to Washington. Perle probably would not have been in France had he accepted the job the new Bush administration had in mind for him: undersecretary of defense for policy. But he was making far too much money from his various business dealings and would have never gotten around objections from Leslie. (When I asked if she thought her husband would ever return to government, she replied, "Not with this wife.")

Doug Feith was given the position, while Perle accepted an appointment as chairman of the Defense Policy Board (DPB) Advisory Committee, a heretofore benign assembly of unpaid consultants who would meet four times a year for a day and a half per meeting. The board would hear briefings from various officials on the status of defense programs either planned or in the pipeline, debate the merits, and come up with recommendations for the secretary of defense, who would appear on the final afternoon. Perle had been a member of the board since resigning as assistant secretary of defense in 1987; it was something of a tradition that cabinet and subcabinet members in the DOD were asked to sit on the board, and Perle had been reappointed by both Clinton defense secretaries William Perry and William Cohen, a fact of which Perle was quite proud.

In the Bush 43 administration, Rumsfeld picked the members, and he turned this board into a celebrity chamber, featuring Henry Kissinger, James Schlesinger, Newt Gingrich, Harold Brown, Tom Foley, Jim Woolsey, Richard Allen, Ken Adelman, Fred Ikle, and Charles Horner. These members hardly needed a getting-to-know-you reception, since they'd been moving in the same circles for years. Although Rumsfeld knew whom he wanted, he did allow Perle to get his business partner, attorney Gerald Hillman, onto the board. When asked what qualifications Hillman had to be considering defense policy, Perle snapped, "Well, there was a Nobel Prize–winning economist on the board; what were his qualifications? Gerry's a smart guy, analytical. He was an entirely appropriate person for the board."

As chairman, it was Perle's responsibility to draw up an agenda that would be sent to members in advance of a meeting, but for this session, Perle's first as chairman, 9/11 was the agenda. The board met on September 19 and 20 and received briefings from the CIA and Defense Intelligence Agency (DIA) on what was known at the time. "I think we knew by then that it had been Al-Qaeda and that they were sheltered by the Taliban regime. It was a pretty widely held belief among the board members that Afghanistan was probably the most important target first, but that we had to come to terms with Iraq." The rationale for the jump from Afghanistan to Iraq is both critical and convoluted. Of course, Perle and many of his colleagues had been pounding away about Saddam for years, as Iraq had hopped on and off the State Department's bad-guy list with the phases of the moon. In testimony before the Senate Committee on Armed Services a year before 9/11, Citizen Perle had warned, "Unless we find a more effective policy, Saddam Hussein—with the chemical weapons he has hidden from inspectors and sheltered from air attacks—will emerge from the ruins of 'containment' as the ultimate victor in 'the mother of all battles,' and a continuing scourge on his own people and the Gulf region."

To ensure that the converted would receive a proper catechism Perle invited two guests to speak before the board, Bernard Lewis and Ahmed Chalabi. Lewis, a nonagenarian Harvard professor, was perhaps best known for his view that the decline of the Ottoman Empire and other Muslim countries was the result of their cultural arrogance, and sec-ondarily, for his belief that the Armenian genocide was not comparable to the Holocaust because there is no evidence it was planned by the Turks. Lewis had long been an intellectual Svengali for Perle, Harold Rhode, and many others he's entranced. In fact, he was a living, breath-ing testament to Perle's belief that academics "live in a dream world"—unless they share his views.

Lewis could always be relied upon to say something provocative, but at this session he merely noted that the United States should encourage democratic reformers in the Middle East, "such as my friend here, Ahmed Chalabi." With this, Chalabi took center stage to recite the litany of Saddam's crimes, including his stockpiled weapons of mass destruction (WMD). He asserted that a better strategy for the United States would be to ignore Afghanistan and go after Iraq first, explaining that a coup attempt by him and his followers, with American support, would encounter no resistance and would be "a quick matter of establishing a government." When asked why he had invited Chalabi, Perle said, "Because Iraq was clearly a country capable of doing a lot of damage, and because Saddam had cheered 9/11. He was one of the few leaders anywhere, including most of the Muslim world, who made favorable comments about it." While it was not customary for the secretary of state or his deputies to be invited to the DPB sessions, one might have thought that given the extraordinary nature of events it would have been both prudent and professional for the board to have at least informed Colin Powell of the meeting or briefed him afterward. They did not. This would be the first of many snubs and humiliations that would drive Powell to resign in 2004. As one top State Department official told me, Powell "just got sick and tired of Perle trying to ram Chalabi down our throats every day."

At the close of the meeting, Rumsfeld gave his own address, expressing his concern about what he believed was a peculiarly American malady: the habit of pulling back once it is threatened or attacked. No, this time there was a need to "lean forward," and that clearly meant something bigger than simply crushing the Taliban and bombing Afghanistan where there were few worthwhile targets to begin with. Later, in fact, Rumsfeld was downright angry that the CIA paramilitary had successfully coordinated the invasion of Afghanistan with the anti-Taliban Northern Alliance just days after Bush had given the go-ahead. Rumsfeld was reportedly so upset that the first Special Forces mission in Afghanistan was greeted by a CIA man that he told his underlings, "This is the last time our people will be met by the CIA."

"The CIA really did Afghanistan, not the military," said former Colin Powell aide Larry Wilkerson. "The military was a day late and a dollar short. And when they finally did get there, they didn't have the kind of wherewithal they needed to get bin Laden. And when [General] Tommy Franks [commander of U.S. forces] was deflected to Iraq, partly because Donald was looking for *his* triumph, it was over. You weren't going to get bin Laden then. They had already lost him. I'm not even sure the president or anybody else in government knew Rumsfeld had shifted things that fast. And when he did that, it was partly out of ire— 'I've got to have *my* war.' "

If indeed Perle and the board had not been fixated on Iraq before the meeting, they certainly were afterward. Just one day later, many of the attendees, including Perle, wearing their PNAC hats again, signed an open letter to President Bush calling for the removal of Saddam "even if evidence does not link Iraq directly to the attack." The letter goes on to warn, "Failure to undertake such an effort will constitute an early and perhaps decisive surrender in the war on international terrorism." Bush is reported to have rejected the proposal because Cheney and Powell agreed there was no evidence so far linking Saddam to the attack.

But that problem would be fixed soon enough. Right after the DPB meeting, Deputy Secretary of Defense Paul Wolfowitz dispatched Jim Woolsey to London, reportedly to meet with the INC and troll for any information linking one of the hijackers, Mohammad Atta, to Iraqi intelligence. Asked about this, Woolsey replied, "I've never talked about that. I was asked by the Defense Department and the Justice Department to accompany an official from each organization to talk with the Brits and share information. Richard could conceivably have suggested it." When police in Wales spotted Woolsey, they phoned the U.S. embassy to make sure he was on official government business. It was only then that Colin Powell and CIA director George Tenet learned of Woolsey's trip. Larry Wilkerson said the general became so angry about State being responsible for Chalabi and his gang that either Powell or his deputy, Richard Armitage, finally told Wolfowitz, "You want 'em? You got 'em. You want the INC? We're sick of them. They spend money, they drive Mercedes, they stay in expensive hotels and they don't do shit except spend our money." Responsibility for the INC was transferred from State to the DIA, but Wilkerson still fumes at the memories. "We wanted out of that business. So finally, we said, 'Take the money and everything.'"

Meanwhile, Wolfowitz had ordered Doug Feith to begin an operation that was more than an echo of the old Team B, a "review" of all data from the intelligence community, especially the CIA, ostensibly to determine whether any links had been missed. Although the names of the various offices and panels either created or assigned to the intelligence review are the subject of some debate (with Feith insisting that Seymour Hersh "got it all balled up" in Hersh's *New Yorker* story on the operation), what is clear is that even before the attacks, in fact, even before his confirmation as undersecretary of defense for policy, Doug Feith was making sure his office contained true believers only. He recruited Harold Rhode in January of 2001, ostensibly to work in the Office of Net Assessment, then run by a Pentagon legend named Andy Marshall. But that assignment appeared to be a cover.

Marshall, another RAND offspring, known as "Yoda" within the DOD, lived in a high-tech world of RMA, or Revolution in Military Affairs, a theory first suggested by Marshall Nikolai Ogarkov, chief of the Soviet general staff in 1982, that holds that technological advances eventually will make ground troops unnecessary, as conflicts will be decided by computers and smart weapons. This theory played heavily into the Rumsfeld view that a relatively small number of troops would be required to take and hold Iraq.

Harold Rhode, whose expertise was the study of the Ottomans, would not have known which end was up in Andy Marshall's office. His real impact was ferreting out personnel who did not share his or Feith's views. Rhode was seen as Feith's hatchet man, purging career defense officials who would not get on board for the target-Iraq mission, "pulling people out of nooks and crannies at the Defense Intelligence Agency," according to one analyst. "They [Feith and Rhode] wanted nothing to do with the professional staff. They wanted us the fuck out of there." Feith and Rhode recruited David Wurmser, the *Clean Break* author, to run the intelligence review, and he in turn was teamed with a technocrat named Michael Maloof, who had worked for Perle at the Pentagon in the 1980s, and had previously been monitoring technology transfers to China. Perle denies having played a role in the staffing of the operation but acknowledges that it was more than serendipity that the major players had all worked for him in the past.

Likewise, Abe Shulsky, a Straussian scholar, RAND man and PNAC charter member who had worked for Perle at the Pentagon, was named director of the Office of Special Plans, an umbrella group that included Wurmser's team. To fully appreciate Shulsky's point of view, one need only peruse an essay he wrote for RAND in 1999, with Francis Fukuyama, the elegant neoconservative and PNAC signatory. The essay, titled "Military Organization in the Information Age," explores what the military could learn from entities such as Wal-Mart and the Wehrmacht: Enable those at the bottom to bypass intermediaries and reach decision makers without the burdensome and time-consuming reviews built into most organizational structures. To buttress their argument, the pair cites studies of the German army in full Blitzkrieg by historian Martin Van Creveld: "Front-line Panzer units, for example, could request air support directly from the Luftwaffe without having to go through higher Army echelons. By contrast, British and French command structures required unit commanders to go through several intermediary headquarters to communicate with supporting units."

Extrapolate from that, and place it against the backdrop of the War on Terror, and the result is: Bypass interagency review, ignore the CIA and the State Department, marginalize or navigate past anyone who disagrees with you. Do not even mention NATO or the UN. As for Wal-Mart, the authors cite the ingenious applications of the bar code: "The information that a particular product has been sold, which is obtained at the checkout counter when the bar code is scanned, is used not only to calculate how much the customer owes but is also transmitted to a companywide database. Without increasing the workload of the checkout clerk, and without burdening other company employees, timely and detailed sales information is collected for processing and use."

Hence the domestic surveillance program scouring millions of credit card and banking records, a story the *New York Times* agreed to suppress for a year, as well as the FBI's scouring of telephone records, which even the bureau admitted went too far.

Fukuyama had been recruited by Paul Wolfowitz to the Johns Hopkins School of International Studies when Wolfowitz was the dean. Eventually Fukuyama was also recruited to assess the long-term effect of global terrorism on the United States, one of more than thirty conservative policy specialists brought in and divided into teams in the fall of 2002. Like Saint Paul, Fukuyama would one day experience a cleansing epiphany, not on the road to Damascus but on the road to his publisher, where he would deposit *America at the Crossroads*, a repudiation of benevolent hegemony, an intellectual's equivalent of *Saturday Night Live* star Gilda Radner's "Never mind." After immersing himself in the material for three months, he and his team concluded that the United States must avoid overreacting to the events of 9/11 and must resist military incursions that would "lead to a world in which the U.S. and its policies remain the chief focus of global concern." His group's report, which was never published, recommended that while some military response was necessary, America's focus should be on winning the hearts and minds of the vast majority of Muslims who genuinely admired America.

This think tank exercise reflected Wolfowitz the academic and utopian; the Doug Feith Office of Special Plans (OSP) operation reflected Wolfowitz the avenger, whose lifeless, monotone testimony before congressional committees in the run-up to the war made him seem cold-blooded and ruthless. In fact, there was more than one Pentagon official who considered Wolfowitz the most dangerous of all Rumsfeld's advisors, despite the fact that the deputy and his boss were barely on speaking terms. Rumsfeld and Wolfowitz were never comfortable with each other, partly because of Wolfowitz's seeming obsession with the safety and security of Israel, a goal Rumsfeld shared only when it suited him. One State Department official said that if Wolfowitz wanted to find out what subjects were on the agenda for the Defense

Policy Board, he had to call Powell's deputy, Richard Armitage. "Rumsfeld wouldn't even talk to him," the official told me. "He wouldn't talk to Paul. So, putting that together with other comments from other people in DOD, I knew the deputy secretary seemed to be out of the loop lots of times on key issues that I knew Rumsfeld was very much in the loop on."

If Rumsfeld wasn't speaking to Wolfowitz, what was Wolfowitz doing in the deputy's job in the first place? "Waiting to become secretary of state," former Perle aide Bruce Jackson told me. "I know they offered Paul the agency [CIA]. But he refused because his aspiration was to become president of Harvard or Princeton or some other major university and the unwritten rule is that if you ever served in the agency, the academics won't accept you. So they gave him the most prestigious of the deputy slots and Paul assumed he'd be there for two years and then move. But war broke out and he had to stay."

Perle also knew that the Rumsfeld-Wolfowitz relationship wouldn't work, given Rumsfeld's ego and unwillingness to share the stage. "I can't imagine an institution run by Donald Rumsfeld that could have more than one decision maker. Paul had a platform from which to try to influence Rumsfeld, but he didn't have a platform from which to make decisions. Their relationship got worse over time, and Paul's influence declined."

While Cheney had his own man, Wurmser, involved in the intelligence mining, Rumsfeld had Stephen Cambone, his highly trusted and darkly ambitious aide, keeping an eye on the process. In fact, Cambone tried on at least one occasion to take the operation away from Feith, a move prevented only by protests from Wolfowitz. As one player described the scene to journalist Andrew Cockburn, "That was one fight Steve didn't win. There were so many webs being woven. Cambone was in charge of intelligence. Perle was feeding in stuff. Chalabi was feeding in stuff. The CIA had their own bunch of bullshitters. Everyone had their favorite guy who would tell them what they wanted to hear."

Chris Carney, a political science professor, naval reserve officer, and now a congressman from Pennsylvania, was recruited to OSP from the

DIA, where he was on reserve duty. Carney replaced Wurmser, who went to work for Cheney. Among OSP's main objectives, perhaps *the* main objective, was challenging the conventional wisdom that Saddam Hussein, the tyrant and secular autocrat, would have had nothing to do with Osama bin Laden, the radical fundamentalist who had repeatedly denounced Saddam as an infidel. "I was always open to the possibility that terrorists who hated the United States would make common cause when it was convenient to do so," Perle told me. "The CIA was not, and they just wouldn't look at evidence that suggested they might. So the decision was made to bring in people with fresh eyes to review the intelligence that the CIA and other agencies had collected. The mandate was to review, not to go out and get new intelligence, which they were not capable of doing anyway."

The "fresh eyes," of course, were more jaundiced with respect to the CIA. As with Richard Pipes's original Team B, which the Senate Intelligence Committee found had been stacked with those skeptical of CIA estimates of Soviet strength, the OSP was hardly a dispassionate review panel, and in due course it indeed produced what it saw as links between bin Laden, Al-Qaeda, and Saddam Hussein that the CIA had either missed or discarded. Richard Perle said he had seen the evidence.

Have you ever seen the Bayeaux Tapestry? It's a medieval tapestry in the French town of Normandy. It depicts scenes and it goes all the way around the room. Well, this evidence was like that. It had been laid out by Chris Carney on what looked like butcher paper, brown paper which had been draped around the inside of his office. It went all around the room on this brown paper, and it had boxes connected with lines that were color-coded so you could tell...a green line from box A to box B meant that the individual in box B had intercepted phone conversations with the individual in box A. A red line meant they had met and had been physically present in the same place. It looked like the design of a computer chip, with lines and boxes everywhere, and it was clear there was a lot of interaction, people going to meetings with one another, people being part of organizations that carried out terrorist acts. It was a pretty compelling case of exactly what you would expect…which is that there were relationships.

But if the evidence was so strong, why didn't the administration present it to the American people?

"I don't know," Perle said weakly. "There was one leak in the piece Stephen Hayes wrote for *The Weekly Standard*, and Cheney referred to that. He said, 'If you're looking for evidence, read that.' Part of the problem is that the Hayes piece leaked information that was highly classified. It's always a struggle whether to violate the rules and go ahead and leak."

"Case Closed," Stephen Hayes's essay on Al-Qaeda and Saddam, was indeed cited by Cheney as a "must read" for skeptics. Published in November of 2003, the article was based on a memo from Doug Feith to Senators Pat Roberts and Jay Rockefeller of the Intelligence Committee and contained classified intelligence reports outlining an effort by bin Laden to forge a link to Iraq through Sudanese strongman Hassan al-Turabi. It also asserts that hijacker Mohammad Atta had not one but four meetings with Iraqi intelligence, a claim supported, the document says, by Czech intelligence. The Czechs later backed off of that claim, and the DIA, the Defense Department's own intelligence arm, later backed off claims by a captured Al-Qaeda figure who had acknowledged an Al-Qaeda–Iraq connection but later recanted. If the Hayes article was the administration's way of making its case, it was a thin reed indeed. While the Justice Department either threatened to or in fact did prosecute news organizations for publishing classified information leaked to them, no one issued so much as a murmur about how Hayes or the *Weekly Standard* had received Feith's memo.

For his part, CIA director George Tenet was trying to have it both ways, telling the president the evidence was solid while calming his own people who were insisting it wasn't. Tenet's behavior made Perle apoplectic. "He was saying there was a connection only after the evidence had been assembled by outsiders and placed in front of him. The honest response would have been, 'Gee, I guess you're right.' It was an embarrassment because they missed it completely. And as far as I know, you can't find anywhere the conclusions the CIA accepted after the work that was done by this tiny little group."

Just how much of the information the OSP was Cuisinarting into its reports, and Carney was stringing up on butcher paper was coming from Chalabi or the INC, is one of the enduring debates of the period. David Wurmser insists he and his colleagues deliberately set aside intel from Chalabi and the INC to avoid criticism of its veracity.

"Whatever we advocated in terms of intelligence on the war was done on the basis of information provided to us by the intelligence community because we understood that was the language they could understand. The moment we went outside their sources of information, they could attack us, and our sources would be challenged. So when they say we got it all from Chalabi, it's simply not true. I formed that special unit and I never used anything Chalabi gave me, not once, for precisely that reason."

As far as Doug Feith was concerned, all the hoopla over a review of available intelligence on Iraq and Al-Qaeda was overblown. There was, he insists, nothing at all secret about what his people were doing, that of course Richard Perle was aware of it, and that information from Chalabi and the INC was treated the same as information from any other source. He adds that this entire endeavor was not among his areas of expertise.

> We got information about Iraq from multiple sources. Virtually every one of these external organizations had some arrangement for providing information. I am not the world's leading expert on this, but I've heard a fair amount and I've talked to a lot of the people, and I would urge you to talk to people who really have expertise in this. My understanding of this is that all of these programs through which these groups were providing information to the United States were a mix of good and

bad information. And that's always the case. I mean there's no such thing as an intelligence program where all the information that comes in is solid gold. There's not an American newspaper that meets that standard. And when people say Chalabi sold us a bill of goods, I don't think that's correct and I don't think that the intelligence people who worked on these things would bear that out.

Actually, most of them would. As part of the multimillion-dollar Iraqi Collection program, the INC supplied defectors to the mainstream media in the United States and the UK. They produced a long list of stories about secret projects from development of long-range missiles to mobile laboratories loaded with chemical and biological agents. None of them led anywhere.

Throughout this process Perle was using his position as chairman of the DPB to spread the word about what the operation had unearthed, telling the friendly Fox News Channel that "substantial links" between Saddam and Al-Qaeda had been found, and telling the British House of Commons that the United States would attack Iraq even if UN weapons inspectors found nothing. "I cannot see how Hans Blix can state more than he can know," Perle told the MPs. "All he can know is the results of his own investigations, and that does not prove that Saddam does not have weapons of mass destruction." Although not a member of the administration, Perle spoke as though he were, and that gave him all the credibility without any of the accountability, a situation that enraged Colin Powell. Time and again, Powell implored Rumsfeld to rein Perle in, and time and again Rumsfeld would nod and do nothing.

But it was an episode Perle orchestrated in July of 2002 that created an international incident and got everyone's attention. Perle invited an obscure RAND analyst and French national named Laurent Murawiec to deliver a lecture to the DPB on the general subject of fighting the war of terrorism. Murawiec had been a follower of the neocons' enemy Lyndon LaRouche, convicted felon and serial presidential candidate, and had been an editor of LaRouche's *Executive Intelligence Review,* which regularly railed against Jews, Israel, and the neocon "cabal." He had also worked as a consultant for the Rich Foundations, established by the fugitive financier Marc Rich.

At the DPB meeting, Murawiec unveiled a twenty-four-slide PowerPoint presentation making the case that Saudi Arabia, not Iraq, was a far more significant enemy, and that the United States must "target" the Saudi's oil and financial holdings and even its holy shrines until the Wahhabite royal family either flees or is forced to change its ways. The presentation was, from all accounts, an eerie exercise in which Laurent "of Arabia," as he was dubbed once news of the affair leaked out, used his slides dramatically, like Ravel's *Bolero*, to build to a crescendo of evidence against the Riyadh regime. But the final slide left his audience scratching their heads. It read, "Iraq is the tactical pivot...Saudi Arabia the strategic pivot...and Egypt is the prize."

Say what?

While the evidence is overwhelming that Saudi Arabia has for decades financed terrorist groups, including bin Laden's Al-Qaeda, to just leave them alone, the reality on the ground is that since the Gulf War, the United States has maintained a military base in the kingdom and relies on the Saudis to temper the more impulsive actions of other oil-producing states. Beyond that, the Bush family has had close ties with the Saudis going back at least to George W.'s grandfather, Prescott. Both sides have used each other and have held their noses while doing it. Going after Saudi Arabia while trying to make the case for going to war in Iraq was, to say the least, off message.

The lecture set off a major row in which Colin Powell rushed to reassure the Saudi ambassador that the show-and-tell was something akin to a high school prank and certainly did not represent the views or the position of the White House. Henry Kissinger left the meeting mumbling gravely, "I don't consider Saudi Arabia to be a strategic adversary of the United States. They are doing some things I don't approve of, but I don't consider them a strategic adversary." Just weeks later, Murawiec spoke by telephone to a reporter from *Arabian Business* magazine, and while he claimed he was barred from speaking about his briefing in

Washington, he did have a few observations about the Saudis: "My experience with your part of the world is that most people hate the Saudis' guts, not to make too fine a point about it. Everybody knows they are bunch of lazy assholes that are arrogant, too big for their shoes, and behave in a constantly disgusting manner. People in your region have told me that for 20 years. But I'm not telling you anything new."

Murawiec not only denied making those remarks; he also denied ever having spoken to the reporter, calling the story "spurious and void." That held up for just as long as it took the reporter to produce the audiotape of the interview. While not acknowledging that the voice on the tape is Murawiec's, his boss at RAND, James Thompson, issued a statement repudiating the remarks "in the strongest terms" as "offensive and repugnant."

As for Perle, the man who invited Murawiec and who has never denied his animosity toward the Saudis, he claims he hadn't seen the presentation before inviting the Frenchman to Washington. "RAND had a contract to do research on terrorism. I was invited to participate in a little panel, and that's where I met Laurent. He gave a presentation and I was impressed by it. And I wasn't alone in being impressed by it." But, Perle claims the slide show he saw at RAND was not exactly the same show Murawiec put on for the DPB. "The truth is I reviewed his presentation beforehand and I might have said, 'Look, there are a couple of slides here that are pretty inflammatory. You should take those out.' But I didn't. And, by the way, there was discussion afterward by the entire board and nobody said, 'That last slide is ridiculous...it's inflammatory,'"

But what does "Egypt is the prize" mean?

"I'm not sure I fully understood that either. But it was not of great importance. Often with these presentations, particularly when you get to the end, the presenter is running out of time and he rushes through things. I didn't even remember the 'Saudi is the target...Egypt is the prize' thing. But, of course, the Saudis went crazy. They just went berserk."

It is difficult to believe that Perle, a savvy gamesman, would have invited a man he barely knew to appear before several dozen of the country's most powerful men and give a speech he had not vetted down to the last slide. The more plausible explanation was that Perle wanted to fire a missile at Riyadh, a red, white, and blue rocket with the trailing message, "Don't get too comfortable." Perhaps he remembered when he and Dickie Fosdick were denied visas by the Saudis on the assumption that they were both Jewish. Perhaps the years of listening to Saudi apologists Kissinger, George H.W. Bush, and Brent Scowcroft had finally convinced Perle that someone in power needed to say "Screw the oil...these people are not our friends."

"They have done tremendous damage in the world and they keep on doing it," he said. "There are thousands of mosques all over the world where young kids are being taught that it's their mission in life to wage holy wars and kill infidels, and they're financing it for their own selfish reasons. It's a handful of people living obscenely ostentatious lives at the expense of everybody else, and all they care about is remaining in power. And the damage they do to the rest of the world? They couldn't care less, as far as I can tell." But they cared mightily about the PowerPoint show.

For Colin Powell it was yet another episode in which Perle, from his little perch atop an obscure advisory board, was shaking down the thunder, stirring the pot, grabbing the gutless and guileless by the lapels and slapping them silly. To Powell, it was like fighting a fifth column, with snipers like columnist Charles Krauthammer taking shots from the outside, Wolfowitz and Feith getting their shots in from the inside, and Perle straddling both sides of the firing line. There was anger, to be sure, but sadness as well. Perle and Powell had once been good friends, back in the Reagan years when Perle worked for Cap and Powell was Weinberger's military liaison. They had traveled the world together, the Brooklyn boy keeping an eye on the kid from Hollywood High, making sure Perle didn't do or say anything that might make Cap gag on his morning coffee. As Powell told a friend, "We used to have major problems when Richard would wander off the farm and be caught doing things that were not consistent with the policies that Weinberger and Shultz were trying to implement. And that was Richard's great skill."

Powell wasn't worried about Perle dispensing military advice; even

Perle knew that was not his bailiwick. It was Perle's ability to influence decision makers, the brazen self-confidence of his arguments mixed with charm, that concerned Powell the most. Because Perle, as much as anyone inside or outside of government, was pushing the country toward a cataclysmic event the outcome of which no one could possibly foresee. It was what Powell and many others saw as Perle's smug certainty about a conflict neither he nor his son would have to fight that almost brought Perle to blows with author Tom Clancy. "Perle was saying how Powell was being a wuss because he was overly concerned with casualties," Clancy recalls. "I said, 'Look…he's supposed to think that way!' Perle just didn't agree with me. People like that worry me."

Of course, had it been up to Perle, Colin Powell would never have had to make that fateful speech before the UN Security Council on February 6, 2003. Perle's contempt for the United Nations and most other international institutions was well-known, and it mattered little to him what Powell would say to make the case for war. The Russians, the Chinese, the Germans, and the French…*especially the French*…would ignore the facts and insist that Hans Blix and his inspectors be given more time.

But it mattered a lot to Lieutenant Colonel Wilkerson, who, just one week before the scheduled speech, was handed a forty-eight-page report that constituted the administration's case for going to war. Where did all this stuff come from? From just about everywhere. Had anyone really checked out the material? Well…sort of. The file had been put together by I. Lewis "Scooter" Libby, Vice President Cheney's Chief of Staff and was essentially the product of the OSP operation. Wilkerson took one look at the file and thought seriously about resigning on the spot. But a soldier couldn't walk out on another soldier. As he packed for what would be seven straight days and nights of excruciating pain trying to separate the wheat from the Wheaties, he said to his wife, "This will be my undoing. I'm not going to succeed here." When Barbara Wilkerson scolded him for having a poor attitude, he replied, "You don't understand. Adlai Stevenson did this with satellite photographs!"

Wilkerson was referring to the epochal moment in 1962 when then UN ambassador Stevenson shocked the Soviets and the rest of the world with satellite photos, projected onto a large screen before the Security Council, that clearly depicted missiles and missile launchers being assembled in Cuba. Standing in front of the screen, silhouetted by the stark, unambiguous evidence, Stevenson asked Soviet ambassador Valerian Zorin for an explanation. Receiving nothing but silence, Stevenson said, "You can answer yes or no. You have denied they exist. I want to know if I understood you correctly. I am prepared to wait for my answer until hell freezes over, if that's your decision." Powell wouldn't have slides like Stevenson's. The audio and video evidence that Wilkerson had to work with was, put charitably, interesting but hardly compelling. He knew this would not be a Stevenson moment. It wasn't so much what was in the file; he hadn't even read it yet. It was the time…seven days to vet everything.

Just a few weeks before, the president had told the nation and the world that Saddam had tried to purchase uranium from Africa, pinning the claim on British intelligence. The sixteen words were shoehorned into the State of the Union address even though the claim was phony and lots of people in the administration knew it. Wilkerson wondered why Powell had to deliver this speech. Why not UN ambassador John Negroponte? Why not…and then Wilkerson answered his own question: because Colin Powell was the only man with poll ratings like Mother Theresa's. No one else could sell this case with a straight face, and be believed, except Perle's old friend Powell.

What transpired over the next week could have been written for the Marx Brothers. Think of that hilarious scene from *A Night at the Opera* in which Groucho explains a contract to Chico. To each of Groucho's "now, the party of the first part" Chico responds, "Nah, dats-a no good," and Groucho tears it from the page. When they reach the "Sanity Clause," Chico objects: "Ah, everybody knows there's no Santy Claus." A sanity clause might have put Larry Wilkerson's effort out of business. After about eight hours of arguing over the genesis of each factoid, Wilkerson looked at George Tenet and said, "We can't do this. We'd been through one page and it's taken all day. And George said, 'Let's go to the NIE,' and I said okay." The NIE was the latest National

Intelligence Estimate, the CIA's best guess as to who was doing what all over the world.

Using that as a source for composing the speech would certainly save time. But, as Wilkerson knew only too well, the NIE was crammed with stuff as faulty as anything in the file he'd been given. Others involved in the preparation, especially Will Toby from the NSC staff and John McLaughlin from CIA, kept arguing for inclusion of the most dramatic but least trustworthy claims. Cheney even called Powell to suggest that he "take a good look at Scooter's stuff." Libby himself approached the secretary to lobby for inclusion of his suspect material, only to be told, "No. I want to use what Larry's been working on." Wilkerson thought his military training and his ability to stay awake for seventy-two hours straight would force the others to give up, but he was only partially right. McLaughlin finally gave in to sleep, but Toby stayed with Wilkerson and fought him on every phrase, every comma, every adjective.

Then came the final rehearsal, attended by NSC chief Condoleezza Rice, her deputy, Stephen Hadley, Tenet, McLaughlin, and Powell's deputy, Richard Armitage. After every few sentences, someone would stop Powell and ask, "Why was this taken out?" or "Why did you change that?" Powell, understandably, became frustrated. When Hadley asked why the alleged Muhammad Atta meeting with Iraqi intelligence had been dropped from the speech, Powell stared directly at the NSC deputy, who was sitting just two chairs away, and said, "We took that out and it's not going back." Powell would repeatedly pull Wilkerson aside, out of earshot of the others, and say, "This is not really convincing." As Wilkerson told me, "He'd look at me like I was supposed to make it convincing. And I wanted to say, 'Fuck you, boss. I'm leaving, I'm outta here, I'm gone. But I had the same problem he did about loyalty."

There were debates about aluminum tubes, about mobile weapons labs, about the context of remarks heard on NSC intercepts, and a debate about unmanned aerial vehicles that Saddam supposedly had. The air force had knocked down that claim as phony, but it still made it into Powell's speech because no one told him the information had probably been obtained by torture of an Al-Qaeda operative and was unreliable. No one told him that the CIA's top source, an Iraqi code named "Curveball," being held by the Germans, was delusional and therefore unreliable. In Powell's mind, there were three pillars to the argument: (1) Iraq's nuclear ambitions; (2) the connection between Baghdad and Al-Qaeda; and (3) the existence of mobile labs for biochemical weapons. In the weeks and months to come, he would watch each pillar rattle and fall under the withering assault of the truth police.

On the morning of the speech, Powell was calm, his aides having secured the quiet top floor of the U.S.-UN mission in New York and created a mock-up of the Security Council, complete with place cards. The night before, they had managed a run-through with only one or two interruptions, at which Powell would turn to ask Tenet, "Are you sure?" and with the director of central intelligence (DCI)'s assent he would proceed. It was not Tenet's idea to be sitting directly behind and to the left of Powell when he made the speech; Powell insisted on it. He wanted to make sure the television audience saw that the head of the U.S. intelligence community was literally behind everything he said. When Wilkerson watched the final run-through, with no interruptions and no distractions, he says he got up and walked out into the cold, damp air of February in New York and muttered to himself, "Failed, failed, failed...that was all circumstantial bullshit. It can be interpreted ten different ways."

Sitting at home, Richard Perle watched Powell's performance with admiration. Of course, Perle was in full agreement with the thrust of the secretary's argument, so a thumbs-up for his old friend was not surprising. But, by any reasonable standard, this was not an Adlai Stevenson moment. Inconclusive photos and dubious audio intercepts left knowledgeable viewers with the sinking feeling: This is all they've got? That's it? The CIA's Tyler Drumheller was watching in his office and called his aide to ask, "Did we send him the wrong speech? We redacted a lot of that stuff. Did he get the wrong speech?" The aide replied, "No, they just didn't listen to you. And that shows how much influence you have." Drumheller had called his boss, McLaughlin, in an effort to wave

Powell off of a number of key points in the speech for which there was no credible corroboration. McLaughlin later denied having had any such conversation with Drumheller. "He says he doesn't remember," Drumheller told me. "He says I wasn't on his calendar that day, which is baloney. I was a division chief and I could see him anytime I wanted to." Mention of McLaughlin makes Wilkerson steam. "Tyler said he talked to John for thirty minutes! He detailed all his doubts about Curveball and everything else! And John's supposed to be the intelligence professional, the guy who's got thirty years in the agency!"

After the speech, Wilkerson walked for blocks in the drizzle on Manhattan's east side, with his aide Peggy Cifrino in tow, finally sliding into a noodle shop for the first passably decent meal either had had in days. Cifrino said, "You feel better now, don't you?" "I don't feel worth a shit, Peggy," Wilkerson said. "That was terrible. That was a terrible presentation." Fortunately, the overnight press was inexplicably impressed, with Richard Cohen of the *Washington Post* describing the presentation as "bone chilling." Had he and the rest of the mainstream media been watching the same speech? No, Wilkerson believed, it was the mesmerizing effect of Powell. "His making the presentation made it effective. It was all him. That's what did it." Wilkerson gave each member of his exhausted staff a special award for their efforts, much like the Order of the Golden Palm given to Mr. Roberts (played by an idealistic Henry Fonda in the 1955 movie of the same name) by his crew for his many efforts to contain the deranged captain of their ship and the captain's obsession with a potted palm tree (with James Cagney at his truculent best). When Powell asked, "Where's yours?" Wilkerson replied, "I don't want one."

Sitting in his cramped office at George Washington University, the highly decorated career military man stared down at his clasped hands and told me, "He saw the look on my face. I didn't feel good about it at all. But I was not prescient enough or smart enough or expert enough to realize just how badly we had done. I knew in my heart of hearts that if people felt it was effective it was because of Powell. Remember, this is the same man who, in November of 2002, walked into my office and said, 'I wonder what would happen if we put a half million troops in Iraq, go from one end of the country to the other, and don't find a damn thing?' "

As expected, the Security Council rejected the U.S. position, so the United States went about the business of trying to cobble together a "coalition of the willing," a kind of protean amalgam that to many old-hand diplomats foreshadowed the end of NATO and the European alliance that had held for half a century. This would be the first test of the exceptional nation in a unipolar world, or so it was believed. This was about the ethics of conscience and the new rules for justifying a war ex post facto; certainly we will leave the Iraqis better off, it was asserted, than if we did not act, and therefore the war is just. Perle publicly advocated that the United States invade even without a single ally.

Just weeks before the start of Shock and Awe in Iraq, Perle received a strange call from his protégé, Michael Maloof, suggesting that he meet with a Lebanese-American businessman named Imad Hage. Perle invited the pair to his home, where Hage identified himself as a man interested in peace and prosperity in the Middle East and especially in furthering U.S. interests. "It was kind of a vague presentation," Perle recalled. "He didn't ask for anything; he didn't have a specific proposal and wasn't looking for anything as far as I could tell." The meeting broke up and Perle assumed it was the last he'd hear from Hage. But the businessman called days later and asked if Perle would meet with Syrian officials either in Damascus or in a city of Perle's choosing. Perle declined. "And, by the way," Perle added, "he offered me a substantial amount of money." Asked why he didn't report such a contact to someone in the government, Perle said, "I didn't report it because I didn't take it anywhere. I simply turned it down. He said, 'We'll send a private airplane and we'll pay you a lot of money,' and I just turned it down."

Later, Hage received a visit in his Beirut office from Hassan al-Obeidi, chief of foreign operations of the Iraqi intelligence service. According to Hage, al-Obeidi, who was in ill health, complained that Iraq did not want war and was prepared to make deals to avoid it. "He said, 'If this is about oil, we will talk about U.S. oil concessions,'" Hage recalled. "If it's about the peace process, we can talk. If this is about weapons of mass destruction, let the Americans send over their people. There are no weapons of mass destruction." Hage telephoned Maloof, a fellow Lebanese American, to make him aware of the contact, and to try to get the message to anyone of consequence in the U.S. government.

After another meeting with al-Obeidi in which the offers were repeated, Hage agreed to come to Baghdad, where he met with Tahir Jalil Habbush, the head of the Iraqi intelligence service and number sixteen on the U.S. list of most-wanted Iraqis. Habbush ran down the offers again, and added a sweetener: extradition of Abdul Rahman Yasin, who had been indicted in the United States in connection with the 1993 World Trade Center bombing. Meanwhile, Maloof had been passing the information on to Jaymie Durnan, a top aide to Paul Wolfowitz, who told Maloof to keep working the channel, but "keep this close hold."

The next thing Perle knew, Hage was on the phone again, this time explaining that he had been to Baghdad and had an urgent message from intelligence chief Habbush. Perle said he was not about to jump on a plane to Beirut or anywhere else in the Middle East, but that he would soon be in London on business and would meet Hage there. In an office in Knightsbridge, Hage laid out what he said was an offer that had come through Habbush from Saddam Hussein himself. Call off the invasion and Iraq would allow an unlimited number of inspectors to search wherever they wanted, UN-supervised free elections, oil concessions to U.S. companies, and the extradition of Abdul Rahman Yasin. Perle told Habbush he would have to take the offer to a higher level. He then telephoned perhaps the only friend he had at the CIA, Buzzy Kronegard. Kronegard had been recruited by Tenet in the late nineties and became executive director in 2001. Perle ran down details of the Hage meeting and Kronegard told him to wait for a response, He didn't have to wait long. "Tell him we'll meet him in Baghdad," Kronegard told Perle, shorthand for "The show is on and the time for talk is over."

Thinking back on the episode with Hage, Perle remembers being wary of the kind of trap only he could have thought up, one in which he or someone from the government agrees to meet with Habbush or al-

Obeidi, only to have word get out that the Americans are talking to the Iraqis about massive oil concessions in exchange for canceling the war. "That would have undermined everything we were trying to do," he said. "And to this day, I don't know if it was on the level or not."

On March 20, 2003, the war began.

X.
CITIZEN PERLE (2)

THERE WERE A few problems on the war's takeoff. The Turks, whom Perle, Feith, and many others had spent years cultivating, were under a new and tenuous government, a government buffeted by a wave of extreme nationalism. Polls in Ankara showed the Turks wanted no part of this American war, and with even the possibility of a new Kurdish state forming in Iraq's northern province, the Turkish parliament voted to deny the use of Turkish soil from which American forces could drive south to Baghdad. Bruce Jackson was hanging around the parliament in the run-up to the vote and felt like a vegan at a barbeque. Not a single member of the Bush administration had come to Ankara to cajole the Turks into giving the United States clearance. In fact, Jackson was the only American there. This was bad, and Jackson understood why.

As the son of William Jackson, the nation's third national security advisor, who served under President Eisenhower, Jackson had grown up in the world of foreign affairs and realpolitik. At the Jacksons' home in Princeton, New Jersey, George Kennan was not only a frequent guest; he was also the next-door neighbor, dropping by with the likes of Paul Nitze, Dean Acheson, George Ball, and Walt and Eugene Rostow. Once, when he asked his father about all those people living in their barn, Jackson was told, "They're our chauffeurs." Actually, they were Hungarian freedom fighters who had somehow made it to America, and they really did live in the Jackson barn for almost a year.

After realizing that he was "a second- or even third-rate poet," Jackson became a military intelligence officer, as his father had once been. He was imbued with a sense of responsibility: If you were lucky enough to be living the good life, which he unapologetically was, it came with an IOU to the rest of society. Jackson wanted to give back, but not in the manner of his young contemporaries on the protest marches. "Even in 1968," he told me, "I knew that 99 percent of everything we were hearing was absolute crap, although it was a good way to meet girls and not go to school. So, if you're asking if I had a classic neoconservative moment, I think that's probably not correct. I was pretty much a conservative from the beginning. I mean, Princeton liberalism really gets under your skin. According to the academics at Princeton [Perle's graduate alma mater], the United States hasn't done anything even remotely correct for the last sixty or seventy years. I mean, even Kennan became one of the great handwringers of the world. He claimed he had basically championed every single view and everybody else was wrong. Well, there are two incorrect things about that statement: One, everybody else wasn't wrong, and two, he didn't champion any views. It was all ex post facto."

In 1984, Jackson was splitting his time in the military with doctoral work at Johns Hopkins School of International Studies, where the erudite former Carter defense secretary Harold Brown was teaching. He became Brown's assistant and chief researcher on a study of the effect of strategic defenses on nuclear stability and deterrence theory funded by the Carnegie Foundation. In the course of his research, Jackson interviewed virtually everyone in Washington whom he might like to work for after the project was over. When it was, Jackson still had a two-year service obligation, and when Brown asked what assignment he could try to arrange for his assistant, Jackson replied, "You know, I'd really like to work for Richard Perle." According to Jackson, Brown looked at him and said, "Where have I failed?" He was hired as an aide to Perle and Fred Ikle in the Office of Strategic Defense, writing memos and position papers for the arms negotiating team.

In the years to come, Jackson would become not only one of Perle's closest friends but also one of the most influential and effective proponents of Perle-backed foreign policy in Washington. One neoconservative described him as "the nexus between the defense industry and the neoconservatives. He translates us to them and them to us." As vice president for strategy and planning for Lockheed Martin, he helped the world's largest defense contractor become larger when Poland, Hungary, and the Czech Republic were admitted to NATO in 1997. Jackson was the prime mover of the U.S. Committee on NATO expansion, which was hugely successful. In that capacity he engineered what became known as the Vilnius Ten Declaration, a letter supporting the Iraq War and signed by the representatives of Romania, Bulgaria, Slovakia, Slovenia, Croatia, Albania, Macedonia, Latvia, Lithuania, and Estonia. Jackson was later accused of enticing those representatives to sign with the implied promise that their applications to join NATO would be given special consideration, a charge Jackson denies.

Just six months before the start of the Iraq War, Stephen Hadley, then assistant to NSC advisor Rice, asked Jackson to do his committee thing with Iraq, that is, to frame an intelligent argument for going to war. Thus was born the Committee for the Liberation of Iraq. "This administration, like most administrations, is lousy at public diplomacy," said Jackson. "They couldn't communicate or educate if they tried. Karen Hughes is the proof of that rule. If you look back at the history of this country, Woodrow Wilson and Franklin Roosevelt spent many years talking to the country about what was at stake. These were agonizingly slow decisions. And clearly, as we now know, we were hugely behind in our thinking about was required: explaining the danger of Iraq and what would be required to fix it. And they never did get the second question answered."

Actually, they didn't get the first question either. As an intelligence officer, Jackson was surprised that his friend Hadley and his colleagues had gotten caught up in CIA estimates of Iraq's nuclear capability. "I mean, everybody knows it's unreliable, and Steve Hadley certainly should have known that for the past twenty or twenty-five years. He got caught saying this was the truth when he knows perfectly well it's never the truth. In some of those years, I had to write parts of the intelligence estimates. And some years we would put in some stuff and some years it was so preposterous we would take it out. So, it was just whimsical as to whether something was a threat this year or wasn't."

And so, with the war just days away, Jackson found himself alone with the Turks in Ankara, as they voted against allowing the United States to attack from their soil. "That was sixty thousand troops out in the first day," he said with some bitterness. "That's when I started to think, as others did, that these guys didn't know what they were doing. And that's why we shut the committee down, because I couldn't really have that." Jackson knew from the Romanian and Bulgarian experience that one of the easiest entities to reform in a post-totalitarian country is the military. But, to his astonishment, the Iraqi military was being disbanded. "We never would have made that mistake. That's just kindergarten in my field." When Jackson says "we," he means the 175 members of his committee, which included people like Václav Havel, the hero of the Czech Republic, and former Swedish foreign minister Carl Bildt—people who knew something about fixing broken societies. Everyone that Jackson, Perle, and their colleagues recruited had experience in Central and Eastern Europe in the post-Yugoslavia break up. But, as Jackson put it, "We got screwed. The bottom line is we were promised that we were going to be consulted about the conduct of the war and the reconstruction efforts, and we were lied to. Rumsfeld just slammed the door."

While the battle for Baghdad was beginning, Jackson saw that Perle was being drawn into a battle of his own, over the very same issue that had dogged Jackson during his years as a Lockheed big shot by day and a foreign policy lobbyist by night: the appearance of conflicts of interest. Just days before the war, the *New Yorker* magazine published an article by Perle's nemesis, Seymour Hersh, titled "Lunch with the Chairman." The article described in detail a meeting in Marseilles attended by Perle, Saudi industrialist Saleh al-Zuhair, and the notorious Saudi arms dealer Adnan Khashoggi. Khashoggi, who had brokered billions of dollars worth of arms deals over his colorful career, had been the prime weapons contact for Oliver North during the Iran-Contra scandal. His appearance in this episode would add to the growing list of Iran-Contra figures who would eerily reappear, like Flying Dutchmen, almost twenty years after the scandal: Khashoggi, Ghorbanifar, Ledeen, and Elliott Abrams, to name a handful.

On its surface, the article suggested that Perle, the staunch anti-Saudi, was attempting to solicit funding for a private investment company he and a partner had set up. The company, Trireme, had been registered in November of 2001, just two months after 9/11, and, according to a prospectus, intended to invest both in technology and in goods and services related to homeland security. The brochure high-lighted the fact that three members of Trireme's "management group" were also members of the U.S. Defense Policy Board: Perle, his partner Gerald Hillman, and Henry Kissinger. In fact, Kissinger was not a mem-ber of management but of the firm's advisory board; when negative press began to appear, the Kissinger PR machine swung into high gear and flooded media outlets with a press release saying, in effect, that the liv-ing legend had merely leant his name to the business and knew nothing about anything.

Apparently, a Trireme official named Christopher Harriman, whom Khashoggi had known previously, had sent an introductory letter to the arms dealer inviting him to invest in the company. The letter reportedly said that $45 million had already been raised, including $20 million from Scoop Jackson's favorite company, Boeing. This was followed by a meeting in Paris at which Khashoggi, Zuhair, Harriman, and Hillman discussed the Saudis' making a large investment with, of course, the assurance of a healthy return. According to Hersh's account, Zuhair was more interested in averting war than in making some short-term profit, telling Hillman, "If we have peace, it would be easy to raise a hundred million. We will bring development to the region." Hillman then agreed to arrange a meeting between the Saudis and his partner Perle.

By Perle's account, there were actually two meetings, the first in Belgium, and the second in Marseilles, the meeting Hersh wrote about. "They said they were eager to talk to me about the situation in Iraq," Perle told me. "And I said, I'm not going to travel to Paris for this. So we agreed to have lunch in Marseilles [a forty-five-minute drive from Perle's place in Provence]. The entire conversation was about Iraq, and it began with this fellow al-Zuhair making a passionate plea for us to engage in a dialogue with him. It was basically an argument about whether one could do business with Saddam Hussein. But he wasn't an emissary, and that was it. There was no discussion of business of any kind. Not one word. Not a word. And I got a letter from both Khashoggi and al-Zuhair to that effect." Indeed, even in Hersh's piece, Zuhair is quoted as saying that throughout the lunch Perle made it clear that he was "above the money" and that he had stuck to his idea that "we have to get rid of Saddam." Khashoggi added that as Zuhair made his case, "Perle politely listened and the lunch was over."

But Hersh's piece went further, claiming that when news of Perle's meeting became known to high-ranking Saudis, they "reacted with anger and astonishment." Either Hersh contacted Saudi Arabia's influential ambassador to the United States, Prince Bandar bin Sultan, or Bandar contacted Hersh to say that from what he had heard, the lunch was all about business, not about averting war. "There is a split personality to Perle," Bandar told Hersh. "Here he is, on the one hand, trying to make a hundred-million-dollar deal, and, on the other hand, there were elements of the appearance of blackmail—'If we get in business, he'll back off on Saudi Arabia'—as I have been informed by participants at the meeting."

It turns out that just a week prior to the meeting in Marseilles, Hillman sent a lengthy memo to Khashoggi outlining a dozen steps Iraq would have to take to avert war, including an admission that it possessed weapons of mass destruction, after which Saddam would be allowed to resign and leave the country. The memo, and a similar note sent just a day before the Perle meeting, was signed by Hillman. When contacted by Hersh, Hillman said his partner had nothing to do with the memos and was not even told about them until after they had been sent. Hersh writes, "The views set forth in the memorandums were, indeed, very different from those held by Perle, who had said publicly that Saddam would leave office only if he is forced out, and from those of his fellow hard-liners in the Bush administration." Then, inexplicably, Hersh adds, "Prince Bandar's assertion that the talk of peace was merely a pretext for some hard selling is difficult to dismiss." Why? Nothing in the article, especially the quotes from the participants, supports Bandar's assertion.

Not surprisingly, the Hillman memos and news of the luncheon made it into the Saudi-owned newspaper *Al Hayat*, where the affair was characterized as a "negotiation" between the Americans and the Saudis to avert the Iraq War. The Beirut daily *Al Safer* published Arabic transla-tions of the memos, attributing them to Perle. Obviously, the conclusion drawn in Washington and elsewhere was that Perle was freelancing as an ambassador and trying to make some money in the bargain.

Perle threatened to sue Hersh, calling him "the closest thing American journalism has to a terrorist," but later thought better of it. The expense and the slim odds of success made the exercise quixotic. But in the end, Perle's threats and bluster made him appear, as Slate's observer Jack Shafer put it, simply as "a gasbag." Years later when Hersh and Perle found themselves sharing a greenroom at the Charlie Rose show, Hersh reportedly extended his hand, but Perle refused to shake. As Perle described it, "He came in and said something one would say to a friend, and I didn't say anything. Then he said, 'Wow, I suppose we can agree never to speak again,' and I said, 'That would be just fine.' He is obviously under the mistaken impression that I would want to talk to him." "Lunch with the Chairman" had a huge and damaging effect, coming as it did at the start of the war. Perle is convinced that Hersh was encouraged to write the piece by the Saudis as payback for the infamous PowerPoint lecture Perle had arranged for the DPB by Laurent Murawiec. "I think the Saudis decided, 'We're going to get this guy one way or the other.'"

Had the Khashoggi affair been the only incident enveloping Perle, he doubtless would have survived it. But it was only the beginning. At about the same time, Perle and the DPB heard a classified briefing by the DIA on the situations in North Korea and Iraq. Three weeks after that brief-ing, he was the featured speaker on a telephone investment seminar sponsored by Goldman Sachs titled, "Implications of an Imminent War: Iraq Now, North Korea Next?" As if orchestrated, Perle's other business interests suddenly began appearing in the press worldwide. In San Francisco, protesters marched outside the offices of Autonomy Corporation, a UK-based firm that makes software for monitoring e-mails and phone conversations, which had contracts with the Office of Homeland Security. The protesters were demanding the resignation of Richard Perle from Autonomy's board.

Then came news that the bankrupt telecommunications company Global Crossing had hired Perle to help win government approval for the sale of the company's fiber-optics network to a Chinese firm with close ties to the Beijing government. Perle's fee was a reported $750,000, for what the company described as his "unique perspective on and intimate knowledge of the national defense and security issues that will be raised by the [review] process." Not to be outdone, the *International Herald Tribune* published a story that Perle had also been hired by American satellite maker Loral Space and Communications to help it respond to federal charges that it had improperly given secret technical data to China. The cumulative effect of these stories in the opening weeks of a controversial war made Perle a symbol to war critics and conspiracy theorists who believed that the neocons' primary motivation was greed. Calvin Trillin felt obliged to write another poem: "On Richard Perle, Lobbyist, Businessman and, Perhaps Not Coincidentally, Chairman of the Defense Policy Board":

> The plans to start this war were laid
> Within the Sissy Hawk Brigade—
> A band of Vietnam evaders
> All puffed up now as tough crusaders.
> Yes, now, as then, they love inciting
> A war that others will be fighting.
> In recent weeks, there been much talk
> Of Richard Perle, a sissy hawk.
> There've been some articles about
> Just whether Perle has used his clout,
> While fighting evil hell for leather,
> To profit. (Hawks have nests to feather.)
>
> A pity that some lads who fought
> In Vietnam were later brought
> Back home again in body bags
> Adorned with battle stars and flags:

They missed the fruits that dedication
Can bring to those who serve their nation.

At the State Department, Colin Powell was complaining loudly and frequently that Perle had become a major liability and should be removed from the Defense Policy Board. When he thought he had finally succeeded in ousting him, Condoleezza Rice informed Powell, "We compromised." "What do you mean, 'compromised'?" Powell asked. "He's no longer chairman but he's still on the board," Rice replied. Powell was incredulous. "Condi," he said, "that's not the problem. The problem is he still has the title. So he's not the chairman—he's still an advisor. You're going to regret this."

Indeed, on March 28, 2003, Perle resigned as chairman, saying he did not want the adverse publicity to affect the work of the defense board. The news triggered another devilish poem by Calvin Trillin:

> And so for Richard Perle was writ
> The second graph of his obit:
> The soaring bird of hawkish myth
> Was grounded when discovered with
> His talon in the cookie jar
> While reaching for a small pourboire
> To use Old Europe's language, French,
> May seem to hawks contrarian.
> Pardon. Our friends have changed too fast
> For me to learn Bulgarian.

An investigation by the Defense Department's inspector general (IG) cleared Perle of any wrongdoing, but his troubles did not end there. In the summer of 2003, Perle coauthored an op-ed column in the *Wall Street Journal* praising a proposal by Boeing to lease tanker jets to the air force as a cost-effective way of solving one of the Pentagon's chronic problems. He did not disclose in the column that Boeing had already invested $20 million in Trireme, leaving the *Journal* embarrassed and apologetic.

Sitting and listening to my recitation of the incidents one after another, Perle chuckled and shook his head. "You know, when you string them together like that, it sounds like I'm a complete dolt!" Or worse. He then conceded that, given his notoriety, he should have been more circumspect about the overlap between his business dealings and his unpaid position on the DPB. "But," he admitted, "I don't live my life that way." For all of his strategic brilliance and his reputation as a consummate insider, Perle appears extraordinarily naive concerning the appearance of conflicts of interest. Either that or the "Who, me?" is just an act.

The Boeing affair is a case in point. According to Perle, he was contacted by Denny Miller, an old crony from the Scoop Jackson days. Miller asked Perle if he would hear a pitch from a client, Boeing, about leasing tankers instead of buying them. "If it had just been someone from Boeing calling, I probably would have said no," Perle said. "But this was an old friend. So these guys came over and gave me a PowerPoint presentation and it sounded pretty good. It sounded sensible because a lease instead of a buy would solve the air force's cash-flow problems. Then Tom Donnelly [a PNAC member and former Lockheed executive] called and said, 'Why don't we write something together?' And I said, 'Sure.' Tom did the first draft; I revised it; and we sent it off. The idea that Boeing was a potential investor in Trireme, that somehow I was doing this to please Boeing—"

"What did you expect people to think?" I cut in. "Twenty million dollars is serious money."

"The two things were so completely unrelated that it never occurred to me. I didn't feel I had any ties to Boeing at all." When the plan to lease one hundred 767s was analyzed and dissected, critics concluded that the arrangement would amount to a bailout of Boeing, which was trying to save more than three thousand jobs, and a big bill for the taxpayer. After two years of wrangling, the DOD finally agreed to lease twenty aircraft and buy the other eighty.

On the Goldman Sachs telephone seminar, Perle says he had no knowledge of how the investment firm was advertising the teleconfer-

ence, and, in any event, he had not and would not have disclosed classified information. "I was there to talk about Iraq. I began the call by
saying, 'What you are going to hear from me is my view of the situation.
I'm not going to disclose any privileged information.' There's a recording
of that conversation. It's quoted in the IG's report. They went through
every line in it and concluded that, indeed, I had not disclosed any privileged information, and on North Korea I had almost nothing to say."

The Global Crossing affair is a bit more complicated. According to
Perle, another lawyer friend of his approached him for help on structuring the sale of the fiber-optic network to Singapore Electronics and a
Hong Kong–based company, a transfer that would have to meet strict
technology transfer guidelines. Since Global Crossing was in bank-
ruptcy (having nothing whatsoever to do with Perle), and Perle's fee
would come out of the sale, it had to submit an affidavit to the bank-
ruptcy court explaining its actions. It was that affidavit that described
Perle's "unique perspective on and intimate knowledge of the national
defense and security issues that will be raised by the [review] process."
Perle says that when he read that sentence in a draft of the affidavit, he
told the company to take it out. While packing for a trip, Perle says a
notary public arrived with the twenty-six-page document, which he
signed, not realizing that although the phrase had indeed been removed
from the first few pages, it appeared again later in the document. As he
was riding in a taxi in Manhattan, he received a cell phone call from a
reporter from the *New York Times* inquiring about the document and
reading the words Perle thought had been deleted.

"I said, 'I never signed that.' And he's got it in front of him, so he concluded that I'm lying. Believe me, I was blown away when I discovered
it was in the document." Perle insists he did no lobbying for Global
Crossing. Instead he says he impressed upon the company's management that in order to comply with national security concerns, the sale
would have to be beyond squeaky clean; it would have to be challenge
proof. "I advised them to set up the most draconian structure that had
ever existed for separating the new owners from the management of the
company. I said, 'You're not going to build the Great Wall of China;

you're going to build a combination of the Great Wall and the Israeli Middle East Wall. It's going to be stainless steel, and you will be afraid of it.'" In fact, Perle said publicly that the company had done a poor job of structuring the deal and that he would oppose any sale that did not comply with regulations.

Still, the Global Crossing episode, given the fact that it involved a China connection, made Perle seem even worse than a greedy opportunist; it made him look like a traitor, as did the case of Loral Space and Communications. Loral already had been caught violating technology transfer regulations by providing the Chinese with data to help them determine why one of their rockets had blown up after launch. That transfer required a license that Loral had not obtained, and their failure to do so resulted in a large fine and other penalties, which the company eventually paid without admitting guilt. Perle was brought in to negotiate with, of all people, his good friends at the State Department, on the size of the fine and other acts of restitution. "They screwed up," Perle told me. "It was as simple as that. The data they gave the Chinese was not sensitive data, but it required a license. They were wrong, and they paid a very heavy price for it, including having a lot of potential sales frozen. So I made one phone call, which I make no apologies for, to the Department of State just to see where the case stood. Not to pressure anybody to come out a certain way, but just to find out where it stood."

As for the formation of Trireme, Perle admitted that the prospectus, which he said he never read, would lead a potential investor to believe that the fund managers were well connected. But the fund was set up to invest in new media, not the defense industry, until the NASDAQ bubble burst. Then he and Hillman decided to focus on the field of homeland security, a target-rich environment in the post-9/11 world. "The policy board doesn't make decisions," he said. "It doesn't do procurement of any kind. It's basically a seminar to talk about broad policy ideas. So, I didn't see a conflict and neither did the IG. Now, in retrospect, maybe I should have said to myself, 'People are going to try to invent a conflict and therefore I should choose between a business life and the board.' Maybe I should have done that. It wasn't so important for me to be on the DPB. It wasn't that important to me to be chairman. I enjoyed doing it. The issues are issues that, to this day, continue to interest me deeply. And it was a way of keeping a hand in."

Perle's interest in new media had begun with his recruitment by Conrad Black, the flamboyant and extravagant CEO of Hollinger International, which owned hundreds of newspapers worldwide, including the *Chicago Sun-Times*, London's *Daily Mail and Telegraph*, and the *Jerusalem Post*. Black, a bombastic Canadian who gave up his citizenship so he could become Lord Black of Crossharbour, and about who, one wag remarked, "he does a wonderful imitation of a great man," was best known in some circles for charging his company somewhere between $42,000 and $62,000 for a birthday party for his glamorous spendthrift wife and for stockpiling influential Americans for his board, including Perle, Henry Kissinger, former Illinois governor Jim Thompson, former Sotheby's CEO Alfred Taubman, and Perle's old sparring partner Rick Burt.

Perle says he met Black in the early 1990s while going through the revolving door of a hotel in Davos, Switzerland, the site of the annual international economic conference. "I was going in and he was coming out," Perle recalled. "He recognized me and introduced himself." Perle said Black remembered an appearance Perle had made at another conference in which he debated Canadian prime minister Pierre Trudeau on the always thorny subject of missile defenses. After Trudeau made his case against the American plans, Perle rebutted point by point. "So, Conrad remembered that talk and said, 'You eviscerated Trudeau. It was exquisite. You just cut him up into little pieces.' And my vague recollection was that he was right. Trudeau didn't know what he was talking about and I did." Perle says Black then began reciting specific sparring matches Perle had had with the likes of Les Aspin and Ted Kennedy, mostly from televised congressional hearings. "I was astonished by his recall. I'd never seen anything like it. He had a photographic memory."

Not long after that, Black asked Perle to join Hollinger's advisory board, which included Kissinger, Margaret Thatcher, Paul Volker, Lord Carrington, George Will, and David Brinkley; and in 1994, Perle joined

Hollinger International's executive board. This board, according to Perle, functioned as a quick-response team when an immediate approval of some action was necessary and the full board could not be convened promptly. On one such occasion, Perle says he had to negotiate a deal in which he represented the shareholders and Black was the "related party." Perle chaired the special committee of independent directors who oversaw the process. "We hired lawyers and we hired bankers to examine all the terms. For every penny more that Hollinger got, Conrad had to give up a penny. The bankers had given us a dollar figure which they thought would be fair to the shareholders. But, and I guess it's the negotiator in me, I was determined to do better than that. And I did. I got Conrad to pay more than the fairness figure, which he didn't know. I was pretty pleased with that; that's what you're supposed to do when you're an independent director."

While Perle was also a member of Hollinger's audit committee, he sent a memo to Black imploring him to take the Internet seriously because of the effect it was having and would continue to have on the newspaper industry. Perle predicted that within five years, urban dailies would lose a third of their revenue base because classified ads would move to the Internet. Therefore, he suggested, Hollinger should be investing in Internet companies that would benefit from the trend. Black agreed and the board voted to set up a subsidiary called Hollinger Digital. According to Perle, the entity was supposed to be run by Black's twenty-seven-year-old nephew, Matthew Doull, who had once tried unsuccessfully to interest his uncle in a start-up called Netscape. Had Black listened, his initial investment would have been worth millions.

With the young man now considered a genius in Black's eyes, he was put in charge of Hollinger Digital, and, as Perle tells it, managed to alienate practically everyone within forty-eight hours. "He started telling editors and publishers what to do, and there was a kind of rebellion." Black then asked Perle to be chief executive, an offer that would represent a major transition for Perle, who had never run a company before. Perle agreed and, on the advice of company counsel, resigned from the audit board. But he did not also quit the executive board, a decision that would come back to haunt him when Black's house of cards came tumbling down. (Black went on trial in March 2007 and was found guilty by a Chicago jury on four felony counts in July.)

In February of 2001, Black threw a lunch for Donald Rumsfeld to celebrate his confirmation as secretary of defense. It was a typically lavish Black affair, held at historic Decatur House across Lafayette Square from the White House. Naturally Perle was at a star-studded table, bracketed by Margaret Thatcher and Giscard D'Estaing. According to one guest's account, Rumsfeld spent most of the affair paying homage to Perle, "almost as if Perle was some sort of guru—I would even describe Rumsfeld's attitude as obsequious. There was a lot of 'Richard, what do *you* think?'"

When shareholders began complaining about Black's lavish lifestyle, a special committee began looking more deeply into the company's financials. What they found were numerous questionable transactions, including three specific dealings in which the executive committee had given approval by written consent in lieu of a full board meeting. There were three signatures on the consents, Conrad Black's, partner David Radler's, and Perle's. "In each of these instances," Perle explained, "it is alleged that Black and Radler got money they shouldn't have received. I never received anything. The consents I signed authorized the management to enter into transactions. Nowhere do they say, 'Oh, and help yourself to improper payments.' These were absolutely garden-variety vanilla consents." Perle insisted that the alleged improper activity took place *after* he signed the approval to proceed with the transcations.

In the fall of 2003, Black and Radler were charged with bilking Hollinger shareholders out of hundreds of millions of dollars, and using a rubber-stamp board to get away with it. The machinations were complicated, but as the *Chicago Tribune* explained, "Black and Radler borrowed money from Black and Radler to pay Black and Radler for not competing with Black and Radler." The allegations triggered federal charges and a $400 million shareholders' suit, as well as an investigation by the Securities and Exchange Commission. Perle, whose compensation was an estimated $5.4 million, was among the directors described in a company audit as being part of "a corporate kleptocracy"; Perle himself was described as "a faithless fiduciary," who never bothered to read and evaluate transactions before signing off on them, a charge Perle vehemently denies. "With the notable exception of Perle," the report charged, "none of Hollinger's non-Black group directors derived any financial or other improper personal benefit from their service on Hollinger's board."

The audit recommended that Perle return the $5.4 million. It also mentioned Hollinger's $2 million investment in Trireme, as well as the $63.6 million invested in eleven new media companies Perle recommended during the dot.com boom, gambles that had lost $50 million. One company that Hollinger Digital invested in, Interactive Investor International, was taken public by Credit Suisse First Boston in February of 2000. At the end of trading on the first day, the options Perle was owed as a bonus would have been worth some $40 million. But, as he was required to wait six months for his bonus, the options ended up being worth just about $1 million, as close as Perle had ever come to being truly rich.

Perle dodged two bullets when first the SEC cleared him, and then federal prosecutors indicted only Black and Radler, informing Perle and the other directors that they might be called to testify as witnesses for the prosecution. Perle was not called. After a lengthy trial, Black and three co-defendants were found guilty of three counts each of mail fraud; they each face a maximum of 35 years in prison plus a maximum fine of $1 million. This still left Perle as the subject of the civil suit. Through his attorney, Perle denounced the charges contained in the company's internal report as "factually and legally wrong."

Numerous e-mails by Black included in the company report and placed into the trial record reveal that Black saw Perle as an operator just as devious as he. In one, apparently a reference to the Trireme investment, Black wrote, "As I suspected, there is a good deal of nest-feathering being conducted by Richard, which I don't object to other than there was some attempt to disguise it behind a good deal of dissembling and obfuscation." In another, sent to a Hollinger executive in

January of 2003, Black writes, "I have been exposed to Richard's full repertoire of histrionics, cajolery and utilization of fine print. He hasn't been disingenuous exactly, but I understand how he finessed the Russians out of deployed missiles in exchange for noneventual deployment of half the number of missiles of unproven design." In an astounding example of pots screaming at kettles, the report also included a letter from Black to Perle complaining about the $1,000 to $6,000 a month Perle was billing the company on an American Express card, for which, according to Black, "there is no substantiation....These items include a great many restaurants, groceries and other matters. This is not a system that conforms to the standards being imposed in every area of this company." The report said it could find no reply from Perle.

To Perle's critics, the Hollinger case is a clear example of arrogance morphing into greed. Leslie Gelb, who rarely agreed with Perle during Gelb's walk-ons at the State and Defense departments and as a columnist for the *New York Times*, read the affair with typical self-righteousness: "Richard has always been willing to take the highest risks, playing for the highest stakes on policy issues over the years and often winning. But this is also really a story of being seduced by money. When you are touched by lightning and manage to get into the inner sanctum to make money, the opportunities are delicious."

But Jonathan Perle, a lawyer who has watched these episodes unfold for years, believes that if his father is guilty of anything, it is of failing to look both ways when crossing what to others is an ethical divide. "I do say that to him a lot, actually," Jonathan told me. "I do now. I wouldn't have been as aware of it ten years ago. But now I do say, 'Maybe you better not have that meeting,' or 'Are you sure you want to do that interview with so and so?' And he'll either say, 'That's a good idea,' or 'I know what I'm doing.' It's his call to make."

"They think we're rich?" Leslie Perle said with genuine surprise. "Really? I'm a butcher's daughter. What do they mean by rich? I always find it interesting when other people are counting my money, and I wish we had as much as they think we do. I'm not complaining, but I wonder why they think I worked all those years at civil service jobs. There

203

were times that I used to get really upset about this. But I can't do anything about it. I'm amazed that people think he would take foreign policy positions for monetary reasons. Go back to the Jackson days, to the days in the Pentagon. His views haven't changed."

But the world around him had. The series of events, the litany of accusations, became too much for Colin Powell. He went to Rumsfeld and told him that Perle had become a major embarrassment for the administration, not just for his business dealings but because of his constant appearances in the media around the world making remarks that were often at variance with stated policy while being presented as an administration spokesman. In February of 2004, Perle resigned from the DPB entirely.

XI.
BAND ON THE RUN

A year from now, I'll be very surprised if there is not some grand square in Baghdad that is named after President Bush. There is no doubt that, with the exception of a very small number of people close to a vicious regime, the people of Iraq have been liberated and they understand that they've been liberated. And it is getting easier every day for Iraqis to express that sense of liberation.

—Richard Perle, AEI keynote speech, 9/22/03

GIVEN WHAT WAS unfolding in Afghanistan and Iraq, Perle's resignation from the DPB might have been fortuitous. Bruce Jackson let out a long sigh at the thought of what might have been. "I think we're all somewhat relieved that we weren't at the Defense Department and it all wasn't happening on our watch, because I don't know if we could have done anything better. I didn't see a civil war under the surface, so I guess you never know what's under the surface. They sure as hell didn't consult anybody and they sure as hell didn't reach out to anybody. And boy, did they screw the pooch. It's sort of unbelievable."

Bruce Jackson doesn't think like an intelligence officer; he thinks like a *good* intelligence officer, factoring in both historical caveats and basic human psychology when analyzing an event and its particular signature. Unlike some of his politically like-minded friends, he always leaves room for doubt. When the first 9/11 plane hit, he was in his office at Lockheed Martin speaking on the phone to a Senate staffer. "She told me a plane had just hit the Trade Center. And I told her, 'Let's keep going.' A few minutes later she said, 'We're being evacuated.' At that point, I walked down to my CEO's office and recommended that all our people stay at their posts. Some wanted to go home to their children. But I just felt that if we were needed, and I have no idea for what, we should be at our posts." From his time working under Perle at the DOD he knew what was supposed to happen next. The interagency process would gear up, with each branch of the security establishment sending their top guns to meetings in which the merits of various actions and responses would be picked over like fish-market mackerel on a Friday morning, with the bad stuff being tossed and the good stuff being packed and wrapped for delivery. But that never happened and Jackson could understand why. It took too much time.

"These guys had been hit by two Pearl Harbors on the same day, on their watch. In addition to the casualties, there's a huge sense of guilt and failure. And I think they just maxed out. They had to deal with a whole new world they had never seen before in one afternoon while half the building is still smoking and there are a hundred or so dead on the other side of the E-ring. Of course they skipped steps. Rumsfeld wasn't a detail guy."

Moreover, Rumsfeld was a man of astonishing vanity, having little interest in the psychological state of those who reported to him. "Stir the pot!" was his standing order to deputies, meaning the act of shaking things up was of far greater importance than the benefits that might accrue from frantic pot stirring. Did he know or care that one of his key subordinates was going home each night after a sixteen-hour day to a domestic situation that was so volatile that he had to stay awake all night? After the first flush of victory, after that Saddam statue was pulled down, it almost certainly didn't matter. And neither did the constant nudging from Richard Perle to "hand the keys" over to Ahmed Chalabi right away so the United States could get out of Dodge before the blowback hit. Rumsfeld did nothing to support Perle's case, telling him at one point to "let the cream rise to the top," meaning let the best man emerge as the new Iraqi leader.

The only problem with that strategy, as Perle saw it, was that there was no cream in Iraq to rise. There would be no Nelson Mandela or Lech Walesa or Václav Havel to appear triumphant to jubilant crowds in Baghdad, because Saddam Hussein had killed everyone who had ever aspired to such heights. Mandela had been jailed, Walesa and Havel contained for a time, but they hadn't been executed and lived to fight another day. The best Perle could offer was the Jay Gatsby of the Middle East, but Rumsfeld, taking his cue from Bush, would have none of it. Chalabi was not their guy, and the Iraqis would decide in due time who was. For Perle, this was the beginning of the end. "We needed something immediately," he said. "As you know, I wanted something even before. I wanted to recognize a government in exile so there would be a seamless transfer of authority from the invading force to the Iraqis themselves." Perle paused and sighed. "But you can't replay it. I'm convinced that it could have been and should have been a radically different situation today if we had done that."

Perhaps what U.S. Marine Corporal Eddie Chin did in Firdos Square, Baghdad, on April 9, 2003, set the ominous tone for all that was to come. But neither he nor those of us watching the live satellite feed at CBS News in New York had any way of knowing that at the time. When Chin climbed a statue of Saddam Hussein and covered its face with an American flag, someone in our room said to no one in particular, "Uh-oh. Bad idea. Not good." Sure enough, within seconds Old Glory was replaced with a pre-Saddam Iraqi flag, lest the world receive the impression that dictatorship was being replaced with colonialism. Chin's patriotic intentions, pure though they certainly were, were both harbinger and caveat, unheeded amid the hoopla. (But Chin's sister did make it on to the *Today* show the next morning.)

Needless to say, a review of headlines and news accounts of the spring of '03 is embarrassing not only to those quoted but also to the reporters and headline writers doing the quoting. The Taliban had been routed in Afghanistan, and something resembling a representative government was being formed. There was looting in Baghdad, yes, but as Donald Rumsfeld infamously remarked, "Stuff happens," marking the first of what would be a long list of glib, smart-ass rejoinders to all those naysayers who surely were now eating crow, or humble pie, or their words, or their dinner as cable news trumpeted the takedown of the statue. So what if the scene had been staged, and most of the small crowd consisted of journalists? The images were designed to convey a "higher" truth, which was that the Earp brothers and Doc Holliday had arrived in Tombstone, and the next stop for Saddam and his murderous posse was Boot Hill. The *Jerusalem Post*, on whose board Perle sat, headlined a story "Perle of Wisdom," and the lead line from reporter Melissa Radler read, "It turns out Richard Perle was right. As jubilant crowds of Iraqis welcomed US troops into Baghdad as liberators and helped topple a massive statue of Saddam Hussein, Perle, a member of the Defense Policy Board who is widely viewed as an architect of the war, sounded triumphant. The liberal media elites, with their talk of a Vietnam-like quagmire, were wrong and Perle, to their surprise, was right."

For the cinematically inclined, the scene was meant to be match-dissolved to the removal of one of the many Lenin statues by crane during the collapse of the Soviet Union in 1991. Ms. Radler was certainly not alone in missing the point. The reality was that after a period of euphoria, Moscow was left with gaping holes in its society that were gradually filled by gangsters and nuclear wheeler-dealers, leaving its people only marginally better off. The pain of transformation doesn't make for stirring video. As the *New Yorker*'s David Remnick, quoting Polish Holocaust survivor Stanislaw Lec pointed out, "When smashing monuments, save the pedestals—they always come in handy."

Saddam was captured just before Christmas 2003 hiding in a hole in the ground. But still no WMD and still no bin Laden. Never mind, said Perle; the WMD was not the sole reason for the invasion. And as for bin Laden, his time would come. As a kind of ambassador without portfolio, Perle made the rounds of talk shows and editorial-board interviews suggesting that Syrians, Iranians, and North Koreans should not be making long-term plans. While he constantly repeated that attacks on these countries were not currently on the Pentagon's schedule, he said, all options were and should remain open.

As the Paul Bremer–led occupation in Iraq stretched from weeks into months, far longer than anyone had imagined it would, Perle continued his "if only they'd listened to me" mantra about Ahmed Chalabi and the need to "turn over the keys" to the Iraqis quickly. As the violence escalated, so did the expressions of unconcern by the administration, with Rumsfeld dismissing the incessant suicide attacks and car bombings as the work of a few "dead-enders."

With the publication in 2003 of *An End to Evil: How to Win the War on Terror*, Perle and Bush speechwriter David Frum laid out the argument for an open-ended campaign against evildoers worldwide. With typical understatement, the tome is prefaced by the declaration "There is no middle way for Americans: it is either victory or holocaust. This book is a manual for victory." First, the Perle-Frum plan would require an American military on steroids, a much larger and more muscular force nimble enough to fight and win multiple conflicts in far-flung places. It would require that the American people accept the notion that many of our traditional allies, specifically France, are not really our friends at all and that their support should neither be assumed nor welcomed if offered. It would also require the overthrow of regimes in Syria and Iran, and a blockade of North Korea. Few of those who reviewed the book considered it much more than a neocon fantasy, and not a foreign policy that was either desirable or realistic.

As the Bush administration entered its second term, much of Washington was debating who would be asked to stay on and who would be shown the door. To no one's surprise, Colin Powell was the first to go, having endured four years of mostly losing battles and the unshakeable feeling of having been used. He declined all interview requests until an article appeared in the *AARP* magazine. Asked about the UN speech, the absence of WMD, and his role in selling the war, Powell said, "It hurt...when it turned out that part of that information was wrong, the spotlight was on me and I'm disappointed. When people ask me, 'Is this a blot on your record?' Yeah, okay, fine, it's a blot on my record. There it is. It's there for everybody to see forever."

Perle already had weighed in with his view that the mess Iraq had become almost two years after the invasion could be blamed in part on

Powell for having opposed handing Baghdad over to Chalabi right after Saddam's statue had fallen. Of course, Rumsfeld hadn't stood up for Chalabi either, but that was different: Rumsfeld was Defense and Powell was State and you don't knock your own in public. As for Powell's replacement, Wolfowitz could keep knocking but he couldn't come in. The confirmation votes weren't there to give Wolfowitz the kind of job that would lead to a university presidency, so when an opening at the World Bank appeared, Wolfowitz asked and received, choosing to ignore the obvious parallels with another failed brainiac, Robert McNamara, who had bailed as Vietnam auteur and then landed in the safety and security of the World Bank. George Tenet had been given a more dramatic sendoff, with the president bestowing upon his bruised and battered CIA director the Medal of Freedom, the nation's highest civilian honor. This act of kindness served only to make cynics wonder what honors Tenet might have received had the prewar intelligence he signed off on been true and accurate. On other fronts, there were reports that Chalabi had been feeding information to the Iranians, and the Larry Franklin–AIPAC spy case had also broken. The death toll for Americans in Afghanistan and Iraq had passed two thousand and there were increasing signs that a civil war in Iraq was all but inevitable.

Congress's growing frustration boiled over at a meeting of the House Armed Services Committee in April of 2005. Three years earlier, Perle had gone before the same committee and blithely dismissed the concerns of retired general Wesley Clark as "hopelessly confused," and characterized the general's warnings about trouble to come in Iraq as "fuzzy stuff" and "dumb clichés." Now Republican congressman Walter Jones of North Carolina had summoned both Perle and Clark back to the hearing room to give Perle a piece of his mind and Clark the hope of an apology from someone. Curiously, Perle placed a copy of chef Anthony Bourdain's book *Kitchen Confidential: Adventures in the Culinary Underbelly* on the witness table, just in case his testimony was interrupted by a quorum call. Jones, his face red with rage, thundered at Perle, "It is just amazing to me how we as a Congress were told we had to remove this man but the reasons we were given were not accurate. To me, there should be somebody large enough to say, 'We've made a mistake.' I've not heard that yet."

He would not hear it from Richard Perle, who heaped blame on the CIA for "appalling incompetence" and then produced a head-scratching theory: "There is reason to believe that we were suckered into an ill-conceived initial attack aimed at Saddam himself by double agents planted by the regime. And, as we now know, the estimate of Saddam's stockpile of weapons of mass destruction was substantially wrong." (Perle told me the information that had led to a particularly destructive air strike before the invasion came from Iraqi nationals known as "the rock stars," for reasons unclear. According to Perle's sources, they gave specific information on Saddam's whereabouts, leading the president to order the strike, thus launching the war, ahead of schedule. Apparently, the rock stars' information was wrong. "I suppose it could have been an innocent error," Perle told me, "but my friends were convinced we had been set up.") Representative Jones, who said he had signed more than nine hundred letters of condolence, held up a copy of Perle's remarks and said, "I went to a Marine's funeral who left a wife and three children, twins he never saw, and I'll tell you, I apologize Mr. Chairman, but I am just incensed with this statement."

When committee chairman Duncan Hunter of California tried to look on the bright side, suggesting to Clark that Bush's Middle East strategy was similar to Ronald Reagan's in Eastern Europe, the general shot back, "Reagan never invaded Eastern Europe." And so it went.

While debate about the war increased, a less violent but still noteworthy battle was taking place at the Corporation for Pubic Broadcasting (CPB), the funding arm of the Public Broadcasting System (PBS). Long perceived as a bastion of liberalism, the PBS faithful had successfully fought an attempt to cut its budget by 25 percent but had not been able to stop the Bush administration from installing two of its own at CPB: Ken Tomlinson as chairman and Patricia Harrison as president and CEO. Tomlinson wasted no time in declaring that PBS's liberal bias needed a makeover, and among his first acts was signing off on a documentary featuring Richard Perle.

It would not be a film about Perle, but rather a platform from which Perle could make the case not only for the war in Iraq but for other neocon complaints as well, such as the pervasive influence of those "lefties" in Hollywood. And, in an in-your-face exclamation, the film would be produced by Brian Lapping, Perle's old friend from his London School of Economics days, and his neighbor in Provence. To be sure, Lapping was an accomplished filmmaker, as his docudrama on Reykjavik would attest. But green-lighting a public television film about such a controversial figure as Perle and then asking his friend to make it was clearly not an honest attempt to correct a perceived bias. Of course, Lapping didn't see it that way and was surprised at the howls of protest that were heard before he had even shot a frame. "I think it was all bollocks. I couldn't understand it. If you're making a film about elephants and you can't stand going anywhere near elephants, then you'll make a bad film. And there is no way the view of a particular person to be represented in the film will be well put if the person making the film is not sympathetic with the central character."

Lapping explained that he was contacted in London by Michael Pack, a conservative filmmaker acting as an emissary for Tomlinson. Pack said he was looking for programming that would counter the perceived leftist views of most PBS shows. "Of course," Lapping told me, "when you have an American with funds to spend on films, you don't refuse to have lunch with him." Over lunch, Lapping mentioned that he was a friend of Perle's, and that got Pack's attention. "He said, 'Oh, Richard's the kind of person whose point of view we'd like to put across,'" Lapping told me. "At that point, Richard had ceased to be chairman of the Defense Policy Board and I thought he would like to put his arguments for the president in a better manner than the president manages it himself. So I rang him up and said, 'Do you fancy that?' And he said, 'Why not?'"

The war and those who supported it began to generate a series of films in which Richard Perle was a focal point, becoming, however unwittingly, the personification of everything that was wrong with the

Bush administration. In September of 2005, PBS broadcast a massive, three-part film produced by the BBC titled *The Power of Nightmares*, which purported to demonstrate how the neocons had exploited the fears of the American people, first about the Soviet Union and later about practically all Arabs and Muslims. Among the points made is the refusal by the United States of a Soviet offer to leave Afghanistan if the Americans agreed to stop supplying the mujahideen. Gorbachev warned that continued support would not lead to democracy in Afghanistan but to a more radical form of Islam. He was right, and the rejectionists, including Perle, were wrong.

As the film traces events through 9/11, Perle makes the case that what the Taliban and Al-Qaeda represent is not fundamentally different from what the Soviet Union had been: evil attempting to triumph over good. "It isn't a war on terror," he says; "it's a war on terrorists who want to impose an intolerant tyranny on all mankind, an Islamic universe in which we are all compelled to accept their beliefs and live by their lights, and in that sense this is a battle between good and evil." Perle continued to express his astonishment that practically no one believed in a connection between Al-Qaeda and Saddam Hussein:

Interviewer: There really is evidence?

Perle: There really is evidence.

Interviewer: So, when people say there is no association between Al-Qaeda and Saddam Hussein, they're wrong?

Perle: They're flatly wrong.

The filmmakers suggest that policies in the post-9/11 era were being shaped by an idea first developed by the Green Movement in the 1980s. Called the "precautionary principle," it held that if one believed the world was being threatened by, say, global warming, and there was little scientific evidence at the time to support it, governments still had an obligation to act intuitively on these fears to save the world before it was too late. As Bill Durodie, director of the International Center for Security Analysis at Kings College, explains using a triple negative: "The precautionary principle says that not having the evidence that something might be a problem is not a reason for not taking action as if it were a problem. It requires imagining what the worst might be and applying that imagination upon the worst evidence that currently exists."

This theory bears a strong resemblance to *The One Percent Doctrine*, laid out by author Ron Suskind as Dick Cheney's belief that if there exists just a 1 percent chance of something happening it should be treated as though it were certain. The narrator of *The Power of Nightmares* concludes, "But the fear will not last, and just as the dreams that politicians once promised turned out to be illusions, so too will the nightmares, and then our politicians will have to face the fact that they have no visions, either good or bad, to offer us any longer." And on that cheery note, the credits roll over the song "Raindrops Keep Falling on My Head." The *New York Times* called the film, "awfully tendentious," and described its understanding of geopolitics as "curiously thin."

Perle also appears in *Why We Fight*, a film by Eugene Jarecki that won the Grand Jury prize at the Sundance Festival in 2005. The fulcrum of the film is President Eisenhower's farewell address in which, as most every high schooler knows (or used to) he warns against the pervasive influence of the military-industrial complex. The thrust here is Chomskian: We fight because it's good for business. It's good for Lockheed Martin, good for Haliburton, good for Boeing, good for everyone. After George W. Bush is shown declaring his doctrine of preemption, Perle appears and wonders what all the controversy is about: "If you saw a missile about to be launched and you could kick it over before it could be launched, you'd do it, of course. If you saw someone about to shoot at you and you thought you could shoot first, you'd do it. It's common sense. I don't know anybody who wouldn't agree with that. So what's the big fuss about preemption?"

In the section dealing with the influence of Lockheed Martin, McDonnell Douglas, Boeing, and the other mega contractors, Perle defends the no-bid contracts given to Haliburton for the Iraq War: "Someone has to do this work. And the Haliburton thing is just an outrageous effort to associate the vice president with the activities of a company with which he has no connection. No connection at all....If I am sure of anything, I am sure of this: Vice President Cheney had nothing to do with the awarding of any contract to Haliburton. He wouldn't pick up the phone; he wouldn't whisper in someone's ear. I know him. He just wouldn't do it." Of course, he probably wouldn't have had to, but that would be a question for the phalanx of government investigators who began crawling all over the financing of the war once the bills began coming in.

After a long and brutally effective sequence of how technological arrogance made the United States believe that it could strike the evildoers while sparing women, children, and other noncombatants, Perle appears for the last time and states: "The world has changed. We're not going back to where we were. One of the sillier ideas, and you hear it all the time, is that American policy has been hijacked by a handful of people and as soon as they're out of there we can go back to the way it was. And they're wrong about that. Because we are not the same people we were before."

That last sentence was the assumption that drove everything Perle and his compatriots had envisioned about America's role in the twenty-first century. If we were not the same people we were before, just who had we since become? Were we less tolerant, less willing to accept a role as a mere player, rather than leader of the band? Were we more willing to compromise our values and limit our way of life to feel more safe and secure? Were we prepared to not only accept but embrace the role of global sovereign and all that it entailed? Did the attacks on the World Trade Center and the Pentagon alter our DNA to make us forget our anticolonial roots and our knockabout individualism?

The film ends with two sound bites, the first from Bush's 2002 State of the Union address: "For too long our culture has said, 'If it feels good, do it.' Now, America is embracing a new ethic and a new creed: 'Let's roll.'"

The second comes from someone who appears to be an Iraqi farmer: "America will lose because its behavior is not the behavior of a great nation."

Nassir Sabah was a twenty-four-year-old worker in a pastry factory in Samarra about sixty-five miles north of Baghdad. When the bomb blew the top off the gilded dome of the Askariya shrine on February 22, 2006, Nassir left his job to join his friends in the black-clad Shiite militia, rallying with their Kalashnikov rifles and grenade launchers outside the home of the forbidding cleric Muqtada al-Sadr, Iraq's own Prince of Darkness. "This is a day we will never forget," Nassir said. Although no one was killed, the bombing of one of the Shiites' holiest places was their 9/11, and retribution was swift. More than twenty Sunni mosques were bombed, strafed, or torched. In Basra, gunmen in police uniforms broke into a jail, seized twelve Sunni men, and executed them. If there was a tipping point in post-Saddam Iraq, this might have been it, although reprisal killings were already rising beforehand. Had all of those experienced and well-educated strategic planners missed the tribalism lurking just below the surface? Absent a Milosevic to make Noel Malcolm's case that conflicts of this sort were the makings of a few bad men, was Robert Kaplan's nightmare vision of collapsing nation-states and warring tribes now validated?

Writing in the op-ed pages of the *New York Times*, reporter Hussain Abdul-Hussain described a conversation he had with a former schoolmate in Iraq named Ayad who told him he had no problem with the establishment of Iranian-style Shiite government in Iraq, and that it would set a good example for Shiites of Lebanon who number about a third of the population, and in Bahrain, where they are the majority. "But we are Iraqis," Hussain protested, making the sharp distinction between Arab Shiites and the Persian Shiites of Iran. "We are Arabs. We have our cultural differences with the Persians. We don't even speak the same language!"

Doesn't matter, said Ayad. "When we fought the Persians during the 1980s, we were wrong. We're Shiites before being Iraqis. Sunnis invented national identity to rule us." And then there was an extraordinary column by conservative David Brooks titled "Same Old Demons." The column quotes extensively from an essay written in 1970 by an Iraqi Jew named Elie Kedourie, author of such books as *Democracy and Arab Political Culture*, who recounts the history of the Iraq the British tried to establish more than eighty years ago. It is a place of unspeakable barbarism, mayhem, and murder, where tribal wars destroy families and the rule of law is subservient to the rule of warrior clans, where a former prime minister is grabbed on the street by a mob and killed, and his body reduced to pulp by cars running over it. Kedourie quotes a British official's report that "the political ambitions of the Shia religious headquarters have always lain in the direction of theocratic domination. They have no motive for refraining from sacrificing the interests of Iraq to those which they conceive to be their own." That report was written in 1923. Kedourie wrote, "The collapse of the old order had awakened vast cupidities and renewed venomous hatreds."

Kedourie concluded in 1970 that Iraq faced only two alternatives: "Either the country will be plunged into chaos or its population should become universally the clients and dependents of an omnipotent but capricious and unstable government." Again, Kedourie was writing this nine years before Saddam Hussein seized power. Why were these realities obvious to everyone except those in the Bush administration and those who were influencing its policies?

In the coffee shop of Washington's Mayflower hotel, I asked David Wurmser, Cheney's Middle East advisor, if he had read the Brooks column. He hadn't. But listening to my summary, he dismissed the notion that the elimination of a central power, even a malevolent one, might create a conflagration among ethnic groups whose hatreds had been suppressed along with their freedoms. "It was never for sure that the Iraqi people would come together. But that's okay. Once you start creating competing nodes of power, you're beginning to have the foundation of a civil society. And I think tribalism is a little overdone, by the way. You have a sectarian divide in Iraq which is very real. On some level, we're accused of being pro-Shiite. That's probably true. I'll own up to that. In terms of the classic blood-feud tribalism, though, the Shia elites have departed from that. A lot of them couldn't tell you where they came from with their tribes. But I thought tribalism would be useful in the long run if harnessed, if these various nodes of power were harnessed."

But the leap from forcibly removing a dictator to harnessing nodes of power in a volatile society with a long history of sectarian violence was never part of the stated U.S. goals. This was not mission creep; this was, from any rational point of view, insanity. In the end, someone had to get the people to stop killing one another long enough to ensure that the electricity and the water stayed on. Bruce Jackson shook his head at the thought. "How did we get to guaranteeing we could build democracy and all sorts of other things like infrastructure and security and urban renewal and art museums and the oil industry? Any strategic planner would have said, 'Where does it say we can do all these things?' Markets build those things. Governments don't. Was it utopianism? Absolutely. Reagan never did this. We would go in and drop one bomb or another, and then we were out. If we didn't like the situation in Mogadishu or Beirut, we got out. Reagan understood intuitively that democracies can fight where they want to fight and don't have to fight where the other guy wants to."

But the axiom "When you're in a hole, stop digging" was lost on men such as Wurmser and on Perle as well, as evidenced by his arranging a meeting in his living room between Ahmed Chalabi and Farid Ghadry, a Syrian exile who had left his country when he was ten and who now headed up something called the Syrian Reform Party. Perle was telling anyone who would listen that Bashar Assad "has never been weaker, and we should take advantage of that." When asked whether he was trying to achieve with Ghadry in Syria what he had failed to achieve with Chalabi in Iraq, Perle told me, "Farid is a decent person who's trying to rid his country of this awful dictatorship. He hasn't succeeded in getting much support. The administration seems to be moving toward working with the kind of people the CIA always prefers to work with: people who are not decent guys. They don't like decent guys. They will refer to decent guys as boy scouts and treat them with derision. In the

CIA's view of the world, the only people who can get things done are as brutal as the ones you're trying to replace."

Why, I wondered, did Ghadry join AIPAC, making him perhaps the only Arab in the Jewish lobby and a poster boy for Zionist conspiracy theorists? "I don't think that's good for his image either," Perle said. "But he's his own man. I don't always understand what he's doing and why he's doing it."

On another front, overthrowing Iran, Perle had befriended a dashing young dissident named Amir Abbas Fakhravar, who claimed to have escaped from Iran's notorious Evin prison and was being whisked around official Washington by American Enterprise Institute types promoting him as an Iranian Chalabi. "I met him on the telephone originally through an Iranian American living in Los Angeles," Perle told me. "He doesn't speak English and I didn't want to keep him on the phone for very long because the last thing I want to do is be on the phone with someone when the police come and arrest him." Fakhravar's story is Hollywood material. In and out of prison as a dissident in Iran since he was seventeen, he telephoned the promonarchy, antiregime radio stations broadcast by satellite from Los Angeles. The station put him in touch with Perle, who somehow managed to bring him to America, where he was feted by the AEI at a lunch attended by officials from the Defense and State departments. In an interview with the neocon-friendly *New York Sun*, Fakhravar said of Perle, "In my eyes I saw the Prince of Light. I could see in his eyes he is worried for our people as well as the American people and this is very important and this is very special."

But other dissidents, and journalists who have checked into Fakhravar's background, tell a different story, one of a young man who was not jailed for political acts, who was allowed to use a cell phone while in jail because he acted as a snitch for the police; who did not escape from Evin prison but went AWOL during a temporary prison furlough; who did not make a dramatic getaway from Iran despite a shoot-on-sight order but took a regular flight from Tehran to Dubai where Perle was waiting for him; and who realized he could become a celebrity with the help of gullible neocons. Naturally, Fakhravar and his supporters dismiss these charges as political smears spread by jealous dissidents on the Left and proregime operatives on the Right.

In any case, as with Chalabi, Perle had once again lent his name to a dissident of questionable background, not exactly a Mandela, Sakharov, or Sharansky. "I think the best way to bring about regime change is to help decent people who for the right reasons want to bring down a regime and who are powerless without outside help," Perle said. "For a very long time I've supported people like that almost always without results. But I have a soft spot for political prisoners."

Apparently so do Wurmser and Liz Cheney, the vice president's daughter and top dog on the State Department's Iran-Syria desk. Cheney filed the required report disclosing she had received a Persian carpet valued at $4,000 from the woman who put Fakhravar in touch with Perle, Los Angeles–based Iranian Manda Shahbazi. Shahbazi is the daughter of Yaddolah Shahbazi, who served as an advisor to the Iranian prime minister during the end of the shah's reign and who put together Iranian and Israeli investors in a shipping company that employed Manucher Ghorbanifar.

In 2006, Wurmser and Liz Cheney held numerous meetings with Syrian dissidents including Farid Ghadry to talk up a possible overthrow in Damascus. But how did Cheney and Wurmser know they were not being conned? "He's not asking for money and we're not advocating money for him," Wurmser said of Ghadry. "As for him getting power, yeah, I'm sure he has his agenda also. I'm sure Ahmed Chalabi thought in his mind, 'You know, I could be prime minister.' But that said, it didn't matter. This is where you go back to the Soviet Union because it's the same question that we always work with, from Lech Walesa to Václav Havel. The issue was, Did they have an understanding of the malady and danger posed by the totalitarian regime in their country?" Of course, any schoolkid in Damascus had that understanding. But were Farid Ghadry and Fakhravar and Chalabi of the same moral stuff as Walesa and Havel? If you invoke the names of the sainted, shouldn't your charges live up to the comparison? Or was the bar being lowered for the sake of expediency?

When Francis Fukuyama bailed on the neocons, few outside of the cozy world of *Foreign Affairs* subscribers understood the significance. Fukuyama was perhaps the brightest light, the most intellectually nimble of the new-wave conservatives. He had made his mark with his 1992 book *The End of History and the Last Man*, which argued that the collapse of the Soviet Union signaled an end to mankind's ideological evolution and "the universalization of Western liberal democracy as the final form of human government." But in surveying the world fourteen years later in *America at the Crossroads*, Fukuyama saw not the end of history but the end of a failed policy that was bankrupting the country economically, politically, and morally. In the chapter "After Neoconservatism," Fukuyama writes, "There are clear benefits to the Iraqi people from the removal of Saddam Hussein's dictatorship, and perhaps some positive spillover effects in Lebanon and Syria. But it is very hard to see how these developments in themselves justify the blood and treasure that the United States has spent on the project to date. The so-called Bush doctrine that set the framework for the administration's first term is in shambles....Successful pre-emption depends on the ability to predict the future accurately and on good intelligence, which was not forthcoming, while America's perceived unilateralism has isolated it as never before."

Fukuyama then points out that at least two of the founding principles of the neoconservatives were in conflict: an agnostic view of social engineering to solve societal problems, lest such attempts produce unintended consequences, and the use of American power as a moral agent to spread democracy. This dilemma was never resolved with the sort of rigorous debate Richard Perle always welcomed. Nor was a dialogue established with our allies about the justification for preemptive action, a concept to which the United States would certainly have objected—and loudly—had it been asserted by the French, the Germans, or even the Brits. Our argument, never stated as such, was that our moral superiority was sufficient to sanction such actions, and that our intentions were not colonial or even economic but humanitarian. This, Fukuyama judged in elegant prose, would not fly and in fact had crashed and burned.

Richard Perle was not convinced. Appearing in London on the BBC Radio program *Today*, hosted by heavyweight commentator John Humphries, Perle was asked whether he conceded the point made by Zbigniew Brzezinski and others, that a U.S. attack on Iran would make America an outlaw state and so damage international relations that it would take twenty to thirty years to repair. "No American president who believes that there is a last opportunity to prevent Iran from becoming a nuclear weapons state is going to be deterred by derision. He will do what he believes to be in the best interests of the protection of those who might come under attack from an Iranian nuclear weapon including the United States."

Elsewhere in the world, the current seemed to be flowing away from America. Hugo Chávez, aka Fidel with oil, had been reelected in Venezuela by a wide margin and was thumbing his nose at Washington while nationalizing energy companies. Daniel Ortega, the bête noire of many in the Reagan administration, was alive and grinning as President-Once-Again of Nicaragua, a reminder of America's utter policy failures in Latin America. In Africa, the United States had cast its lot with the repressive Ethiopian regime as the best of the worst choices to combat the warlords in Somalia. In Darfur and Chad, the killing machine ground on with only limp protest from the United States and what was left of its allies. In Thailand, an uprising by the Muslim minority in response to alleged murders by the police threatened to spill over into Malaysia and destabilize the region. In Afghanistan, which Americans had mostly forgotten about in 2006, reports of a resurgent Taliban and a weakening Karzai government called into question the American military's shift out of the country as soon as it had. And, in yet another example of unintended consequences, free elections had placed Hamas in power in the West Bank and given Hezbollah a substantial foothold in Lebanon, presaging an inept campaign by Israel's Ohlmert government to drive Syrian- and Iranian-backed forces out of southern Lebanon.

As the Iraq death toll climbed and the president's approval rating plummeted, Ahmed Chalabi weighed in on the absence of WMD he had insisted were there. "We are heroes in error," he declared. "As far as we're concerned we've been entirely successful. The tyrant Saddam is gone and the Americans are in Baghdad. What we said before is not important." Chalabi turned out to be so popular in Iraq that his INC party failed to win even a single seat in the parliamentary election. A half dozen former U.S. generals called for the resignation of Donald Rumsfeld and a new strategy for the troops. They would get their wish on Rumsfeld just two days after the November 2006 midterm elections; no new strategy for the troops was in the offing, just a "surge," a troop increase of more than twenty thousand, which peaked in the summer of 2007. It did not stem the violence. The stench from the disaster in New Orleans was still in the air far beyond the bayou, the appalling corruption and ineptitude of the relief process mirroring the appalling corruption and ineptitude of the Iraq relief process, as was the odor from the Jack Abramoff lobbying scandal that had ensnared several top Republicans. Abu Ghraib, torture at Guantánamo, a possible My Lai at Haditha; there were scandals aplenty,

It was becoming painfully clear that had this administration been in power in 1861, America would now be whistling "Dixie." Nor was the near future rosy for the neoconservatives, as the constant clatter of RIP articles, talk shows, blogs, and op-ed columns would attest. But it was an article that appeared in *Vanity Fair* just days before the midterm election that helped to seal the administration's fate. Cleverly titled "Neo Culpa," the feature consisted of interviews by writer David Rose with some of the key players in the selling of the Iraq War, including, most prominently, Richard Perle. Perle had agreed to the interview with the stipulation that his remarks would be embargoed until after the election, a condition *Vanity Fair* had agreed to. But, after reading the remarks of the various subjects, the magazine's editors decided it was of such overriding interest that it must appear before the election, thus violating the agreement. The article, scheduled for the January issue, was posted on the magazine's Web site on November 3, just four days before the voters went to the polls. For Perle, it was another episode in his long-running love-hate relationship with the press. As a master leaker, he knew how to charm, cajole, and manipulate the press to his advantage, a fact with which I had been keenly aware from the start of my work on this book. But he also knew the press could be fickle and disingenuous when it suited its needs.

In any event, there he was, under the "Neo Culpa" headline in an extremely flattering photo by Nigel Parry, a slight smile playing on his lips as he holds his chin in his hand. Rose writes that Perle looks into his eyes, "speaking slowly and with obvious deliberation...he is unrecognizable as the confident hawk I once knew."

"The levels of brutality that we've seen are truly horrifying, and I have to say I underestimated the depravity," Perle said in the article. "The decisions did not get made that should have been. They didn't get made in a timely fashion....At the end of the day, you have to hold the President responsible....I don't think he realized the extent of the opposition within his own administration, and the disloyalty." Disloyalty? By whom? Colin Powell and George Tenet did everything they had been asked to do, even actions with which they had disagreed, before being shown the door. Rumsfeld would be dumped in a few days, after having receiving Bush's total support. Cheney? No. That would leave Condi Rice among the major players, and she had already heard it from Perle with both barrels in a *Washington Post* op-ed column titled, "Why Did Bush Blink on Iran? (Ask Condi)". Asked if he would again support an armed invasion of Iraq, Perle replied, "I think if I had been Delphic, and had seen where we are today, and people had said, 'Should we go into Iraq?', I think now I probably would have said, 'No, let's consider other strategies for dealing with [the threat].'"

Ken Adelman, whose use of the word "cakewalk" in the run-up to the invasion was widely criticized (he says he was referring only to the act of taking Baghdad, not to bringing democracy to Iraq), all but pronounced neoconservatism dead in *Vanity Fair* with no hope of a phoenixlike revival for at least a generation. "It's not going to sell," Adelman told Rose. Asked what he would do with a mulligan, he said he would write an article declaring that although Bush's arguments for invading were right, they were also worthless because his administration could not execute the plan. "You just have to put [those arguments] in the drawer marked CAN'T DO. And that's very different from LET'S GO."

Only Jim Woolsey chose the sunnier side of the street, insisting that the war's outcome was still not known, but agreeing that the administration had made many of the same mistakes the United States had made in Vietnam. As soon as the article was posted, Perle and others quoted issued a rebuttal on the *National Review* Web site, pointing out that an agreement had been broken and claiming that some quotes had been taken out of context, a charge the magazine denied. All signed the protest except Ken Adelman, who e-mailed Rose, "I totally agree with you. Why keep issue #1 behind closed doors until the American people have a chance to vote? That's why I am the only one not giving a rebuttal despite being asked and pressured to do so, since I think it's just fine to get word out when it could make a difference to people."

Of course, there is no way to measure what effect the piece had on the electorate, but the Democrats hardly needed any help, retaking both houses of Congress and gaining subpoena power to hold hearings the Republicans had stonewalled on everything from Iraq to Katrina to the Abramoff scandal to the shameful lies told about the death of army Corporal Pat Tillman and the hyped rescue of Private Jessica Lynch. But ascertaining the truth at this point would involve some heavy lifting. The Pentagon had outsourced its propaganda campaign on the war to a company called the Lincoln Group, which spent $130 million of U.S. taxpayers' money planting stories in the foreign press. Add to that the 108 stories the INC bragged it had planted in the American and British press, and the tens of millions spent by the Rendon Group, and it's no wonder the optimism about Iraq had lingered as long as it had. Some thirty-five years before, another RAND graduate, Daniel Ellsberg, the man who leaked the Pentagon Papers, remarked that it was a sign of the Pentagon's respect for the American people that it knew they had to be lied to so the Vietnam War could continue.

As 2006 came to a close, Saddam Hussein was hanged in Baghdad. The Iraqis even managed to bungle the execution, as cell phone video recorded guards taunting the doomed dictator and chanting the name of

Muqtada al-Sadr. And as the wars in Iraq and Afghanistan lumbered forward, the totals for both stood at 2,961 American dead, 22,565 wounded. Estimates of Iraqi deaths ranged from 47,016 to 793,663. No one really knew for sure.

XII.
FAR AND AWAY

THE VILLAGE IS what the French would call "typique" of the beloved region in the south, a glorious still life pulsing with rich earth tones of clay, rust, olive, and chartreuse, where plant life and stone meld in intelligent design. The fruit from rows of gnarly saplings is just arriving, along with the first brigade of French tourists sporting their standard-issue backpacks, baggy shorts, and earbuds, looking just like clueless tourists from anywhere else. On this particular spring day, the second round of elections for a new French president was taking place, a race featuring a conservative son of an immigrant, Nicolas Sarkozy, versus the mandatory socialist required in all European elections, in this one Madame Ségolène Royal. The French do not worry about the "middle" holding, since there is no middle in France. Perhaps this is why the French are described as being "in decline" in the Western press. After twelve years of Jacques Chirac socialism, the French face a national debt proportionally as large as that of the United States, an economy barely moving forward while Britain and China have jumped ahead, unemployment topping 20 percent among French youth, who led three weeks of riots in 2005, and a third party candidate, Jean-Marie Le Pen, who intended to solve France's immigration problem as Pat Buchanan would solve America's: by building a wall around the country. Sources of French pride have been few and far between in the recent past, namely Chirac's opposition to the U.S. invasion of Iraq and the unveiling of a high-speed train that broke the world record at 367 miles per hour. The French hope to sell it to the Chinese.

Back in the United States, the early presidential field features the first woman with a real chance to win, the first black with a real chance to win, the first Italian American with a real chance to win, the first

Hispanic American with an outside chance to win, and the first Mormon, period. There is a "middle" somewhere among these candidates, even though, as Mort Sahl used to say, "The middle is like putting twin beds together and trying to sleep in the crack." In this case the crack is Iraq.

In an echo of the late sixties, a candidate's stand on the war defined his or her candidacy and framed the national debate. The Iraq War had already claimed Tony Blair's legacy. As the sun set on his time at 10 Downing Street, Londoners were treated to a West End play with the unwieldy title *Called to Account: The Indictment of Anthony Charles Lynton Blair for the Crime of Aggression Against Iraq—a Hearing*, in which one of the witnesses called to testify is that infamous American hawk, Richard Perle.

"It actually wasn't bad," Perle told me. "The actor used my quotes just as I had said them in my interview. Of course, the one thing they highlighted is when I was asked if I thought the evidence we had was sufficient to go to war over, and I said, 'It was bad…but sufficient.'" We were talking over dinner on the patio of his perfect Provençal home to which he and Leslie had come, sans their dog Reagan, to steal a vacation week in late April after a stop in London for a business meeting and to take in the play. The reviews were generally positive, with one critic gushing that his biggest thrill of the evening was seeing the real Richard Perle shaking hands after the show with the actor who played him.

Maison Perle is the sort of vacation home one sees in tony magazines. The extended and remodeled main house is surrounded by an acre and half of meticulously managed gardens, which ring the swimming pool. Festive lights are strung through the trees, and the soothing quiet mingles with the sounds of chirping birds and the comforting flow of water through the mouth of a gargoyle on a wall fountain. The kitchen, like the one in his Maryland home, is built for the serious chef. When the Perles first bought a share in the house, with ownership divided among five individuals who put up $50,000 a piece, the kitchen was the size of a walk-in closet—unworkable for major-league foodies. Obtaining the required permits to alter the house is as difficult in

France as it is in most places in the United States. But, as usual, Perle had a plan. After buying out the other partners, he invited the village's mayor over for dinner and staged an eight-course feast. The Perles deliberately stacked the dirty dishes as high as they possibly could in the tiny kitchen and then invited the mayor to take a look at their plight. The permits arrived shortly thereafter.

Above the main house is Perle's study, a cozy, inviting rectangular room with the feel of an Aspen ski lodge. Large windows on one side offer an impressive view of the valley beyond the gardens. A projector for watching big-screen DVDs sits on a table surrounded by comfortable chairs and a long sofa. At the front of the room is a bank of computers and sundry electronic equipment for keeping in touch with the rest of the world. It was in this room that Perle wrote *An End to Evil*, the post 9/11 blueprint for the war on terror he coauthored with former Bush speechwriter David Frum, the man who will forever be known as the author of the "axis of evil" line in Bush's 2002 State of the Union address. The irony, of course, is that it was from this idyllic setting in the South of France that Perle blasted away at the French in his book, recommending that (1) all "important" NATO business be conducted by NATO's military council, on which France does not sit; (2) the European Union resist and oppose the protectionist agricultural policies championed by the French and decline to purchase "expensive and ineffective weapons whose only merit is they are made in France;" (3) European governments should be forced to choose between Paris and Washington, rejecting French arguments that beneficial relations with both can exist simultaneously; and (4) both NATO and the European Union (EU) be enlarged because "the bigger the EU grows, the less amenable it will become to French aspirations to boss other states." It is no wonder Perle's resignation from the Defense Policy Board was celebrated as a victory for France in the French press.

As if on cue, the serenity of the lazy afternoon is shattered by the teeth-rattling screech of a Mach 2 jet fighter here and gone in a thunderous flash. "The French air force," Perle muttered as he sliced a zucchini. "Now we can all feel safe." We had joked the night before about how Americans must feel so much safer now that their toothpaste tubes are being confiscated at airport security checks, as mine had been before my flight to France.

"Why are you taking that?" I asked the security inspector.

"It's too big."

"I have large teeth."

A woman behind me in line assured me, "It's for our own good."

Of course, post-9/11 America was no laughing matter. The FBI had been caught using what were supposed to be antiterrorist laws to rummage through the telephone records of millions of Americans. The administration had gone after the *New York Times* for its follow-up reports on searches of individual bank accounts and credit card records despite the fact that the president had actually announced the effort in a Rose Garden speech. There were the prisoners held for years at Guantánamo without being charged, and others who had been spirited away to black sites in countries that practiced torture. Under a Republican Congress, the power of the executive branch had been expanded beyond what even some Republicans thought prudent. Now the newly emboldened Democrats, fueled by the voters' frustration over the war, were beginning to roll back at least some of the power the White House had either assumed or been granted since the attacks by an enabling Congress.

Perle's mentor and spiritual father, Scoop Jackson, had been a hawk all right, but he was also a libertarian who abhorred unchecked power, particularly power employed by the executive against its own citizens. What would Scoop have made of the Patriot Act and the suspension of habeas corpus for suspected terrorists, including Americans?

"I don't know," Perle replied. "He certainly would have been unhappy about the abuses that have come to light. But I don't think the Patriot Act went beyond what is reasonable. If the government violates that, you have to come down like a ton of bricks. If you have a statute that allows wiretaps in order to catch terrorists, and in the course of that you find out someone's running an illegal gambling operation, my view is 'tough luck.' You cannot use that information to go after him for illegal gambling. You weren't authorized to collect information for that purpose. But is it reasonable to tap the Algerian embassy's phone and listen to every conversation? Yes. The Saudis' phones? Yes. And there are Saudi organizations throughout the U.S. and I would tap those too."

As the dinner table was being set, I asked him how he read the 2008 presidential race. He answered with a question: "What do you think of Fred Thompson?"

"I thought he was really good in *The Hunt for Red October*," I replied, and that was the end of it. But it seemed to me that Perle had indicated his preference.

While Perle was in France, American TV audiences were tuning into *60 Minutes* to hear George Tenet's explanation of how the CIA was simultaneously responsible and not responsible for the prewar intelligence, a carnival side-show act akin to walking barefoot across hot coals while juggling bowling balls. It was Tenet's first stop in an orgy of overexposure to promote his book *At the Center of the Storm: My Years at the CIA*, which begins on the day after 9/11 when Tenet says he ran into Richard Perle coming out of the White House. Tenet wrote that Perle placed blame squarely on the Iraqis and urged an attack. Correspondent Scott Pelley mentioned this opening passage but did not question it, choosing instead to spend the next twenty minutes or so jabbing as Tenet bobbed and weaved around the truth. I e-mailed my former boss, Jeff Fager of *60 Minutes*, and said, "Nice piece...well done. But Perle wasn't in Washington the day after 9/11. He was in France. Maybe someone might have mentioned that." The next day lots of people, including Perle, did. Tenet insisted that while he might have gotten the date wrong, the conversation had indeed taken place. Tenet-bashers used this to question the veracity of everything else in the book, as though discrediting an already discredited player would somehow matter in the grand scheme of things.

Of course, Perle had never met a DCI that he liked, and when asked who he would appoint in a fantasy world, he told me, "I think it should be a Newt Gingrich, someone who is very, very smart, and Newt is brilliant, with a lot of insight and historical depth and knowledge of politics because there's a lot of politics in this, and with personal courage, and I think Newt has that." One could only assume Perle was not referring to the same Newt Gingrich who discussed divorce with his bedridden wife while she was hospitalized with cancer, and who admitted having an extramarital affair while presiding over the House effort to impeach Bill Clinton in the Lewinsky affair. "It takes someone like Gingrich. I actually thought Rumsfeld would have been a good choice. But it's going to take someone eight years to [reform the agency] and it'll take a strong president who knows what needs to be done."

So, one could add George Tenet to the scrap heap of ruined careers and reputations left in the wake of the war. Valerie Plame's career as a CIA agent was ruined when the administration leaked her identity to discredit her ambassador husband for writing an op-ed column questioning the so-called Niger-Saddam connection. Now she was suing. Scooter Libby's career was ruined when he was convicted of lying about the leak. The president commuted Libby's two-and-half-year sentence, which Bush claimed was too severe. That followed a deluge of letters to the judge pleading for leniency for Libby from Washington's political elite, including Richard Perle. Judith Miller's career lay in ruins after her editors at the *New York Times* concluded she had become a virtual mouthpiece for the administration's WMD claims, many of which proved to be false, and had pushed her editors to jump on the Valerie Plame story that Scooter Libby had touted to her. She and the *Times* parted ways in November of 2005.

Larry Franklin, with his wheelchair-bound wife and five kids, was ruined when he pleaded guilty to trying to pass classified war information to AIPAC, and now he was looking at twelve years in prison. Doug Feith was run out of government on a rail, the main villain of a Defense Department inspector general's report that concluded that Feith's Office of Special Plans was used to bypass the normal interagency process and embellish questionable intelligence on an Al-Qaeda–Saddam connection. While it concluded that no laws were broken, the report described the Feith operations as "inappropriate." Watching his protégé being grilled and bullied on C-SPAN by Senate Armed Services Committee chairman Carl Levin, Perle fumed, "It's an exercise in power that reminds me of McCarthy." Feith escaped to Georgetown University and is currently writing his own book. When George Tenet discovered that his new office at Georgetown was in close proximity to Feith's, he asked to be moved.

Paul Wolfowitz was ruined when, after retreating from the Pentagon to the World Bank, he was ousted in what some believed was a scandal involving alleged preferential treatment for his girlfriend, an economist at the bank. Perle shook his head in disgust. "The willingness of people to destroy careers…and over what? Because they didn't like what they think he did when he was deputy secretary. He did not deserve the treatment he got." Perle revealed that he had not spoken to his old friend since Wolfowitz joined the bank, suspecting that Wolfowitz wanted to turn a page in his life and leave the past, as well as his old friends, behind.

The president chose Wolfowitz's intellectual compadre, former U.S. trade representative Robert Zoellick, to head the bank, which in Bruce Jackson's mind was just as well, since the president never cared much for having intellectuals around. "It's a Texan thing." Jackson shrugged. "I mean Zoellick can't answer a question in under twenty-five minutes. When he was on my board I would say, 'Bob, just shut up already.' Condi and Hadley are much more Bush's style." Wolfowitz finally emerged from seclusion long enough to tell Charlie Rose that he, like Perle, "was not the architect for anything," leading many to wonder if the war had actually produced itself, *sui generis*.

Then there was another onetime Perle friend, Colin Powell, of whom little had been heard since his unceremonious departure from the State Department. At the mention of his name, Perle nodded toward the still covered swimming pool in his Provençal garden and said, "Colin Powell used to swim in that pool. He is a very smart man, very capable. But I don't know why he feels he must go around the country apologizing for that speech. He used the intelligence he was given, just like everybody else."

So much wreckage, so much rubble and debris from the decision to go to war. Quite apart from the atomization of an entire country, from the unspeakable grief of families and loved ones and the anger and bitterness of those who tried to halt or reverse fateful decisions, there remained all of those broken people who had come to Washington in hopes of making the world better.

"Look," Perle said, "it's a tough town, no doubt about it. And a lot of people who go there…honest, capable people…they don't anticipate this. They've never had to deal with anything quite like it. It's the personal attacks. And a number of people have said to me, 'I don't see how we're going to get people to come into government.'"

But Richard Perle, now a grizzled veteran of the Beltway battles, would not retreat for good to academia or the anonymity of the think tank, or even to the serenity of Provence. He had to be out there, "in the arena," as Richard Nixon was so fond of calling it, where he could confront, confound, and confuse the naysayers and the Roundheads and the Philistines. Back in the United States, a tavern-restaurant hard by the Harvard Yard in Boston was the venue for an informal chat with members of the Harvard Business School's Century Club, a kind of frat for tomorrow's tycoons. This was the front end of a doubleheader for Perle, a few remarks followed by some Q and A with the Century clubbers, and then a screening of the controversial PBS film *The Case for War*, starring Perle and produced by his friend Lapping, at a multiplex near Emerson College on Boylston Street. It was a somewhat surreal scene at the Grafton Street Pub, where the dining area of the restaurant had been cleared for Perle and the students but the bar was open and packed with the Red Sox Nation as the beloved Beantowners played their home opener on the big-screen TVs.

As Perle munched on mini-quiche, for him a gastronomic grotesquery, and mingled with the fresh-faced entrepreneurs, one could hear a medley of Perle's greatest hits overlapping with the play-by-play: "That's because negotiators are too anxious to get an agreement and don't think about the long term"…"First and third, nobody out"…"It was a risk-management decision, and just because we didn't find WMD doesn't mean going to war was foolish or dishonest"…"And that liner hooks foul, right in front of the Pesky pole"…"If it had been up to me,

I would have turned it over to Chalabi and the INC." Finally, Perle departs for the theater with these words for the students: "If you can get a job working for a good senator or congressman, take it."

The audience for the film screening and panel discussion to follow would not be nearly as friendly as the one at the Grafton Street Pub. Here, Perle would have to deal not only with students and faculty members of the all–liberal arts Emerson, but also with invited panel members, including Abdul al-Bari Atwan, editor of the independent newspaper *Al-Quds al-Arabi*, a kind of one-man truth squad often paired with Perle by PBS to drum up publicity for *A Case for War*, as well as the other seven films in the ambitious America at a Crossroads series. During the audience question period, Perle was confronted by a young man who declared, "I think you should be tried by the International Court of Justice as a war criminal." This sort of business Perle had heard many times before, and he simply chose to ignore it. And he had heard it all before from Atwan too: "You broke it, and now you can't fix it!" Perle just sat there like Jabba the Hut and let the angry Arab flail away. He looked tired and bored.

As for the film itself, which would air nationally in a few days, it delivered exactly what it said it would deliver: Richard Perle traveling the world and making the case for the Iraq War. There was no pretense at balance. This was never intended to be a documentary in the traditional sense, and the hue and cry over its airing made the liberals appear childish and petty. How could one hour in a series of eleven hours of independently-produced films constitute a "sellout" by PBS, as many bloggers whined? Yes, Ken Tomlinson's ham-fisted, Boltonesque, bull-in-the-china-shop tactics were reprehensible, and he paid the price, resigning as CPB chairman in November 2005 after a CPB inspector's report accused him of misusing taxpayers' funds for political purposes and running his horse business out of his government office. Throw another career on the fire. But letting Perle have his say and make his case did not threaten the republic; some viewers would agree, some would disagree, and most would just watch something else.

Brian Lapping described his effort this way: "It's a competently made film. It's quite lively and quite funny. Richard goes to quite a few interesting places and encounters some rows. He talks to people on the other side and is quite often gently persuasive with them, even though some of them are quite rude to him." Indeed, as Perle wanders into a crowd of antiwar protestors in what is an awkwardly contrived scene, he encounters one of the protest's organizers, whose husband served in Iraq. Her anger is assuaged somewhat by Perle's calm and respectful recitation of the war's rationale: the elimination of an evil man who had evil intentions regarding the United States and the rest of the free world. Telling the woman "I did not hear statements that Iraq was responsible for 9/11" no doubt enraged many viewers, but the woman let it pass unchallenged. Amir Abbas Fakhravar, Perle's leader-in-waiting for Iran, appears, looking like the very young shah, and comparing Khomeini and Ahmadinejad to Hitler. Of course, no mention is made of Fakhravar's controversial past.

Perhaps the most telling moment in the film comes in another awkwardly contrived scene in which Perle pays a call on Pat Buchanan, isolationist to the stars, who believes that Perle and the neocons have hijacked the Republican Party. As he sits down across from Buchanan, Perle remarks with a hint of jest, "There's got to be *some* advantage to being a superpower," to which Buchanan responds, "This sounds like a neocommenter. That was the Soviet Union's idea…that what is ours is ours and is not negotiable, and we will reimpose our ideology if it's overthrown and we have a right to change your government. And to me, that is not a traditional American foreign policy." Perle then points out that more than half of the population of Iran is under twenty-five, and that most among that group embrace American culture. Why not help them to overthrow their repressive regime? Buchanan replies, "This reminds me of what we allegedly did in Hungary. We said, 'Rise up, folks; this is a dreadful regime you've got.' And the people rose up and the Americans weren't there and they were cut to pieces. And the same thing happened in Tiananmen Square. And so you have to tell these folks the truth, which is, I think, that if you're gonna be free you're gonna have to do it yourselves and you're gonna have to maintain it yourselves because we're not gonna do it for ya. My problem, Richard, is with democratic imperialism, the idea that we're gonna democratize the world that Bush put in that Russo-istic inaugural he delivered, and that we're gonna eliminate tyranny from the face of the earth. Is he kidding?"

Pat Buchanan as the voice of reason? Who would have thought?

Perle waited until the ides of May 2007 to drop the hammer on President Bush himself. In a speech in New York at the Hudson Institute (founded by Herman Kahn, who wanted "a classier RAND"), Perle said of Bush, "He came ill-equipped for the job and has failed to master it. I do not meet the president, but from the people I meet who are close to him and from his speeches, I believe the gap between the president and his administration is without precedent." He then went on to beat those thoroughly dead horses, Condi Rice, the State Department, and those "keys" that should have been handed over to Ahmed Chalabi right after the Saddam statue came down.

Since the war had now entered its fifth year, the wonder was what took Perle so long to conclude that George W. Bush was not up to the job. "It's just gotten worse and worse," he told me. "I actually have a lot of sympathy for Bush. I think he's a decent guy who has been courageous and is trying to do the right thing. But he just can't execute. He can't run the government. He's proven again and again he can't get his arms around the government for which he takes responsibility. And on the issues I care most about, it has gotten substantially worse since Condi went to the State Department." For Perle, Rice's style and substance were uncomfortably closer to Madeline Albright's than to Jeanne Kirkpatrick's, and Perle wasted no opportunity to opine in public and private that she was in dangerously over her head.

Naturally, Perle's criticism of Bush was big news, but it was actually not new news. Shortly before Christmas 2006, Larry Wilkerson was a guest at the embassy of a foreign government in Washington where Perle was a guest speaker at a no-press-allowed event. "I'm sure Richard thought I was going to fall out of my chair," Wilkerson told me, "because for five solid minutes all he talked about was the ineptitude and incompetence of this administration. I was just agog that he'd finally woken up to this fact. But then he cuts to the second part of his speech, and I realized why he said what he said. The Europeans were concerned that we were going to cut and run, so Perle then went into, 'But this president is absolutely resolute,' blah, blah, blah. What he was doing was showing them a little leg, acknowledging the incompetence and the bad decisions, but adding, 'There's no way this guy's going to cut and run.' And when they turned to me, I tried to blow him out of the water. I said, 'We're not going to cut and run; we're going to turn and walk. We're going to blame the Iraqis and then get out.'" For Wilkerson, it's all past hearing now. Once, when he and Perle were standing outside the French embassy after a similar forum, Wilkerson turned to Perle and said, "Richard, you make me sick sometimes, you know?" According to Wilkerson, Perle replied, "Well, I won't respond to that."

So Perle had now publicly and privately trashed, in no particular order, Rice, Powell, Tenet, and Bush. Yet he had been virtually silent about two of the main players: Donald Rumsfeld and Dick Cheney. "I don't fault Cheney because I think by and large, Cheney's been right. I know this is not a popular view at the moment because he gets blamed for a lot of things."

What about Cheney's declaration that Rumsfeld was the greatest defense secretary in the nation's history? "I had said that earlier," Perle replied. "He was innovative. He understood the need to bring a military establishment that was oriented to the cold war into the new world that we were facing. Cap came in with a very strong president and a strong mandate to rebuild American defenses. Rumsfeld had a more daunting task. He had the concept right. He knew what needed to be done, which was to transform a military establishment that had not adapted to the way the world had changed." Perle showed me an unpublished report he wrote with Cheney in the early 1990s about the structure and capabilities of the military establishment. It was pure RMA, Revolution in Military Affairs theory, with the focus on high technology as the way to simultaneously reduce the defense budget and increase military effectiveness…as utopian a concept as one could imagine. "In the real world, you end up choosing between labor and capital," Perle told me. "And the labor is expensive, about $70,000 per man per year. You can buy a lot of technology for the price of a hundred thousand soldiers. I'm in favor of boots on the ground, but efficient boots on the ground are better than inefficient boots on the ground."

This was vintage Perle. One could easily see him laying it all out in front of a Senate committee, just daring some smart-ass to challenge his argument, just waiting to beat the intellectual bejesus out of him. But even he knew that his days as the dreaded Prince of Darkness inside the Beltway were nearing an end. In the past two years he had lost three friends and supporters: Cap Weinberger, Roberta Wohlstetter, and Jeanne Kirkpatrick. This, he thought, was what Jonathan didn't understand. These people were giants, and now there are only pygmies.

About now, the only thing certain in Perle's mind was that he and Leslie would spend even more time in Provence, far and away from that town without pity. He might write another book, and then again he might not. That's a lot of work, and Perle has never been a workaholic. Mulling over his future, the ideas and images flashed through his mind so fast that he became, momentarily, strangely, inarticulate. "I've got a lot of...every day there's news...and I read the papers or I listen to someone make a statement and I have a reaction to it...It's a lot of ideas about what we should be doing in the world and how we should go about it. I'm more than unhappy with...I don't like the influence of money in our politics. A lot of other people don't either, but a lot of the solutions can't be made to work because of constitutional concerns. It's a real dilemma. I haven't forced myself to think hard about that, but somebody should. I don't know."

Sitting now on the front porch of his home outside Washington on a spectacular spring afternoon, Perle spoke of the need to get tougher with Vladimir Putin, of how we should not look favorably upon a man who, according to a biography, took pleasure in killing rats.

"It beats raising them," I said.

"It was a very revealing biography," Perle replied, with the certainty of perhaps the only person on the planet, besides Putin's mother, who had read it. "I came away with the impression that this is a bad guy and I have Russian dissident friends who share that view." Just what America needed…another bad guy. It must have been of some comfort to Perle that the world would never run out of bad guys, leaving him, like a Supreme Court justice or a tenured professor at Princeton, fully employed for life. But the nature of the bad guys was changing. The game Perle understood and played with skill was the Jets and the Sharks at the schoolyard; your guys against my guys. But now there were so many other players playing by so many different sets of rules that, as Churchill said, "This pudding has no theme." Things were so much clearer and easier when all that confronted America was a Soviet scowl.

The irony of a globalized world is that while by necessity it draws nations closer in the day-to-day business of business, it diffuses the power of the once powerful, much as cable television and the Internet sapped the long-held dominance of the three broadcast television networks. America can still do high-tech better than anyone and can still rattle the largest saber when the spirit moves, but when the priciest sports coat on the rack at Nordstrom is made in China, it is time to accept the inevitable reality that sometime soon, perhaps real soon, the United States will no longer be the world's number one economic power. This does not concern Richard Perle in the slightest. "I don't care if we're number one or number three," he said. "What matters is whether our economy is effective and whether our citizens are living a decent life and whether we are protecting our interests. Inevitably, China will have a larger economy than ours, but it will be a long time before they have per capita income greater than ours. And what I'm hoping is that as the country gets richer and as power is diffused from the central government into the hands of the private sector, and as the private sector seeks the value of ordinary citizens, which is more freedom, not less, more information, not less, that that will have an influence on the government."

Soon Perle would be off to the Bilderberg conference, the super-secret-yet-everybody-knows-about-it annual gathering of the world's most influential people. There was little doubt that somehow he would manage to make news there, as he did at the annual conference in Herzliya, Israel, in late 2006 when he offered his opinion that George W. Bush was ready, willing, and able to join Israel in bombing Iran if it showed the slightest evidence of getting close to building a nuclear weapon. He neither discussed nor cleared that statement with anyone in the U.S. government. "Even when I was in government I never cleared anything," he said with a smile. "It's why I almost never, ever prepare a text. Because, when I was in the Pentagon, if I drafted a speech it had to be sent around for approval. So I just stopped doing it. It drove some people crazy, but it left me free to say what I wanted to say."

For the exclusive conclave that is Bilderberg, you know you've been chosen when you receive luggage tags in the mail bearing a large *B* so you will not have to bother with your designer bags at whichever airport you arrive. Even one's toothpaste passes through unmolested. The 2007 gathering is in Istanbul, and, as with every year's conference, it will be certain to enrage the Chomskyites and LaRouches who are convinced that the world is run by elitists and fascists, a permanent world government, elected by no one. At last year's affair in Ottawa, a reporter who somehow managed to get past the phalanx of security asked Perle as he was walking by, "Are you going to set the price of oil?" Perle laughed and replied, "If I were able to do that, I'd be *trading* in oil."

"It's not a big deal for me," Perle said, as we sat on his porch in Chevy Chase. "The meetings are held in very nice places. It's relaxed and comfortable. There are some people I see only once a year and I see them at Bilderberg. But it's not what it's cracked up to be." And neither, he believes, as he slouches toward his sixty-sixth birthday, is his image and perceived importance. "Look," he said. "I'm a realist and I had a choice to make in my career. I've known for a long time that I was too controversial for the kind of career that would land me in some very powerful position. And I made a decision a long time ago that I wanted to say what I thought and do what I wanted to do, and if that meant I would never be secretary of this or that, that was okay."

He paused to allow a particularly noisy truck to exit his neighbor's driveway. A gust of wind further disrupted his already tousled hair, and he turned to his side, placed his elbow on his knee and his fist under his chin, and stared as the truck pulled away. "I'm not interested in legacy," he said. "I'm really not. You do what you can while you're alive and you like to think that the people who knew you when you were alive formed a good opinion of what you've done. But after that ..." He let the sentence hang with a shrug. "What's persuaded me of that is watching people who really have done great things in their lives, people like Scoop Jackson. And now I talk to a lot of young people, and they don't even know who Scoop Jackson was.

"It doesn't last very long."

EPILOGUE

THE TWO ITEMS arrived almost simultaneously, on Memorial Day weekend no less. The first was a review of a book written by Ali Allawi, an Iraqi exile who returned to his country after the invasion to become defense minister and then finance minister in the series of revolving-door governments formed every six months or so in Baghdad. The second was the release of the much anticipated Senate Intelligence Committee report on what had been the prewar predictions of the U.S. intelligence community. It's no wonder it was released on a Friday, the weekday that attracts the weakest media attention. Taken together, these items lead to a numbingly obvious conclusion: The Iraq War was not an intelligence failure; it was an astonishing failure of intelligence, an abject refusal to absorb, digest, understand, and exploit the most basic truths about the Iraqi people. To wit, it was always about the tribes and never about the flag or even about the family. The template was not the fall of the Soviet Union or even the breakup of Yugoslavia. It was more *Lord of the Flies*.

Allawi, who just happens to be the nephew of Ahmed Chalabi (but guilt here should not be associated), describes a country quite similar to the one sketched by Elie Kedourie, the Iraqi Jew in the David Brooks column, and Hussain Abdul-Hussain, the reporter who finds his old school chum on the day after the Sunnis blew up the Askariya mosque. Their Iraq is not a state as such, but a state of mind, like Chicago in the twenties, a series of walled-off garrisons in which warlords and their bodyguards meet to carve up territory and lucre. The Americans believed that once Saddam was removed, the Grand Ayatollah Ali al-Sistani would stay out of political affairs and use his influence to tend to the spiritual needs of his people as they struggled to form a fair, free,

243

and representative government. But Allawi writes that this was an absurd misread of the old man, that what al-Sistani hoped to achieve from the beginning was a fundamentalist regime along Iranian lines. This misunderstanding folds in uncomfortably with the Intelligence Committee finding that the Bush administration was warned not once, but twice, that a war in Iraq could and probably would set off sectarian violence on a massive scale and unintentionally serve the interests of both Al-Qaeda and Iran. Asked about this, President Bush said, "Going into Iraq, we were warned about a lot of things, some of which happened and some of which didn't happen. And obviously, as I made a decision as consequential as that, I weighed the risks and rewards."

Was the possibility of a civil war truly unknowable, or was the likelihood simply unsought and unwanted? A reporter friend covering the launch of the space shuttle *Challenger* could barely contain himself after the craft blew up. "Fifteen degrees colder than they had ever launched before, *and they went ahead anyway just to stay on schedule!*" Of course, the Bush administration had to stay on schedule as well. It needed to make a big war in a target-rich environment, unlike Afghanistan, where the bombs simply made the rubble bounce.

There must be some advantage to being a superpower.

This remark by Perle to a bemused Pat Buchanan encapsulates the neoconservatives' dilemma. Here was the United States past the cusp of a new millennium, with the collapse of the Soviet Union and a raging stock market fueling national pride and a sense of entitlement, all dressed up with no place to go. The nation needed to seize the moment, to step up, to make something happen, lest historians shake their heads in wonder at the intransigence and timidity of its leaders. Hence the leaked 1992 Defense Department policy draft, supervised by Paul Wolfowitz, which outlined a role for America that Buchanan would derisively dub "Globo-Cop." It was a blueprint for the kind of dominance that would have spurred the United States to war had it been broached by any other country on the planet. The moral underpinning? How about the desire to make everyone free? Who could possibly be opposed to that? It was short, easy to remember, perfect for the six o'clock sound-bite machines, and was so virtuous as to eclipse any concern that might be raised about those military bases that would sprout as a necessary residue of our efforts. Freedom isn't free, the saying goes, and it's often even less free for those who are being freed.

In some quarters, a new intellectual standard emerged regarding just wars. Unadorned, it holds that if the recipients of the intended freedom are left worse off than they were before the effort to free them was made, the action cannot be justified after the fact. Bruce Jackson, the most erudite of Perle's friends, not only can quote Hannah Arendt on the difference between the ethics of conscience and the ethics of responsibility, but he also actually understands what she meant and how it applies to Perle and Iraq.

"Richard came from the ethics of conscience as Scoop Jackson did. And many of those people found themselves in some very senior positions in the 1980s; that was the ethics of responsibility and they did quite well." They did well then because the nature of the threat was unambiguous and their leader was clear in both the premise and practice of the policy. More important, they were active members of the administration, not columnists or talking heads with no chair at the table. All of which goes to the heart of Perle's argument regarding responsibility for the disaster in Iraq, an argument which, from his statements and writings, can be summarized thus: *I was an unpaid advisor and not a member of the administration. I was not invited to nor did I attend meetings of the NSC at which policy was discussed. I have never met privately with the president. While I continue to believe that the decision to remove Saddam Hussein was both legally and morally correct, given his record of genocide and his repeated violations of UN resolutions, I was not involved in the execution of the regime change and its aftermath. Ergo, I apologize for nothing.*

If Richard Perle, the master debater, took on an individual making this argument, Perle would annihilate him. Prior to his appointment as chairman of the Defense Policy Board, Perle was a Johnny-one-note on the removal of Saddam Hussein, along with a posse of notable former government officials. To suggest they had little or no influence on policy makers is to render pointless such activities as the Project for a New American Century. Surely Perle, like Wolfowitz, Rumsfeld, Cheney, Ikle, Libby, Podhoretz, and the others who signed the PNAC "Statement of Principles" and later urged an attack on Iraq had better things to do with their time than sign inconsequential manifestos for their own amusement.

As for the notion that the policy was justified because Saddam was "a bad guy" who violated UN sanctions, it not only raises the question of America's responsibility to the victims of the world's other bad guys; it contradicts the belief of Perle and the others that the United Nations is a feckless obstacle to the pursuit of foreign policy. If the UN shouldn't matter, then neither should violations of its edicts. One could fill several pages with the direct quotes of Perle et al. comparing Saddam Hussein to Hitler and the Clinton policy of "containment" to Chamberlain's appeasement. These hackneyed references not only cheapen and minimize Hitler and the Holocaust but create a moral patina that can be used to cover a broad range of morally dubious policies and actions. Perhaps Perle's participation in this excess can be written off to his cynical use of hyperbole to achieve political ends, but his Zionist friends should know better. Saddam as Hitler is a grotesque distortion of both motive and means, and, as an excuse for war, a shameless exercise in the politics of fear.

Finally, there is the lament that if Bush, Cheney, and Rumsfeld had only listened to Perle and others in the PNAC chorus, the regime change would have been swift and the American getaway clean. There is not a whisper of evidence to buttress the claim that Ahmed Chalabi and his "heroes in error" enjoyed support at any appreciable level among Iraqis. Even Doug Feith's law partner, Marc Zell, bailed on Perle's favorite Iraqi, describing him as "a treacherous, spineless turncoat" who tried to curry favor with Israel and gullible neocons to gain power and then delivered nothing during his brief, U.S.-engineered tenure on the Iraqi Governing Council and as Oil Minister—nothing, that is, if one excludes the U.S. intelligence he was alleged to have passed on to his friends in Iran, a charge Chalabi denies.

The conjuration in which Paul Bremmer anoints Chalabi as interim something-or-other while the Americans hail a fleet of cabs doesn't meet the intellectual standard Perle has always set for his arguments. It is fantasy, as is this analysis from Jim Woolsey: "The Iraqi criminal code and civil code which date from the 1950s was one of the most progressive and well-drafted codes in the Middle East. The British and the Egyptians had worked with them on that. So we didn't need to start from scratch. We could have had an Iraqi government in place that was rooted in Iraq's history." And what history is that? The history of barbarism and tribal warfare described by Ali Allawi and Elie Kedourie? And what progressive criminal and civil code was being observed by those who shot and burned to death four U.S. contractors in Fallujah before mutilating their bodies and hanging them from a bridge before a cheering crowd? Or those who gunned down Andrea Parhamovich, the twenty-eight-year-old woman from Perry, Ohio, who came to Iraq to teach *democracy* to children? Is it the same progressive society that has a word unique to its culture, a word found in no other country throughout the region? As Edward Wong of the *New York Times* noted, the word is *sahel*—and it means to utterly defeat and humiliate someone by dragging his corpse through the streets.

No fast and easy exit was ever in the game plan to begin with. There was no exit strategy because there was no intent to leave, which explains why so many American facilities in greater Baghdad were built not as prefabricated put-up-and-knock-downs but as solid structures that would be around for a while. New defense secretary Robert Gates said as much in early June of 2007 when he told reporters that the U.S. decision to remain in South Korea after the war was a lot smarter than the handling of Vietnam, "where we just left, lock, stock and barrel." He spoke of America having "a long and enduring presence" in the region, ignoring the fact that the U.S. presence in Saudi Arabia was, as Osama bin Laden stated, one of the reasons for the 9/11 attack in the first place. Invoking Vietnam was not a smart idea on Gates's part. A recently declassified CIA assessment of that war written in 1967 was published in *Foreign Policy* with the Vietnam references crossed out and Iraqi references typed in, to wit:

Most would probably agree that the US could achieve its objectives if it persisted long enough and paid the cost. But the compelling position of emerging from the situation would be that the US, acting within the constraints imposed by its traditions and public attitudes, cannot crush ~~a revolutionary~~ AN INSURGENT movement which is sufficiently large, dedicated, competent and well-supported. In a narrow sense, this means more simply that the structure of US military power is ill-suited to cope with guerrilla warfare waged by a determined, resourceful and politically astute opponent. This is not a novel discovery. It has long been suspected.

Five months after this memo was written, the Tet Offensive shocked the U.S. command and almost overwhelmed Saigon. As the Senate Intelligence Committee report on Iraq concluded, it is not as if the administration had not been warned, early and often, about the consequences of its policy.

As for weapons of mass destruction, of course, the world had every reason to believe that they still existed. After all, America had the receipts for many of them, as Perle knew only too well, having argued against their export throughout the eighties. But Perle declared on numerous occasions that the presence or lack of WMD was no longer the primary rationale for the invasion. So what was it? There is little doubt that multiple agendas were at work regarding Iraq and the Middle East long before the Bush team took control of the government. In the end, was it all about oil? Or security for Israel? Or a windfall for Haliburton, Bechtel, Lockheed Martin, FMC, the Duct Tape people and the rest of the burgeoning homeland security industry? Or raging testosterone that would not be assuaged by a drive-by takedown of the Taliban? The answer is yes to all, depending on whose agenda one examines. But for Richard Perle, the evidence shows that none of these motives were causative factors in his steadfast campaign for regime change in Iraq and beyond, as much as that may enrage the legions who revile him and all they believe he represents.

On the subject of oil, Perle has consistently argued for a national policy to reduce dependency on imported oil and rejects the idea that America must kowtow to the Saudis and the Gulf states just to keep the oil flowing. "We protect them. The Saudis are toast without the United States," Perle told me. "They can't defend themselves and they run to Daddy [the United States] whenever they're in trouble." Unlike the Bush family, with long ties to the oil business and the Saudis, and Cheney, whose closed-door huddles with Saudi Arabia's American oil partners throughout the tenure of the administration sent a clear message about his sympathies, Perle has been almost alone in his condemnation of Arab oil money funding a variety of terrorist groups. To him, America's oil gluttony is an unacceptable rationale for ultimately subsidizing hatred and violence against Americans and others.

As for Israel, Perle's excuse that he signed *A Clean Break* without having had much to do with its creation is weak indeed. But to depict him as a Likudnik is inaccurate. To Perle, Israel is a piece on the chessboard—strategically a very important piece, and a piece that had special meaning for his mentor Scoop Jackson—but not a piece worth jeopardizing one's king for. As his son, Jonathan, said when asked about dual loyalties, "I was born in America and there's no Israeli flag flying at my house. There's an American flag. My father is about America first."

Perle as war profiteer is another Internet chestnut. But if Perle saw 9/11 as a chance to make money, he did a poor job of it. From all available evidence, the Perles are comfortable but not rich by contemporary standards of the truly wealthy. Had there been opportunities to profit from the war on terror, as undoubtedly there were, Perle either took a pass or failed to fully exploit them. As a businessman he is a pretty fair security policy analyst.

What Richard Perle is guilty of is of a sadly stupefying resolve. The man the *Washington Post* called "the ultimate insider"—the man who rammed through the Jackson-Vanik amendment when no one gave it a snowball's chance in hell, the man who told George Shultz to just sit there if Gromyko threatened to walk, the man who walked out of Hofdi House in Reykjavik after bluffing with an empty hand—that man was now clinging to an idea that had lost its legitimacy, the idea that America knew the best way for people to live and that American military might could make it happen anytime, anyplace.

He cringes at the word "utopian," but how else can one explain the title of his book? *An End to Evil*? That is the purview of the Almighty. Transforming the region? Who requested that, exactly? It is one thing to have compassion for the oppressed and the downtrodden, as Perle displayed for years by housing Soviet refuseniks who would cook borscht in his kitchen in the middle of the night. It is quite another to bet other people's lives on refereeing a five-sided argument in a pathologically violent place, just because it appears to be the right thing to do. As Mike Tyson once said, "Every fighter's got a plan...until he gets hit."

What seemed to have worked so magically in the collapse of the Soviet Union would not work in Iraq because the driving force for freedom in Eastern Europe came internally, from the shipyards in Gdansk and the balconies over Wenceslas Square. It would not come from the smug face of Ahmed Chalabi. Perle's shrug of a response to anger over various pronouncements and manifestos that bear his name— provocative tracts such as *A Clean Break*, the PNAC open letter to Bill Clinton, papers and movements he claims he had virtually nothing to do with—bespeak a callous indifference to the political impact of his associations. Parrying criticism with the excuse that he was neither an author nor a founder of inflammatory positions and cadres is intellectually dishonest. And Perle's maddening insistence on a link between Al-Qaeda and Saddam Hussein, the "evidence" on Chris Carney's butcher paper tapestry, can be attributed only to a stubborn refusal to concede error. As the great journalist Ed Bradley said of Vietnam, "We made a mistake. And, over the years, we compounded that mistake because we couldn't admit we were wrong. Go tell that to the Vietnamese. And go down to that memorial in Washington and look at those names. What a waste. What a waste."

On May 30, 2007, a blog appeared under the headline "We Had the Very Best of Intentions." It was a dispatch from Britain written by Richard Perle.

I am writing this from the Guardian Hay Bus, a Routemaster that once conveyed people and is now being used to convey ideas. Last night, Philippe Sands and I discussed Iran, Iraq and related issues in a tent nearly filled with a thoughtful, engaged audience of five or six hundred people who had come, I suspect, to hear what could possibly be said in defense of America's policy in Iraq. I tried to oblige.

Did he ever. The scene was not difficult to imagine: Perle under a Chautauqua tent like Frederick March in Inherit the Wind, only this time preaching to the unconverted. This was his meat...a stage, a skeptical audience, a controversy waiting to be thrashed out, just like that scene back in his schooldays in London when he assured the doubting spectators there would be no nuclear war over Russian missiles in Cuba. Only this time, Perle had forgotten what he had told me about his youthful misread of the Cuban missile crisis. "I was too young and inexperienced to take into account miscalculations and errors and misperceptions."

For the Guardian Hay audience, Perle recited the now well-worn path to the invasion and then pivoted to its horrific consequences:

> We should have handed political authority in Iraq to an interim Iraqi government the day Baghdad fell. With the best of intentions, though, we embarked on an ill-conceived and catastrophically flawed occupation aimed at bringing a decent representative government to the long-suffering Iraqis. We didn't know how to do that....We did not go into Iraq to impose representative government on the Iraqis. We went there to manage a threat to our own safety. But now that we are there we are trying to help an elected government achieve a level of safety for its citizens that will allow it to function.

If you buy the premise, you buy the bit. Good intentions, spawned from lordly roots, are of little consequence once the decision is made to unscrew the cap and let the scorpions out of the bottle...on the assumption that it is in their and our best interest. Good intentions? Tell that to the more than two million refugees created by the war, refugees who are not allowed into the United States because of "security concerns." And now it was time to pivot again and look to the future:

> No matter what you think about how we got here, think hard about what we must now do to protect hapless Iraqis and the rest of us from the holy warriors who believe they have a mandate from Allah to destroy a world in which people can gather in a tent and discuss their differences.

But now there were alarming reports that the Turks were massing troops to invade northern Iraq to deal with the Kurds once and for all. Perle helped arm the Turks and his sympathies for the Kurds won't mean very much if the U.S.-supplied Bradleys rumble across Iraq's northern border. In a display of astonishing irony, Defense Secretary Gates was urging Turkey not to take unilateral action because it would be destabilizing. And Perle's old foil, Russia, was rearing its head and making ominous sounds. In late May of 2007, Moscow conducted the first reported test of its new R-24 ICBM with multiple-targeted warheads. According to the spokesman, the warheads successfully struck their assigned targets in a remote region.

This came on the heels of an angry protest by Vladimir Putin of an American plan to install a primitive missile defense system in Poland and the Czech Republic, as well as percolating rage over NATO expansion. In July of 2007, Russia formally announced it would abandon a key cold-war era arms agreement, the Conventional Forces in Europe Treaty, to protest the Bush missile defense plan. With a wave of his hand reminiscent of his cold war heyday, Perle dismissed the Kremlin's displeasure. "He just doesn't get it," Perle said of Putin. "It's a completely irrational view that our missile defense is a threat to them. How could it possibly be a threat to them? Look at what they're doing in Georgia. Look at their support for the last Stalinist redoubt in Belarus.

Look at how they're intimidating the Latvians and Lithuanians. They're doing all kinds of horrible things. There's a lot of thuggery, a lot of brutality, a lot of corruption, and civil society is really being threatened. Condi is the principle influence on our Russian policy, and she got it wrong. By failing to get tough with them, we led them to believe they could walk all over us. And they do."

This soliloquy had a marvelously retro ring, like a clever cover of an Elvis tune. But it was an echo of another time, and resounds with the timbre of decay.

It is dead solid certain that those who live public lives are remembered for the last bad thing they did. It was thus for Richard Nixon and for Dan Rather and for Pete Rose. It will be no different for Richard Perle. His enormously effective career as one of America's premiere cold warriors will be mentioned somewhere down in the intestinal tract of his obituary, along with his courageous championing of the rights of Soviet dissidents and oppressed Jews. He mattered because he could not think of any other way to live but to matter on issues affecting those who could not help themselves. He learned that first from the kid brother born with a handicap and now lost in the world; at Hollywood High where a probing mind could be as seductive to others as a varsity football jersey; and then big time with Scoop Jackson and Dickie Fosdick, who terrorized Capitol Hill with the gravitas of their beliefs. His was a fierce, cunning, rapierlike style that made rivals and enemies twitch. The Prince of Darkness, indeed. But in the denouement of his political life, the notion of America as freedom-giver became so consuming that, like a black hole in space, it sucked in all matter around it. There it was, the unipolar moment, just waiting to be seized. "Yes," said Bruce Jackson. "There was a unipolar moment. It lasted for about thirty seconds and then it was gone." Like the magical missile shield, it was a grand illusion. Empires are made of snow. They melt. Perle was quoted as saying that with the liberation of Iraq, "our children will sing great songs about us." Actually, he never said it.

But does it really matter anymore, now that there is nothing left but silence as the funeral corteges pass by?

Asked if he thought it was fair that Iraq would no doubt be in the first paragraph of Perle's obituary, Ken Adelman paused and stared at the ceiling. "I think it's fair because he and I were supporters. We thought it was the right thing to do, and that it could be done without the ghastly results we've seen. I think it's fair to say that a lot of the advice we gave turned out not to be good. I don't think we were dishonest. We just turned out to be wrong."

In the end, perhaps Perle forgot what it felt like to connect with real people, that glorious rush he felt when he saw, firsthand, the consequences of the Jackson-Vanik amendment he had fought for so tirelessly. Here were people, actual flesh-and-blood people, coming around to Scoop Jackson's office to give thanks for their freedom. For Perle, the dots connected in an emotionally powerful way, the fruits of his labors standing there in the doorway and smiling. Lo and behold, policy initiatives, no matter how complex and contentious, had human consequences. He saw this in the Soviet Union but could not see it in the Middle East. And as the consequences of the policies he helped construct are wrenchingly displayed each day and night on the news, as the toll of dead, maimed, orphaned, and displaced rises without cease, and the impact of fateful decisions he and others clamored for reverberate menacingly throughout the world, Richard Perle is left to contemplate whether the grand vision he championed was worth it after all.

The end of an empire is messy at best
And this empire is ending
Like all the rest
Like the Spanish Armada adrift on the sea
We're adrift in the land of the brave
And the home of the free
Goodbye. Goodbye. Goodbye.

—Randy Newman, "A Few Words in Defense of Our Country"

Acknowledgments

When people give their time to an endeavor such as this they are making an investment with no real hope of return. They sit there, sometimes for hours, answering questions from someone they don't really know and may not really trust. Why? Because somehow it seemed like a good idea at the time. I hope I have not done violence to the words of all those who were gracious enough to endure my interrogations, and I thank them all for granting me the opportunity to hear their views and their recollections. Thanks also to Carl Jay Diesing for his expertise in setting up my database and for his support and good cheer. I am grateful to Walter Bode for his insightful critique and especially to Philip Turner of Sterling for approving and overseeing this project in the first place. A nod of respect and affection to my agent, Sharlene Martin, for agreeing to waltz with me one more time, and to Jeanne, Daniel, and Diana just for being there when I needed them. Finally, a thank-you to Richard Norman Perle for his kindness, his patience, and his willingness to roll the dice when most of his friends advised him not to. I promised him only that I would be fair. I hope he believes I kept my promise.

Notes

I. Prologue

page 1 "He was a British reporter": Perle, interview with the author, 10/21/2006.

page 1 "I never thought I had much hope": Krepon and Caldwell, *The Politics of Arms Control Treaty Ratification*, p. 310.

page 6 "American policy cannot continue": newamericancentury.org, 1/26/1998.

page 6 "The principal objection": Congressional testimony, Federal Document Clearing House, 9/28/2000.

page 7 "Liar! Liar!": AP online, 2/18/2005.

page 9 "I'm so damned tired": David Rose, *Vanity Fair*, January 2007.

page 9 "Yes, I think he is hurt": Wurmser, interview with the author, 11/2/2006.

II. The Imp of the Perverse

page 11 "For a long time, my parents": Perle, interview with the author, 10/21/2006.

page 11 "Consider kids who bullied": Calvin Trillin, *Nation*, 9/16/2002.

page 12 "I suppose Rocco Guntermann": Trillin, letter to the editor, *Nation*, 11/18/2002.

page 12 "Yeah," Trillin laughed: Trillin, interview with the author, 3/13/2007.

page 13 "He was...different": Perle, *Hard Line*, p. 20.

page 14 "I would consider us Bohemian": Zimring, interview with the author, 2/22/2007.

page 14 "During a debate": Horton, interview with the author, 3/14/2007.

page 14 "He learned to stand straight": Perle, *Hard Line*, p. 21.

page 15 "He and I were rather close": Major, interview with the author, 3/15/2007.

page 17 "Despite a widespread belief": Louis Menand, *New Yorker*, 6/27/2005.

page 17 "Prizes for a retaliatory capability": Wohlstetter, rand.org, 11/6/1958.

page 18 "Lang described to me": Wilson, *The Politics of Truth*, pp. 432–433.

page 19 "The struggle for power": Morgenthau, homepages.st.martin.edu.

page 21 "Richard was doing his PhD": Lapping, interview with the author, 3/2/2007.

page 22 "Richard Perle can take": Burt, interview with the author, 11/9/2006.

page 23 "Richard would buy": Feldman, interview with the author, 2/22/2007.

III. The Sorcerer's Apprentice

page 25 "More nonsense has been written": *Washington Times*, 4/2/2006.

page 26 "I don't think in grand": Perle, interview with the author, 2/27/2007.

page 27 "The children of darkness are evil": Niebuhr, *The Children of Light*, pp. 10–11.

page 28 "The atrocities are the most sordid": Kaufman, *Henry M. Jackson*, p. 39.

page 28 "In some ways, this was his": History of Jewish Women in America, American Jewish Historical Library, New York Public Library, Dorot Jewish Division.

page 28 "The hope for peace": Kaufman, *Henry M. Jackson*, p. 133.

page 31 "What impressed me": Ibid., p. 211.

page 31 "such as remembering to file income tax returns, paying parking tickets, and balancing one's checkbook, which they taught him": Winik, *On the Brink*, p. 37.

page 31 "I did that to Cy Vance": Perle, interview with the author, 3/31/2007.

page 31 "He doesn't browbeat": Burt, interview with the author, 11/9/2006.

page 34 "Richard helped make": Feith, interview with the author, 11/2/2006.

page 34 "You could not get him": Feldman, interview with the author, 2/22/2007.

page 34 "The desk I was seated next to": Gaffney, interview with the author, 11/9/2006.

page 34 "He wouldn't come in": Jackson, interview with the author, 2/18/2007.

page 35 "Kissinger had illusions": History of Jewish Women in America, American Jewish Historical Library, New York Public Library, Dorot Jewish Division.

page 36 "It's his ability to use": Adelman, interview with the author, 1/10/2007.

page 36 "He had a scheme": Ledeen, interview with the author, 11/2/2006.

page 37 "We small people": Kaufman, *Henry M. Jackson*, p. 264.

page 37 "If those visas aren't here": Ibid., p. 265.

page 39 "We tried to explain to Jackson": Scowcroft, interview with the author, 1/24/2007.

page 40 "The best thing that could happen": Kaufman, *Henry M. Jackson*, p. 273.

page 40 "a disastrous example": Ibid., p. 277.

page 42 "The remarks attributed to you": *Time*, 5/3/1976.

page 42 "The most likely explanation": Kaufman, *Henry M. Jackson*, p. 334.

page 42 "Jackson had carefully studied": Ibid., p. 300.

page 43 "We have reached an amazing": Winik, *On the Brink*, p. 58.

page 44 "The Jackson-Vanik amendment would not": Perle, *The Forward*, 1/16/1995.

IV. Exile on Main Street

page 45 "During the campaigns": Perle, interview with the author, 2/2/2007.

page 46 "be more careful with foreigners": Kaufman, *Henry M. Jackson*, p. 259.

page 46 "cast no unfavorable reflection": Ibid.

page 47 "I never met anyone": Wilkerson, interview with the author, 2/2/2007.

page 47 "What they really hate": Drumheller, interview with the author, 3/13/2007.

page 47 "Paul sees three possibilities": Weiss, declassified document, U.S. National Archives, 10/7/1970.

page 48 "Intelligence cannot help": *Bulletin of the Atomic Scientists*, 4/1/1993.

page 49 "That was not the purpose": Pipes, interview with the author, 3/21/2007.

page 51 "Albert Wohlstetter made a trip to Iran": Interview with the author, 1/8/2007.

page 51 "Communist World Order": Fitzgerald, *Way Out There*, pp. 83–84.

page 52 "An unsound agreement": Kaufman, *Henry M. Jackson*, p. 360.

page 53 "a first-class polemic": Krepon and Caldwell, *The Politics of Arms Control Treaty Ratification*, p. 292.

page 54 "It sounds very interesting": Winik, *On the Brink*, p. 64.

page 55 "an FBI wiretap": Hersh, *The Price of Power*, p. 322.

page 57 "Carter just did not realize": Kaufman, *Henry M. Jackson*, p. 365.

V. Revolution

page 62 " '*What?*' he said": Feldman, interview with the author, 2/22/2007.

page 62 "He was really smart": Leslie Perle, interview with the author, 4/27/2007.

page 62 "Howard was doing": Perle, interview with the author, 4/27/2007.

page 63 "A lot of people ask": Jonathan Perle, interview with the author, 2/19/2007.

page 64 "enough copper pots": *Washington Post*, 10/5/1980.

page 64 "We had five linear feet": Ibid.

page 64 "Soltam paid Perle": *New York Times*, 4/17/1983.

page 65 "U.S. staging post for Middle East": Marios Evriviades, *Security Dilemmas in Eurasia*: Alliances and Alignments in the Middle East, The Turkish-Israeli Axis. See also: Euripides L. Evriviades, "The Evolving Role of Turkey in U.S. Contingency Planning and Soviet Reaction," Study submitted to the John F. Kennedy School of Government, January 1984.

page 65 "the rise of terrorism": *Foreign Policy Research Institute*, September 1999.

page 65 "Our boys did it!": todayszaman.com, 4/5/2007.

page 65 "The Perle character": Ibid.

page 66 "He's one of the few people": Ledeen, interview with the author, 11/2/2006.

page 67 "There are people who are on": Feith, interview with the author, 11/2/2006.

page 68 In March of 1978: *Nation*, 6/22/1985.

page 69 "with Perle lobbying": counterpunch.com, 2/28/2004.

page 69 "I consider Dr. Bryen": Ibid.

page 69 "I am familiar with the documented": *New York Times*, 4/17/1983.

page 69 "Nevertheless, an investigation by": Ibid.

page 71 "Richard lived on Capitol Hill": Burt, interview with the author, 11/9/2006.

page 72 "It was the height": Adelman, interview with the author, 1/10/2007.

page 73 "At first, Waterman had contempt": Perle, *Hard Line*, p. 5.

page 75 "The air had been cleared": Shultz, *Turmoil and Triumph*, p. 719.

page 75 "a disaster, a total delusion": Ibid., p. 701.

page 75 "The idea of a nonnuclear world": Ibid., p. 705.

page 76 "We must not discuss this": Ibid., p. 701.

page 77 "a look of disbelief": Anderson, *Revolution*, p. 82.

page 78 "clearly talking through his hat": Fitzgerald, interview with the author, 5/17/2006.

page 78 "powerful directed energy weapons": Fitzgerald, *Way Out There*, pp. 127–128.

page 78 "I'm not a rocket scientist": Gaffney, interview with the author, 11/9/2006.

page 79 "Cap handed it to Richard": Bruce Jackson interview with author, 2/18/2007.

page 80 "The good guys won, didn't they?": Fitzgerald, *Way Out There*, p. 39.

page 80 "Even the *New York Times*": Fitzgerald, interview with the author, 5/17/2006.

page 80 "We never believed in the umbrella": Fitzgerald, *Way Out There*, p. 202.

page 84 "I'm not sure": Burt, interview with the author, 11/9/2006.

page 85 "an act that signaled": *Time*, 12/5/1983.

VI. At the Summit

page 87 "I know all about your ideas": Shultz, *Turmoil and Triumph*, p. 589.

page 87 "Leave arguments like that": Ibid.

page 88 "The next time you come to Moscow": Ibid., p. 591.

page 88 "Don't commit to any": Winik, *On the Brink,* p. 384.

page 90 "'In NATO,' he told me": Perle, interview with the author, 2/2/2007.

page 92 "I'm amazed that you would": Shultz, *Turmoil and Triumph*, p. 592.

page 92 "Farmer Jones finds": *National Review*, 3/8/1985.

page 93 "What had happened": Shultz, *Turmoil and Triumph*, p. 700.

page 95 "I thought it was": Adelman, interview with the author, 1/10/2007.

page 96 "I think both Perle": Jackson, interview with the author, 2/18/2007.

page 97 "Be careful now": Transcript, *Breakthrough at Reykjavik*, Grenada Television, 1987.

page 97 "I remember that I just": Burt, interview with the author, 11/9/2006.

page 98 "In my 25 years": Transcript, *Breakthrough at Reykjavik*, Grenada Television, 1987.

page 98 "Wait a minute": Ibid.

page 99 "We should give them": Shultz, *Turmoil and Triumph*, p. 716.

page 99 "Reagan didn't care": Fitzgerald, interview with the author, 5/17/2006.

page 99 "a good man": Shultz, *Turmoil and Triumph*, p. 763.

page 102 "Why do we do this?": Fitzgerald, *Way Out There*, p. 362.

page 103 "No, you are right": Shultz, *Turmoil and Triumph*, p. 773.

page 104 "To them, it was just": Lapping, interview with the author, 3/2/2007.

page 105 "would have been the most painfully": Fitzgerald, *Way Out There*, p. 353.

page 105 "a near disaster": Ibid., p. 353.

page 105 "like an earthquake": Ibid., p. 354.

page 105 "a collection of": Ibid., p. 355.

page 106 "The idea of ridding": Gaffney, interview with the author, 11/9/2006.

page 106 "It was such an enormous step": Adelman, interview with the author, 1/10/2007.

page 107 "simply die on its own": Fitzgerald, *Way Out There*, p. 410.

page 107 "I've only felt it once before": *Time*, 12/21/1987.

page 108 "It was possible, Mikhail Sergeevich": Hoover Institution, *Fond* 89, available on printhis.clickability.com.

page 109 "Summits are wonderful salves": *U.S. News and World Report*, 12/14/1987.

VII. Citizen Perle (1)

page 112 "Who did they think they were": Perle, interview with the author, 2/27/2007.

page 114 "We have 50 percent of the world's wealth": Ohio State debate, 4/12/1988, alternativeradio.org, transcribed by the author.

page 115 "I have sat": Audio of Ohio State debate, 4/12/1988, transcribed by author.

page 116 "Subsequently, over objections": David Hilzenrath, "Washington's Ultimate Insider," *Washington Post*, 5/24/2004.

page 116 "charmed by his manner": Clarke, *Against All Enemies*, p. 49.

page 117 "We'll pay you": Perle, interview with the author, 4/27/2007.

page 117 "Perle's stock options": *Washington Post*, 5/24/2004.

page 118 "As a registered agent of Turkey": Letter from Gene Rossides, American Hellenic Council, to DOD general counsel, 9/6/2002.

page 119 "The Turks and their enthusiastic": justacitizen.com, 11/29/2006.

page 120 "Lockheed sells F-16 fighters": defensenews.com, 5/11/07.

page 121 "In fact, Perle was once": *Washington Report of Middle East Affairs*, 4/1/2004.

page 121 "Actually, the MEK": "Mujahedin-e Khalq Organization," globalsecurity.org.

page 121 "MEK military camps": Ibid.

page 121 "Absolutely false": Feith, interview with the author, 11/2/2006.

page 122 "Even discussion of the Armenian": dissidentvoice.com, 11/18/2005.

page 122 "A 2005 report": bbc.co.uk, 10/6/2005.

page 123 "Iraq employed U.S. military": Bob Woodward, "CIA Aiding Iraq in Gulf War," *Washington Post*, 12/15/1986.

page 124 "The Iranian revolution": Pipes and Mylroie, "Back Iraq," *New Republic*, 4/27/1987.

page 125 "On February 27, 1991": *Air Force*, 3/1/2003.

page 126 "It took columnist William Safire": *New York Times*, 8/29/1991.

page 127 "What the President was saying": Scowcroft, interview with the author, 1/24/2007.

page 127 "There is no main gig": Hilzenrath, "Washington's Ultimate Insider," *Washington Post*, 5/24/2004.

page 127 "The minister of this": Ibid.

page 129 "one of the most despicable": Perle, interview with the author, 3/31/2007.

page 129 "In fact, the administration": antiwar.com, 8/27/2001.

page 129 "We've got more generals": Center for Public Integrity, openairwaves.org.

page 129 "This in turn led to": antiwar.org, 8/27/2001.

page 130 "We went over and taught": MPRI, Inc., Center for Public Integrity, openairwaves.org.

page 133 "is the number one candidate for the job": *Turkish Daily News*, 1/22/1996.

page 133 "like selling our souls": antiwar.com, 8/27/2001.

VIII. Perle and the Jews

page 135 "I want to bash": *Jerusalem Post*, 8/24/2006.

page 135 "The essay, simply": *London Review of Books*, 3/26/2006.

page 136 "a classical conspiratorial": *Nation*, 5/15/2006.

page 136 "piss-poor, monocausal": Ibid.

page 136 "blinding flashes of the obvious": Ibid.

page 137 "*A Clean Break*": 1996, IASPS.com.

page 139 "What makes America powerful?": Wurmser, interview with the author, 11/2/2006.

page 142 "When Perle served as": *PR Newswire*, 7/13/2000.

page 142 "A friend of mine": Perle, interview with the author, 3/31/2007.

page 144 "Bryen allegedly attempted": *Washington Report on Middle East Affairs*, 5/1/2004.

page 145 "Ledeen was also the man": Ibid.

page 145 "Ledeen, who once lived": rollingstone.com, 7/24/2006.

page 145 "that Oliver North had recommended": counterpunch.com, 2/28/2004.

page 145 "What is the most potent": Ledeen, interview with the author, 11/2/2006.

page 146 "a son who wishes": Rhode, interview with the author, 1/10/2007.

page 146 "Those who speak, pay": *Mother Jones*, January–February 2004.

page 147 "Every ten years or so": Attributed to Ledeen by Jonah Goldberg of the *National Review*, from a speech to the American Enterprise Institute in the early 1990s.

page 147 "No more bartering": *Mother Jones*, January–February 2004.

page 147 "constantly on his cell phone": upi.com, 4/30/2004.

page 148 "A sizeable financial interest": *Mother Jones*, July–August, 2006.

page 148 "Michael tells me": Perle, interview with the author, 3/31/2007.

page 148 "Perle thought the call": *Jewish Forward*, 12/31/2004.

page 149 "In April of of 2007": *New York Sun,* 4/17/2007.

page 150 "is like a night flower": lukeford.net.

page 151 Biden "kept repeating": salon.com, 3/16/2007.

page 151 "The sleeping giant": Ibid.

page 152 "The first thing I noticed": rense.com.

page 152 "In the mid-1920s": Krepon and Caldwell, *The Politics of Arms Control Treaty Ratification*, pp. 143–44.

page 153 "The creation of a vast": Fitzgerald, *Way Out There*, p. 79.

page 153 "Democracies will not sacrifice": Ibid., p. 179.

page 153 "In a succession of rooms": *Washington Post*, 5/24/2005.

page 154 "Iraq is not about oil": mondoweiss.observer.com, 6/2006.

IX. The Bayeaux Tapestry

page 155 "All [Rumsfeld] wanted to talk about": Cockburn, *Rumsfeld*, pp. 76–77.

page 155 "Proposing that is": Ibid.

page 156 "I don't remember the circumstances": Perle, interview with the author, 2/27/2007.

page 156 "Among the beneficiaries": *Guardian*, 4/14/2003.

page 156 "An audit found": Ibid.

page 157 "The scale of fraud": Ibid.

page 157 "The Jay Gatsby": Attributed to Noah Feldman, *New Straits Times*, 12/15/2005.

page 157 "Chalabi's daughter": *Wall Street Journal*, 8/7/2003.

page 157 "the de Gaulle of Iraq": *Daily Telegraph*, 2/13/2004.

page 157 "'Dr.' Chalabi's success": petrabank.com.

page 157 "At the end of the Gulf War": Center for Media and Democracy, 10/30/2004.

page 158 "We tried to burn through": Ibid.

page 158 "In the summer of 1991": Center for Media and Democracy, 10/30/2004.

page 159 "He was reporting no intel": *New Yorker*, 6/7/2004.

page 159 "Bay of Goats": Cockburn, *Rumsfeld*, p. 150.

page 160 "American foreign and defense policy": newamericancentury.org.

page 161 "He just needs the Jews": Salon.com, 5/4/2004.

page 161 "Israel has not devoted": forward.com, 7/31/1998.

page 162 "Wearing other hats": newamericancentury.org.

page 162 "He's been vilified": Perle, interview with the author, 4/27/2007.

page 163 "the process of transformation": newamericancentury.org.

page 165 "Unless we find": Federal Document Clearing House, 9/28/2001.

page 166 "a quick matter of": Cockburn, *Rumsfeld*, p. 150.

page 167 "This is the last time": Drumheller, interview with the author, 3/13/2007.

page 167 "The CIA really did": Wilkerson, interview with the author, 2/2/2007.

page 167 "Failure to undertake": newamericancentury.org.

page 167 "I've never talked about": Interview with the author, 2/1/2007.

page 168 "You want 'em?": Wilkerson, interview with the author, 2/2/2007.

page 168 "pulling people out": Robert Dreyfuss and Jason Vest, "The Lie Factory," *Mother Jones*, January–February 2004.

page 169 "They wanted us the fuck out of there": Ibid.

page 169 "Military Organization in the Information Age": *Middle East Policy*, 6/22/2004.

page 171 "Waiting to become": Jackson, interview with the author, 5/22/2007.

page 171 "This was one fight": Cockburn, *Rumsfeld*, p. 167.

pages 171–72 "Have you ever seen the Bayeaux Tapestry": Interview with the author, 4/27/2007.

page 173 "Case Closed": *Weekly Standard*, 11/24/2003.

page 174 "Whatever we advocated": Wurmser, interview with the author, 11/2/2006.

page 174 "We got information": Feith, interview with the author, 11/2/2007.

page 175 "I cannot see how": *Daily Mirror*, 11/20/2002.

page 176 "Murawiec unveiled": pressbox.com, 8/7/2002.

page 176 "I don't consider them": *Washington Post*, 8/6/2002.

page 177 "My experience with your": slate.com, 8/27/2002.

page 177 "offensive and repugnant": Ibid.

page 179 "Perle was saying": AP, 5/24/2004.

page 179 "This will be my undoing": Wilkerson, interview with the author, 2/2/2007.

page 181 "We can't do this": Ibid.

page 181 "Cheney even called Powell": *Washington Post*, 10/1/2006.

page 181 "We took that out": Ibid.

page 182 "Failed, failed, failed": Wilkerson, interview with the author, 2/2/2007.

page 182 "Did we send him": Drumheller, interview with the author, 3/13/2007.

page 183 "bone chilling": politicalcortex.com, 4/11/2006.

page 185 "If this is about oil": *New York Times*, 11/6/2003.

page 185 "close hold": counterpunch.com, 11/10/2003.

X. Citizen Perle (2)

page 188 "Even in 1968": Jackson, interview with the author, 2/18/2007.

page 188 "The nexus": *American Prospect*, 5/1/2003.

page 190 "Lunch with the Chairman": *New Yorker*, 3/17/2003.

page 191 "They said they were eager": Perle, interview with the author, 4/27/2007.

page 191 "There is a split personality": *New Yorker*, 3/17/2003.

page 193 "the closest thing": Wolf Blitzer, *CNN Late Edition*, transcript, 3/10/2003.

page 193 "Implications of an Imminent War": AP, 5/7/2003.

page 193 "In San Francisco, protesters": Knight Ridder/Tribune, 4/12/2003.

page 194 "unique perspective": *Nation*, 4/7/2003.

page 194 "Not to be outdone": *International Herald Tribune*, 3/29/2003.

page 194 "On Richard Perle": *Nation*, 4/14/2003.

page 195 "And so for Richard Perle": *Nation*, 4/21/2003.

page 196 "The Boeing Affair was a case in point": *Washington Post*, 12/5/2003.

page 199 "does a wonderful imitation": *Vanity Fair*, April 2004.

page 201 "almost as if Perle": Cockburn, *Rumsfeld*, p. 103.

page 201 "Black and Radler borrowed": *Chicago Tribune*, 4/29/2007.

page 202 "a corporate kleptocracy": *Washington Post*, 9/1/2004.

page 202 "factually and legally wrong": Ibid.

page 203 "As I suspected": Ibid.

page 203 "I have been exposed to Richard's": Ibid.

page 203 "There is no substantiation": Slate.com, 9/2/2004.

page 203 "Richard has always been": *New York Times*, 9/6/2004.

page 203 "I do say that to him": Jonathan Perle, interview with the author, 2/19/2007.

page 204 "They think we're rich?": Leslie Perle, interview with the author, 4/27/2007.

XI. Band on the Run

page 205 "I think we're all": Jackson, interview with the author, 2/18/2007.

page 206 "Stir the pot!": Cockburn, *Rumsfeld*, p. 110.

page 207 "We needed something immediately": Perle, interview with the author, 4/27/2007.

page 208 "Perle of Wisdom": *Jerusalem Post*, 5/9/2003.

page 208 "When smashing monuments": *New Yorker*, 4/21/2003.

page 209 "There is no middle way": Frum and Perle, *An End to Evil*, p. 9.

page 209 "It hurt...when": AARP/aol.com, 5/2/2006.

page 211 "It is just amazing to me": *Washington Post*, 4/7/2005.

page 211 "There is reason to believe": Ibid.

page 212 "I think it was all": Lapping, interview with the author, 3/2/2007.

page 213 *"The Power of Nightmares"*: Transcript at bbc.com, 10/20/2004.

page 214 "precautionary principle": Ibid.

page 214 "awfully tendentious": *New York Times*, 12/9/2005.

page 214 "If you saw a missile": *Why We Fight*, Sony Pictures, 2005.

page 216 "This is a day": *New York Times*, 4/8/2006.

page 216 "But we are Iraqis": *New York Times*, 5/7/2007.

page 217 "Same Old Demons": *New York Times*, 11/2/2006.

page 217 "It was never for sure": Wurmser, interview with the author, 11/2/2006.

page 218 "How did we get to": Jackson, interview with the author, 5/22/2007.

page 218 "has never been weaker": *News Straight Times*, 12/15/2005.

page 218 "Farid is a decent person": Perle, interview with the author, 4/27/2007.

page 219 "In my eyes": nysun.com, 5/9/2006.

page 219 "But other dissidents": Laura Rozen,"Has Washington found its Iranian Chalabi?, *Mother Jones,* 10/6/2006.

page 220 "Cheney filed the": *American Prospect*, 6/1/2006.

page 220 "In 2006, Wurmser": Ibid.

page 220 "He's not asking for money": Wurmser, interview with the author, 11/2/2006.

page 221 "There are clear benefits": Fukuyama, *America at the Crossroads*, p. 83.

page 221 "Fukuyama then points out": Ibid., pp. 48–49.

page 222 "No American president": *Today*, BBC4, BBC.com 6/3/2006.

page 222 "We are heroes in error": telegraph.co.uk, 2/19/2004.

page 224 "The levels of brutality": David Rose, *Vanity Fair*, January 2007.

page 225 "I totally agree": antiwar.com, 11/6/2006.

page 226 "the totals for both stood at": globalsecurity.org.

XII. Far and Away

page 227 "After twelve years of Jacques Chirac": AP, 4/15/2007.

page 228 "It actually wasn't bad": Perle, interview with the author, 4/27/2007.

page 229 "all 'important' NATO business": Frum and Perle, *An End to Evil*, pp. 249–50.

page 233 "It's a Texan thing": Jackson, interview with the author, 5/22/2007.

page 233 "was not the architect": *Charlie Rose*, 5/30/2007.

page 235 "he paid the price": *Washington Post*, 11/4/2005.

page 236 "Perle pays a call on Pat Buchanan": *A Case for War*, PBS/Lapping Productions, 4/17/2007.

page 237 "In a speech in New York": nysun.com, 5/15/2007.

page 237 "I'm sure Richard thought": Wilkerson, interview with the author, 2/2/2007.

Epilogue

page 243 "The Americans believed": *New York Times Book Review*, 6/3/2007.

page 244 "Going into Iraq": *New York Times*, 5/26/2007.

page 244 "It was a blueprint": pnac.info./index.php.

page 245 "Richard came from": Jackson, interview with the author, 5/22/1007.

page 247 "The Iraqi criminal code": Woolsey, interview with the author, 2/1/2007.

page 247 "where we just left": sfgate.com, 6/6/2007.

page 249 "We protect them": Perle, interview with the author, 1/8/2007.

page 249 "I was born in America": Jonathan Perle, interview with the author, 2/19/2007.

page 250 "Every fighter's got a plan": Attributed to Tyson from numerous sources.

page 250 "We made a mistake": *I Remember: The Fall of Saigon*, CBS News Productions, 1996.

page 250 "We Had the Very Best": guardian.co.uk.commentisfree, 5/30/2007.

page 252 "But now there were alarming reports": *Economist*, 6/7/2007.

page 252 "And Perle's old foil": iht.com, 5/29/2007.

page 252: "This came on the heels": *New York Times*, 2/11/2007.

page 253 "our children will sing great songs": powerof narrative.blogspot.com, 6/2006.

page 253 "There it was, the unipolar moment": Jackson, interview with the author, 5/22/2007.

page 254: "I think it's fair because": Adelman, interview with the author, 1/10/2007.

Bibliography

Anderson, Martin. *Revolution: The Reagan Legacy*. Stanford, Calif.: Hoover Press, 1988.

Arendt, Hannah. *Essays in Understanding*. Edited by Jerome Kohn. New York: Schocken Books, 1994.

———. *Responsibility and Judgment*. Edited by Jerome Kohn. New York: Schocken Books, 2003.

Bronson, Rachel. *Thicker Than Oil: America's Uneasy Partnership with Saudi Arabia*. Oxford: Oxford University Press, 2006.

Brzezinski, Zbigniew, and Scowcroft, Brent. *Differentiated Containment: U.S. Policy Toward Iran and Iraq*. New York: Council on Foreign Relations Press, 1997.

Clarke, Richard A. *Against All Enemies: Inside America's War on Terror*. New York: Free Press, 2004.

Cockburn, Andrew. *Rumsfeld: His Rise, Fall and Catastrophic Legacy*. New York: Scribner, 2007.

Connell-Smith, Gordon. *Pattern of the Post-War World*. Baltimore, Md.: Penguin Books, 1957.

Dean, John W. *Worse Than Watergate: The Secret Presidency of George W. Bush*. New York: Little, Brown, 2004.

Drumheller, Tyler. *On the Brink: An Insider's Account of How the White House Compromised American Intelligence*. New York: Carroll and Graf, 2006.

Evriviades, Marios. *Security Dilemmas in Eurasia*. Athens: Nereus, 1999.

Feffer, John, ed. *Power Trip: U.S. Unilateralism and Global Strategy after 9/11*. New York: Seven Stories Press, 2003.

Fisk, Robert. *The Great War for Civilisation*. New York: Vintage Books, 2007.

Fitzgerald, Frances. *Way Out There in the Blue: Reagan, Star Wars and the End of the Cold War*. New York: Simon and Schuster, 2000.

Fosdick, Dorothy. *What Is Liberty?* New York: Harper and Brothers, 1939.

———. *Common Sense and World Affairs*. New York: Harcourt Brace, 1955.

Fosdick, Dorothy, ed. *Henry M. Jackson and World Affairs: Selected Speeches, 1953–1983*. Seattle: University of Washington Press, 1990.

Friedman, Murray. *The Neoconservative Revolution*. Cambridge: Cambridge University Press, 2005.

Frum, David, and Richard Perle. *An End to Evil: How to Win the War on Terror*. New York: Random House, 2003.

Fukuyama, Francis. *State Building: Governance and World Order in the 21st Century*. Ithaca, N.Y.: Cornell University Press, 2004.

America at the Crossroads: Democracy, Power, and the Neoconservative Legacy. New Haven, Conn.: Yale University Press, 2006.

Fukuyama, Francis, ed. *Nation Building: Beyond Afghanistan and Iraq*. Baltimore, Md.: Johns Hopkins University Press, 2006.

Gabriel, Richard A. *Military Incompetence: Why the American Military Doesn't Win*. New York: Hill and Wang, 1985.

Halberstam, David. *War in a Time of Peace: Bush, Clinton and the Generals*. New York: Touchstone Books, 2001.

Halper, Stefan, and Jonathan Clarke. *America Alone*. Cambridge: Cambridge University Press, 2004.

Hartung, William D. *How Much Are You Making on the War, Daddy?* New York: Nation Books, 2003.

Hersh, Seymour M. *The Price of Power: Kissinger in the White House*. New York: Simon and Schuster, 1983.

———. *Chain of Command: The Road from 9/11 to Abu Ghraib*. New York: HarperCollins, 2004.

Hobbes, Thomas. "On the Citizen." In *Cambridge Texts in the History of Political Thought*. Edited by Richard Tuck and Michael Silverhorne. Cambridge: Cambridge University Press, 1998.

Holbrooke, Richard. *To End a War*. New York: Modern Library, 1999.

Ikle, Fred C. *Annihilation from Within*. New York: Columbia University Press, 2006.

Johnson, Chalmers. *Blowback: The Costs and Consequences of American*

Empire. New York: Owl Books, 2000.

Kagan, Robert, and William Kristol, eds. *Present Dangers: Crisis and Opportunity in American Foreign and Defense Policy*. San Francisco: Encounter Books, 2000.

Kaufman, Robert G. *Henry M. Jackson: A Life in Politics*. Seattle: University of Washington Press, 2000.

Krepon, Michael, and Dan Caldwell, eds. *The Politics of Arms Control Treaty Ratification*. New York: St. Martin's Press, 1991.

Laurent, Eric. *Bush's Secret World*. Cambridge: Polity Press, 2004.

Litwak, Robert S. *Rogue States and the U.S. Foreign Policy*. Washington, D.C.: Woodrow Wilson Center Press, 2000.

———. *Regime Change: U.S. Strategy Through the Prism of 9/11*. Washington, D.C.: Woodrow Wilson Center Press, 2007.

Mann, James. *Rise of the Vulcans: The History of Bush's War Cabinet*. New York: Penguin Books, 2004.

Merry, Robert W. *Sands of Empire: Missionary Zeal, American Foreign Policy, and the Hazards of Global Ambition*. New York: Simon and Schuster, 2005.

Niebuhr, Reinhold. *The Children of Light and the Children of Darkness*, New York: Charles Scribner's Sons, 1944.

Packer, George. *The Assassin's Gate: America in Iraq*. New York: Farrar, Straus and Giroux, 2005.

Perle, Richard. *Hard Line*, New York: Random House, 1992.

Phillips, Kevin. *American Dynasty: Aristocracy, Fortune, and the Politics of Deceit in the House of Bush*. New York: Viking Press, 2004.

———. *American Theocracy*. New York: Viking Press, 2006.

Reagan, Ronald. *The Reagan Diaries*. Edited by Douglas Brinkley. New York: HarperCollins, 2007.

Robinson, Daniel N. *American Ideals: Founding a "Republic of Virtue,"* Chantilly, Va.: Teaching Company, 2004.

Rogow, Arnold A. *Thomas Hobbs: Radical in the Service of Reaction*. New York: W. W. Norton, 1986.

Rosen, Gary, ed. *The Right War? The Conservative Debate on Iraq*. New York: Cambridge University Press, 2005.

Schweitzer, Peter. *Victory: The Reagan Administration's Secret Strategy That Hastened the Collapse of the Soviet Union*. New York: Atlantic Monthly Press, 1994.

Shultz, George P. *Turmoil and Triumph: My Years as Secretary of State*. New York: Charles Scribner's Sons, 1993.

Stelzer, Irwin, ed. *The Neocon Reader*. New York: Grove Press, 2004.

Suskind, Ron. *The One Percent Doctrine: Deep Inside America's Pursuit of Its Enemies Since 9/11*. New York: Simon and Schuster, 2006.

Trento, Joseph J. *Prelude to Terror: Edwin P. Wilson and the Legacy of America's Private Intelligence Network*. New York: Carroll and Graf, 2005.

Turner, Stansfield. *Burn Before Reading: Presidents, CIA Directors and Secret Intelligence*. New York: Hyperion, 2005.

Waas, Murray. *The United States v. I. Lewis Libby*. New York: Union Square Press, 2007.

Walzer, Michael. *Just and Unjust Wars: A Moral Argument with Historical Illustrations*. New York: Basic Books, 1997.

Wilson, Joseph. *The Politics of Truth*. New York: Carroll and Graf, 2005.

Winik, Jay. *On the Brink*. New York: Simon and Schuster, 1996.

Woodward, Bob. *Bush at War*. New York: Simon and Schuster, 2002.

Wright, Lawrence. *The Looming Tower*. New York: Knopf, 2006.

Index

About the Author

Alan Weisman is a former producer for *60 Minutes*, *CBS Sunday Morning*, and the *CBS Evening News*. During his tenure at CBS, he covered the Israeli invasion of Lebanon, the Falklands War, and the Three Mile Island nuclear disaster; produced and wrote segments including "The Last Survivor of 9/11" and "The Fall of Baghdad"; and worked with Charlie Rose, Charles Osgood, Ed Bradley, Morley Safer, Dan Rather, and Walter Cronkite. He is the author of *Lone Star: The Extraordinary Life and Times of Dan Rather*.